LAZY ABOUT
GRILLING

the feet up, hands down

easiest ways to barbecue

Pamela Rice Hahn

Laurel Glen Publishing
An imprint of the Advantage Publishers Group
5880 Oberlin Drive, San Diego, CA 92121-4794
www.advantagebooksonline.com

ISBN 1-57145-799-2
Library of Congress Cataloging-in-Publication Data available
upon request.

First published as *Master the Grill the Lazy Way* by Macmillan
Publishing USA, 1999. The current edition, *Lazy About
Grilling,* has been thoroughly revised.

Publisher: Allen Orso
Associate Publisher: Rachel Petrella
Project Editor: JoAnn Padgett
Production Editor: Mana Monzavi
Design: Duotribe, Inc.
Photography: Renee L. Esordi

Printed in the United States by Von Hoffmann.
1 2 3 4 5   06 05 04 03 02

Are You Too Lazy to Read This Book?

Do you feel pangs of guilt when all your friends invite you to their barbecues and you never seem to get around to asking them back? If you have a moment's time and honesty to spare, take the following quiz to pinpoint how desperately you need help:

1. You have to consult the manual to operate the knobs on your stove.
   ☐ yes ☐ no

2. You think tongs include lyrics. ☐ yes ☐ no

3. You think briquettes are used to build very small houses.
   ☐ yes ☐ no

4. When somebody asks how you prepare your ribs, you name your favorite moisturizing lotion. ☐ yes ☐ no

5. Your idea of grilling pizza is questioning the delivery boy to find out why he took so long. ☐ yes ☐ no

6. You think Marinate is one of the Olsen twins. ☐ yes ☐ no

7. That Simon and Garfunkel song taught you all you know about herbs. ☐ yes ☐ no

8. The closest you've come to grilling lately was that time you forgot to take the foil off the dish in the microwave. ☐ yes ☐ no

9. You use your pantry to store gift wrap and holiday decorations.
   ☐ yes ☐ no

10. Since that embarrassing incident the last time you used a grill, you promised the local fire department you'd study before your next cookout. ☐ yes ☐ no

If you answered "yes" to even one of the above, you need me to show you how to be *Lazy About Grilling*. Without this book, you may never grill at all, which would be a shame. It's really not that much work. Here are the feet up, hands down easiest ways to barbecue.

Table of Contents

Let the others bring home the bacon and fry it up in a pan, I prefer to avoid the cleanup. Whether you plan to use gas, charcoal, a smoker, or your electric countertop, outdoor, or stovetop grill, here's how to maximize your results and minimize effort.

Chapter 1: Simple Staples Sense   1

Must-have items for the grilling gourmet's pantry—and yours, too.

Chapter 2: Effortless Equipment Education   13

These explanations about grill choices will make your selection decisions easier. Plus, I include tips about other gadgets to have on hand to streamline your meal preparation process.

Chapter 3: Get a Grip on Grilling: Some of Us Gotta Have a Map   25

We all dread it, yet we all know we've gotta do it. Getting organized now will save lots of time when you're actually ready to grill. I'll show you that with the proper choice of equipment and utensils, it's not as daunting as it would first appear.

Chapter 4: Sanity-Saving Shortcuts and Tried 'n' True Tips   39

Learn which steps can be done before you fire up the grill. You'll thank yourself (and me!) later if you do.

Chapter 5: Minimizing the Mess   57

Doing the dishes is the inevitable conclusion to every meal. There are tricks that you can do that will give you time to linger over dessert without feeling guilty.

Introduction: The Prehistory of Grilling

I imagine the first cookout occurred one day when, after a thunderstorm, cavemen (and women) from the Bar-B-Clan formed a queue around a wooly mammoth that had been zapped and charred by a bolt of lightning.

Once they tasted that fire-roasted flavor, mammoth tartare just didn't satisfy their palates anymore. Finding a way to duplicate that aroma and piquancy became as important as their hunting rituals. This was a can-do tribe!

So, because they were a forward-thinking group of nomads, they formed a committee. The committee then designated project teams, whose job it was to find ways to grill meat for the next feast. They rounded up herds of animals and trapped them in the valley, while the more limber members on their team danced a rain dance around the perimeter. They herded those animals to different locations, just in case the rumors about lightning strikes frequency were true.

One day—tired and frustrated of being one unsung link in a human fence, and also getting very hungry by this time—a junior member of the team took a break from his daydreams of becoming a freelance consultant and decided to make use of some loose rocks lying in the gully. First he stacked them in a spiral pattern that encompassed his tribe's understanding of their outreaching purpose of life on this planet, sacred geometry, and the Feng Shui dynamic he intended to popularize in a book, as soon as somebody developed a language. Eventually though, growing weary from his task, he stumbled on some loose stones and dropped a rock, which struck some flint, which kindled some twigs clinging to another rock, and the rest, as they say, is history. (Alas, his boss took credit for the discovery.)

However, this breakthrough not only led to expertly grilled meals (and arguments among alpha members of the clan as to whether or not the food was done yet), it also led to smoke signals, which evolved to other means of communication, which resulted in the Industrial Age, which made possible standardized grill construction, which eventually brought me to where I am today—hoping I now have your attention so you will continue not only to read this book, but to savor the recipes, achieve great things with minimal effort, and have a good time in the process. Enjoy!

YOU DON'T HAVE TO FEEL GUILTY ANYMORE!

Being *Lazy About* things usually connotes lack of thought, effort, and preparation. Well, I say, it's time somebody ends this bad wrap lazy gets—and I humbly believe I'm just the person to do it. *Lazy About Grilling: the Feet Up Hands Down Easiest Ways to Barbecue* is here to retire lazy's bad reputation for good. When it comes right down to it, being *Lazy About* planning your work routine is the only way a busy cook can hope to achieve all the flavor without the hassle. That's why being *Lazy About Grilling* is nothing to be ashamed of. It's a skill! An art!

Even with all of the labor-saving devices available today, I know I often feel overwhelmed by the demands on my time. I imagine you feel the same way, too. Just think about it. Every time you turn around, you're given more responsibility, more information to absorb, more places to go, and more numbers, dates, and names to remember (or to lose in your next hand-held computer crash).

Isn't it time we all admitted to ourselves that our minds and bodies are tired of being on overload? Isn't it time that our *Lazy About* tendencies are recognized for what they've always been—the smartest, most efficient ways to work?

Let's be frank—we're all starting to feel a bit guilty about the heaps of dirty laundry, stacks of ATM slips that will never see the light of day in our check registers, and trash bags full of Chinese takeout containers and pizza delivery boxes. Tackling mundane tasks may be necessary, but this doesn't make them any less tedious or exhausting. Seeing that you and your family eat healthier, no-fuss meals isn't meant to be another taxing chore, so don't panic! It isn't the daunting task you probably think it will be; just follow the advice in this book. Being *Lazy About Grilling* is the easy, effortless way to get stuff done (and done right!).

BACK TO BASICS

Everything about grilling says, "recreation"—the great outdoors, casual dress, enjoying the good company of family and great friends. I say let's adapt that attitude for preparing all of our meals! No one should slave over the grill—or anything, for that matter, so in this book I present the most pain-free tricks of the grilling and smoking trade, including tons of shortcuts, timesaving tips, and concise lists of all the stuff you need at your lazy fingertips. The Bar-B-Clan would have wanted it this way, so dig in.

Lazy About Grilling cuts through all of the time-consuming labor you probably associate with cooking by presenting delicious recipes and handy hints to help you save precious grilling and clean-up time for rest and relaxation. I have figured out how to make you look like a grilling genius. *Lazy About* tips and shortcuts will leave you plenty of time to sit back and smugly pity those poor misled suckers who don't know that being *Lazy About Grilling* is a good thing, a true talent! (If you start to feel guilty about thinking of them as "suckers," you can always help spread the word and share a few of the secrets in this book with them. Better yet, set up a book rack beside the cooler next to your lawn chair and earn some extra money selling copies of this book to anyone who stops by.) Here is all you need to go great culinary distances with minimal effort, then devote your attention and energy to the greater pleasures in life. Or, at the very least, visit with your family and friends, instead of having to excuse yourself to babysit the grill or worse, clean up the kitchen.

How to Use This Book

Throughout each chapter, simple, delicious, and hassle-free tricks of the grilling trade appear in the margins to make your life easier. The designer who set my words into print even chose a couple of symbols to draw your eye to these time-savers. Think easy:

Piece of Cake
Easy as Pie

Also in the margins are symbols of better ways to spend your time. These are the little things you can do now to save time and effort later. Remember, being *Lazy About Grilling* does require some forethought, so look for:

A Brimming Family Car Heading for the Beach
The 'Gone Fishin' Signs

Lazy does have its limits, though, so don't be *Lazy About* safety. Text is set in green boxes throughout to mark the importance of handling food and grilling safely. This is fine print to live by, so pay attention, please. No one likes to get sick or to see a grill master's domain go up in smoke. Least of all the kids!

If you're not "married" to making everything from scratch or inspired to brew your own stocks, look to Sources for head-start ingredients and valuable supplier information. Your secret's safe with me! For info on an "as-needed" basis, refer to my Glossary of key grilling terms in the back of the book.

Thank you...

For their help and support, I would like to thank everyone at Laurel Glen Publishing and Advantage Publishers Group: Rachel Petrella, JoAnn Padgett, Mana Monzavi, and Elizabeth McNulty—good luck with your new life among the plants in St. Louis. For all of their hard work and perseverance, I would like to thank my agent Sheree Bykofsky and her associate Janet Rosen. For their efforts in making the earlier edition of this book a reality, I'd like to thank Kathryn Toyer, Amy Gordon, Joan Patterson (for her suggestions and shared laughter over my jokes), Jenaffer Brandt, Marie Butler-Knight, and Keith Giddeon. For my friend who always best understood that I was never lazy, I was just adapting to a new way of doing things, I extend a special thank you to Doris Meinerding. I also want to thank my daughter and joy of my life, Lara Sutton—for letting me fire up your grill for winter lunches and especially for your encouragement and support. Granddaughter Taylor and Grandson Charlie for your help making pizza crusts and for keeping me company outside. Granddaughter Courtney Marie for each and every one of your beautiful baby smiles and cuddly hugs for "Gramma Pam."

Additional thanks go to... For your help with so many of my recipe "experiments," especially when you took your turns doing the dishes, too: my newest "adminstrative assistant" Katie Bonvillian, my niece Nicole Teeters, my former "administrative assistant" and artist friend Michele Nagel, and my nephews Andrew and Tony Rice. For being there: my sister-in-law and "personal shopper" Ann Rice, mom, dad, and the siblings. For your encouragement and sharing the laughter: my photographer friend who makes house calls Bill Grunden; computer guru buddy Don Lachey; my online friends: David Hebert, Eric J. Ehlers, the elusive Bishop Ra Fiki, Jodi Cornelius, Stevie Harris, Ed Williams, Troy More, Dolf J. Veenvliet, Erin Klitzke, and all the other "#Authors on the Undernet" regulars. For reminding me about some of my "creations" that we'd been too busy to grill for far too long: Janet Nelson. For helping me with the Nutribase 2001 software used for recipe nutritional analysis: Ed Prestwood of Cybersoft, Inc. And, for your awaiting big kitchen and appetite: Prince Charming—wherever you are. Have I got a meal planned for you!

Chapter 1

Simple Staples Sense

One of the secrets to being *Lazy About Grilling* is to keep your kitchen inventory under control. Knowing what foods you have on hand makes meal preparation so much easier. When you know what you have available, you can tuck this book into your attaché, carry it with you, and pull it out to search for your next meal's recipe while you wait in line or for the dentist to come into the room. (If you're waiting for the dentist to come in to perform a root canal, I recommend that you prepare a soft food, such as haggis or stuffed mushrooms, as your main course.)

But that's getting ahead of myself. Before that suggestion becomes practical, you must first determine what you already have on hand in your kitchen and what items you need to buy. Stop complaining! This will only take a few minutes, and once you've completed this task, you'll save yourself time later—maybe even enough to indulge in a bubble bath or read something other than a cookbook.

Got that notebook and pen at the ready? Good, because it's inventory time! Ready. Set. Go!

IN THE CUPBOARD AND PANTRY

Putting staples on your shelves doesn't mean tacking the shelf paper into place.

On one hand, some foods you should buy fresh. Foodstuffs, on the other hand, are things that, if you want to be practical, you must keep in stock. As contradictory as it may sound, keeping both of those hands involved now will save you from juggling some steps later.

Bare Necessities

Storage won't be a problem for most of the items on this list because many of them come in their own sturdy containers, designed for just that purpose. Naturally, you can keep baking soda longer than bakery items—otherwise, you'll end up with marbled "wry" bread. Expiration dates are on those packages for a reason. Use those dates and your cooking style and quantity to gauge how much to buy to maintain your "live" stock.

- Arrowroot
- Baking powder
- Baking soda (Keep extra on hand to make a paste to clean the grill. See Chapter 5.)
- Bread, such as crusty loaves of French bread and bakery sandwich buns
- Broth mix or cubes (See Sources for information on my preferred method to make instant broth; I keep my broth bases in the refrigerator, but if you insist on using cubes, it's okay to keep them in the pantry.)
- Canned tomatoes, whole or chopped, can save you time on those days you either don't have fresh ones available or would just

rather devote that chopping time to lounging in the sun.

- Cornstarch
- Flour (The measurements in my recipes, such as those for pizza crusts, call for white or unbleached flour, but there's no reason why you can't substitute bran and stone-ground whole wheat for a portion of that flour, if you prefer.)
- Honey
- Maple syrup, *real* maple syrup for true flavor
- Olive oil (extra-virgin oil for salads and regular for marinades)
- Pasta
- Peanut butter, *natural* peanut butter for a purer, better taste
- Rice (white, brown, or wild)
- Salt (You'll notice as you read this book that I use very little salt. Even when a recipe requires it, I use the minimum amount possible. Keep the shaker at the table so those whose tastes require more can add it. Kosher salt is preferred in many marinades because of its purer flavor; other times I use sea salt. In fact, I never use table salt; I've found it takes less sea salt to achieve the same seasoning results, an important consideration if anyone in your family has high blood pressure.)
- Soy sauce (I stock both Kikkoman and La Choy; each brand has its own distinct flavor, which is why I often blend them to create a subtle, yet distinct, difference in my recipes. Bragg's Liquid Aminos is a lower-sodium substitute for soy sauce and something I also keep on hand; because it isn't fermented, it's safe for most people with mold allergies, too.)
- Sugar (white—I prefer cane—and brown)
- Tahini (sesame seed paste—available in toasted and regular)
- Toasted sesame oil (for adding flavor to Asian dishes)
- Vegetable oil (corn, peanut, canola, sesame, or other poly- or

Gone Fishin'

monounsaturated oil; I prefer olive oil for almost everything, but occasionally a milder oil is called for. Also, peanut oil can withstand high temperatures for those times you want to use an oil to fry something atop the grill in a grill-safe or cast-iron skillet or use an outdoor fryer.)

◟ Vinegar (You can never have too many varieties of vinegar: red wine, white wine, cider, rice wine, flavored and infused, sherry, champagne, and balsamic.)

◟ Worcestershire sauce (For the same reasons I keep different soy sauce brands on hand, I also stock both French's and Lea & Perrins. I also make my own low-sodium variety and will share that recipe with you later in the book.)

Useful Pantry Extras

Even if your home doesn't have a designated pantry area, you can still reserve a corner of your cupboard for special ingredients. Keeping some out-of-the-ordinary items at the ready will help you create extraordinary meals.

◟ Canned peppers, such as chipotle or roasted red pepper (See Sources for the concentrates I use instead.)

◟ Black olives

◟ Canned broth (See Sources for my preferred alternative to canned broth; I use bases instead.) If you choose to go with canned broth, try not to store the unused portion for longer than a few days and remember how delicious rice can be if you use leftover broth in place of some of the water you use to prepare it.

◟ Chocolate chips (semisweet)

◟ Cocoa

- Evaporated milk, powdered or canned
- Hoisin sauce
- Kosher salt
- Marshmallows
- Mashed potatoes, instant
- Molasses
- Nuts, shelled (pecans, walnuts, peanuts, almonds, sesame seeds)
- Oatmeal
- Oyster sauce
- Popcorn
- Raisins
- Tomato paste and purée
- Vanilla (only real vanilla, please, not imitation)
- Wines and liqueurs for cooking (red, white, sherry, Kahlua)

If a recipe calls for a fruit liqueur you don't have on hand, you don't have to rush out and buy some. Simply substitute some frozen fruit juice concentrate instead.

Spices and Herbs

Unless I state otherwise, the recipes throughout this book call for dried herbs and spices. It's not always possible or convenient, but remember that using freshly ground spices, instead of prepackaged, will create a quality taste comparable to freshly brewed coffee instead of instant. Most cooks agree that spices lose their punch after sitting on a shelf for a year; some replace spices every three months. Use fresh spices for my "Old Bay Seasoning" recipe and see for yourself.

- Allspice
- Basil
- Bay leaves
- Cardamom
- Cayenne pepper
- Chili powder
- Cilantro
- Cinnamon
- Cloves
- Coriander seed

- ⸂ Cumin
- ⸂ Dill
- ⸂ Fennel seed
- ⸂ Garlic powder
- ⸂ Grated lemon peel
- ⸂ Grated orange peel
- ⸂ Marjoram
- ⸂ Minced, dried garlic
- ⸂ Minced, dried onion
- ⸂ Mint
- ⸂ Mustard, dry
- ⸂ Mustard seed
- ⸂ Nutmeg
- ⸂ Old Bay Seasoning blend (see recipe)
- ⸂ Onion powder
- ⸂ Oregano
- ⸂ Paprika
- ⸂ Parsley
- ⸂ Peppercorns, black
- ⸂ Red pepper flakes
- ⸂ Rosemary
- ⸂ Sage
- ⸂ Thyme

Old Bay Seasoning

1 tablespoon celery seed
1 tablespoon whole black peppercorns
6 bay leaves
½ teaspoon whole cardamom
½ teaspoon mustard seed
4 whole cloves
1 teaspoon sweet Hungarian paprika
¼ teaspoon mace

1 In a spice grinder or small food processor, combine all of the ingredients.

2 Grind well and store in a small glass jar.

IN THE REFRIGERATOR

If you have kids, you've probably often wondered why you bothered installing an air conditioner, considering how much time they spend standing in front of the refrigerator, supposedly staring at the contents. (I suspect it was once a tip in a fashion magazine, its origination lost in time, but now it's the method teenage girls use to set their makeup so it doesn't run on hot summer days.)

You spend your share of time staring into an open refrigerator, too. But you're looking for answers to that age-old question: Whatever do I fix to eat tonight? Here are some of the things you should find whenever you open the door.

Blanch a package of frozen mixed vegetables and toss them together with some pasta and salad dressing for a quick salad.

Bare Necessities

Just because you store something in the refrigerator doesn't mean you can forget to watch the expiration date. It's funny when someone on a television sitcom grabs "soured" milk off the shelf; it's not quite as humorous when it happens to you.

- Butter (I never use margarine, but it's your call.)
- Cheese (Always have cheddar and Parmesan on hand!)
- Eggs
- Jelly (grape, orange marmalade, red currant, strawberry, apple butter)
- Ketchup
- Mayonnaise
- Milk
- Mustard (Dijon and regular)
- Salad dressing

Don't be afraid to try making your own mayonnaise. It's another way to add that special flavor advantage to a dish. However, to be safe and avoid any possible salmonella contamination, I recommend that you use pasteurized egg products instead of raw eggs.

Useful Extras

I named one of my chapters "Meats that Prove Variety is the Nice of Life" for a reason. Subtle changes can convert your dish from a dull same ol'-same ol' one to something truly special. The ingredients I mention here will help nudge you out of that stuck-in-a-rut cooking mode.

- Buttermilk
- Cottage cheese
- Mushrooms
- Orange or other fruit juice
- Potato flour
- Salsa
- Soda
- Sparkling water

Treat Yourself

Every family has a picky eater. It must be one of the rules. Using the items I recommend here will garner a five-star rating from even the most finicky food critic.

- Cream (Because of its high fat content, cream will keep for weeks. It only takes a small amount to make a delicious difference in your soups and sauces.)
- Nonfat dry milk powder (If you're watching the fat in your diet, I include a "cream substitute" recipe on pg. 284)
- Olives
- Fresh pasta
- Pickles (bread and butter, candied sweet, dill, sweet)
- Sauces and condiments (barbecue, chili, chutney, pesto)

If you know in advance that a certain recipe calls for pasta, get out the pasta machine and make a batch. Or pick up some up from the refrigerator case at your local market. Fresh pasta tastes so much better!

Freeze steaks and pork chops in meal-sized portions.

IN THE FREEZER

Whenever possible, use fresh foods to prepare your meal. But because it's impossible to plan for every possibility (unexpected guests or the kids bringing home a few friends), keeping extra vegetables, fruit juice concentrates, and meats in the freezer will save you unwanted trips to the store. The nice thing about a freezer is that it allows you to buy those products when they're on sale and store them until you need them.

- Bread dough (to use for pizza crust when you don't have time to make your own)
- Chicken (flash-frozen boneless, skinless breasts and thighs)
- Fish fillets
- Fruit juice concentrate (cranberry juice cocktail, Minute Maid 100 percent lemon juice, and unsweetened apple, grape, orange, pineapple, and white grape)
- Ground pork and sausage (See the homemade sausage recipes beginning on pg. 288)
- Hamburger
- Hot dogs
- Ice
- Shrimp
- Steak and pork chops
- Tortillas (flour and corn)
- Vegetables

FRESH VEGETABLES

There are vegetables you can always keep on hand. Others, such as seasonal fresh sweet corn or squash, you'll pick up on the day you need them. The nice thing about most vegetables is, unless I note otherwise, you don't have to store them in the refrigerator.

Bare Necessities

Preparing your meals in the *Lazy About* way doesn't mean you do so at the expense of "the healthy way." Keep crisp, fresh veggies on hand for when you get the munchies or to use in your salads and grilled side dishes. Here are some "healthy way" foods I recommend that you keep in stock.

- Carrots (Store in the refrigerator.)
- Celery (Store in the refrigerator. Even when this vegetable goes limp, it can still be used in most cooked dishes.)
- Cucumbers (Store in the refrigerator.)
- Garlic (Even if you use the prepared sautéed and roasted garlic concentrates I mention in the Sources, you'll still want fresh garlic to rub in salad bowls or to roast.)
- Green onions (or scallions)
- Lettuce (You must keep this in the refrigerator crisper. And don't get stuck in an iceberg rut! Use a variety, such as romaine, Bibb, or fresh spinach.)
- Onions (red, yellow, sweet, and white)
- Potatoes (baking, red, sweet, and Yukon Gold)

Useful Extras

So you can add flavor that you'll savor, include these items on your shopping list, too.

- Cabbage (best stored in the refrigerator, especially after it's been cut)
- Ginger (fresh root or candied)
- Peppers (green or red; refrigerate)
- Shallots

Treat Yourself

Go ahead and buy whatever vegetables are in season. I give plenty of suggestions on how to grill sweet corn, squash, tomatoes, and other special, seasonal vegetables.

IN THE FRUIT BOWL

Unless I tell you otherwise, you can keep most fruit nestled in a bowl, where it not only looks attractive but will also be in view so you and your family will grab it first when looking for a snack, instead of hunting through the pantry for that package of cookies or chips.

Bare Necessities

Fruit isn't just for snacks and desserts. It can be used in grilled dishes, to add pizzazz to salsa, and in other ways, as you'll discover throughout this book. Here are some I suggest.

- Apples
- Bananas
- Grapefruit
- Lemons
- Oranges

Keep a scrub brush next to the sink and use it to wash fruit before you put it in the bowl. Doing so will help prevent pesticide residue from transferring to little fingers or into the meat of the fruit itself, such as when you slice citrus.

Useful Extras

Don't forget about what I like to think of as special occasion fruit. You can either grill the ones I suggest below or serve them fresh for dessert. Everybody likes a treat now and then.

- Grapes
- Kiwi fruit
- Limes (These keep longer in the refrigerator.)
- Pears
- Plums (These keep longer in the refrigerator.)

Treat Yourself

For me, "in season" is dictated by my cravings. Whether you buy these fruits fresh or use them freshly thawed, they'll add a wonderful touch to any meal.

- Blackberries
- Blueberries
- Strawberries
- Raspberries

When you keep your kitchen well stocked, half of the "What'll I cook tonight?" dilemma is already solved. You'll find that a quick peek at what's on hand will trigger menu ideas. When that happens, cooking is no longer a chore, but a pleasure. And everybody likes to have fun. So, have a ball! You deserve it.

Chapter 2

Effortless Equipment Education

With almost any activity or hobby, there are certain items that you "must" have to participate. Of course, there is always the minimum required equipment; it's the extras that usually drop me into debt. I simply have to control myself. Some things are necessary while others aren't.

This chapter will give you ideas on most of the equipment you need to accomplish the grilling techniques explained later in this book. I will also give you a few ideas on some extra equipment that can save you time and worry, and help avoid those occasional instances when you want to drop to the floor kicking and screaming when something doesn't turn out "just" right. (However, because I'm a self-confessed gadget freak, there will be some other equipment items also mentioned in "Chapter 19: Bringin' It Indoors: Indoor Grills and Gadgets." I'll also discuss electric outdoor cooking equipment in Chapter 20.)

Okay, ready? Sit back, lovingly pat your wallet or purse—this won't hurt, I promise (maybe).

FOR WHOM THE GRILL COOKS

I have an easy question for you. What is the most essential thing you need in order to GRILL food? Right! Hey, you're good.

If a grill were just a grill, things would be simple. As it turns out, though, grills come in different varieties and sizes. All you have to do is decide which is best for your needs. Don't worry, it's not as difficult as it might seem at first. I won't be going into great detail about the grills themselves. Everyone pretty much has his or her own opinion about which type is better.

A good place to see many grills side-by-side for your selection is at a local building, gardening, or hardware "superstore" or at a national department store in your area. The salespeople there can answer any specific questions you might have about a certain model or grills in general.

There are basically four types of grills: gas, charcoal, electric (indoor and outdoor), and built-in pits. In this chapter, I am going to limit the discussion to gas and charcoal grills.

There's nothing "lazy" about lugging bricks and mortar around in order to build a pit when you can go out and buy a grill in less than an hour (depending on where you live), so I'll avoid discussing pit grills, too.

TO GAS OR NOT TO GAS? IS THAT A QUESTION?

There are advantages and disadvantages to using a gas grill.

Advantages: Using a gas grill gives you better control over temperature during the preparation of foods. How so? With KNOBS! Some only have one or two knobs, while others look as if they could easily control a starship from your favorite science-fiction show. In

> *A grill is an important tool that you'll own for a long time. Take your time, comparison shop, and look at all the features to get the one that's right for you. Treat yourself by getting the best one your budget can afford.*

addition, gas grills have igniter switches which, well…ignite the gas for you. This is a welcome alternative to hunting down matches or a lighter and then lowering your hand to "danger zone" when lighting the grill. How about that? No more spastic, spine-tingling reactions when the flame ignites!

With a gas grill, you don't have to worry about remembering to buy charcoal and then arranging it. Plus, compared to the cost of charcoal, gas is the most economical choice. You can replace your canister for about $10 and get many uses from it. Charcoal briquettes cost $2 to $5 per bag, depending on quality and size. This cost rises if you get unique briquettes, like the kind with exotic woods included, from a specialty store.

Disadvantages: There are two disadvantages worth noting to using a gas grill. With gas (unless you have purchased materials to counter this problem), you don't get the flavor of charcoal-cooked foods. I will discuss how to overcome this later in the chapter. Secondly, the price of gas grills is well above that of their charcoal counterparts. But, as you've heard time and again, "you get what you pay for." This may or may not be true in some cases, but I believe it is when it comes to grills.

Recommendation: If you can afford the higher price and the addition of wood chips (discussed later) for flavor is not a problem for you, gas grills are the most popular way to go. They cook food evenly and accurately, and with proper maintenance will last much longer than their charcoal cousins.

Some people with chemical sensitivities need to avoid the initial fumes generated when lighting a gas grill. (Starter fluids used on charcoal can cause problems for people with allergies, too.)

Always be sure to have a spare gas tank (filled) or bag of charcoal on hand. Nothing can be more frustrating than running out of fuel in the middle of grilling.

IT'S MY CHARCOAL AND I'LL BUY IF I WANT TO

I hope you're like me and love to grill food with an obsession. However, if you're only a grill chef for special events and aren't faced with housing restrictions that prevent you from using one, a charcoal grill may be your best choice. The low price of most varieties of these grills, coupled with the small amount of maintenance they require, make them an afford-able choice.

DON'T SETTLE FOR THE SAME OLD CHARCOAL EVERY TIME—THERE ARE MANY VARIETIES AVAILABLE. LOOK IN YOUR LOCAL MARKET AND SPECIALTY STORES TO CHOOSE FROM THE MANY VARIETIES OF CHARCOAL AVAILABLE.

THE RIGHT TOOLS FOR ANY GRILL

Simply owning a grill is not enough. Sure, they look nice just sitting there, waiting to be used. But, like a baseball player needs more than a field to play upon, so it goes with the serious grill chef. Some things are necessary while others are just extras—"toys," if you will. In this section, I'll show you a different variety of tools to make your grilling experience more enjoyable. I'll even suggest which tools to always have handy, and mention those you can either get or live without (if you absolutely must do so).

Utensils You Will Need

Unless you're impervious to the pain of heat and flames (unlike me), you're going to need a few items to assist in the turning and basting of food as it sits on the cooking grid. Grilling tools are avail-able in many brands of varying quality. It's usually more cost-effective to buy these in a set instead of individually.

⌣ Tongs are very handy for turning items that are bulky and not necessarily flat, such as poultry and large vegetables like potatoes and eggplant. And using tongs instead of a grill fork avoids the risk of inadvertently puncturing the meat. Tongs come in long-handled varieties that let you stand as far away as possible from the grill to lessen the chance that you'll get singed should there be a flare-up. These are a must-have item.

⌣ A spatula with a long handle is always necessary when cooking hamburgers or any other flat-sided food item. The longer the handle, the better. Remember, you're cooking the food, not your hands and lower arms.

⌣ A long-handled, two-pronged fork is a great item to have around during grilling season, which is year-round, of course!

⌣ An absolute necessity is a good-quality basting brush. Actually, owning more than one might prove to be of tremendous help if you'll be cooking more than one type of meat at once. This also saves you from washing a brush before using it again near the completion of the cooking time; you need a clean brush then to avoid cross-contamination.

⌣ A sauce mop is exactly what the name implies. It looks like a regular household mop, except it's much smaller. It holds much more sauce than a basting brush. This can be very useful when cooking large amounts of ribs or whole birds. A mop isn't absolutely necessary, since you can use a brush, but it can save you some time when there's a lot of basting involved. (I've been known to make my own using 100 percent cotton rug yarn knotted over the "scratcher" end of an inexpensive bamboo back scratcher or over the bent-up ends of a "seen better days" long-handled, grill fork. I clip the knots and discard the yarn when I'm done.)

- Special two-pronged skewers are invaluable when making kabobs. Food is placed on one prong while the second holds it in place with pressure. Food will no longer rotate on the skewer while you're turning it!
- A meat thermometer is an absolute necessity! Not only will using one allow you to tell when food is done, but it's important to be sure the meat has reached the proper internal temperature to kill any harmful bacteria that could cause sickness.

Accessorize Yourself

Using my example from above, what if a baseball catcher entered a game without his protective cup? There's a potential "ouch!" in the making, huh? Well, just like those guys, I need to take some precautions as well. Below is some equipment you should consider acquiring to guarantee your days of grilling are safe ones.

- Grilling mitts are a great way to assure yourself and others that you're cooking what needs to be cooked and nothing else! Grills have a funny way of getting hot in the strangest places.
- Okay, picture it. You've become more daring in front of your grill; there's sauce and meat flying in all directions as you baste and turn food like a true pro! Why not prevent staining your clothes, and possibly getting a few short, stinging burns, by wearing a good apron? Aprons come in several designs and are made of different materials. You decide, cloth or plastic, full- or half-length. Remember, though, keep it tied tightly. You don't want a breeze to whip it into the fire!

GRILL ACCESSORIES

If you look around, you'll find a multitude of grill accessories at specialty and department stores. I will be describing some of those choices in the following sections. These products are designed to make your grilling experience easier by solving specific problems inherent to cooking on a grill. No matter which accessories you opt for, always keep a damp cloth or paper towels handy for quick cleanup. That way, instead of running back and forth, you can relax with a cold drink, family, and friends.

You probably saw Granny using them in her kitchen. They're great for the grill, too. Yep, those old-style and well-seasoned black, cast-iron skillets and pans. What's great about cast iron is that nobody can tell if you scorch the pan. Hey! It's already black!

Toppers and Griddles

Grill toppers are special add-on grids or surfaces that usually have a specific purpose. They have small gaps (none for griddles) in the cooking area and are placed on a grill's cooking surface. They come in various sizes and price ranges. With these you can cook smaller foods like shrimp, vegetables, and bite-sized pieces of fish, pork, poultry, or beef. There are also special toppers for unique foods.

- For those of you who like Asian cuisine, also available is a wok topper that can be used to prepare—you guessed it—your favorite stir-fry recipes.
- How would you like to cook a complete breakfast on your grill? It's not impossible. You see, to keep the eggs from dripping through the grid, there's a simple solution. Pick up a porcelain griddle, which rests on top of the cooking grid, and some egg rings. You'll be creating a smoky-flavored breakfast in no time at all.
- You'll get hooked on the grilled pizza techniques later in this book. Guess what? There's a special pizza topper available just for that!

Internal Accessories

There are many grill add-ons. Here are a few examples to get you started. As you get more involved in grilling, you'll discover others.

- Want to add that "real" grilled taste to gas-cooked foods? Try a smoker box filled with mesquite, hickory, or your favorite soaked wood chips to achieve that perfect dining experience. Simply place the smoker box over the lava rocks (diffusing material) or briquettes in your grill.
- For a larger gas grill, an electric rotisserie kit can be a great addition to save you some time while cooking whole birds, ribs, or whatever will fit on it. The food is automatically turned for you, which leaves you free to sit back and watch your favorite television show. Once in a while (during a commercial, of course) baste the meat if necessary.
- A grill basket lets you place several ears of corn, hamburgers, fish fillets, or any type of food in a manner so you can turn them over at once. If you're careful about using uniform pieces of food—or food sized according to required cooking times, this will help assure even cooking on all items.
- To get even more food on your grill, try a vertical roasting rack. These are great when grilling whole meals at once. One of these could double or triple the allowable cooking space contained on your grill.

External Accessories

If you wish, there are things you can add to the outside of your grill to save time or alleviate any needless worry, such as straining to see your food at night or worrying about gray skies, among other things.

I'll give you some ideas for things you might want to consider to avoid these problems.

WHEN USING ANY ACCESSORY, BE SURE TO READ THE INSTRUCTIONS THAT COME WITH IT. YOU'LL GET THE BEST INFORMATION THERE, SINCE EACH MANUFACTURER TENDS TO DO THINGS A BIT DIFFERENTLY.

Dedicate a shelf near the back door or have a special box to store your grilling supplies. You'll save time trying to hunt these items down, giving you more time to relax.

- While cooking at night, is it difficult to see when checking the doneness of your food? Try a grill light! It attaches to your grill and assures that you'll be able to tell when to make the most important grilling decision: placing the food on the serving plate.
- It's happened to everyone. You've gone beyond a point of no return when cooking on the grill and then rain clouds approach. What should one do? Get a grill umbrella and end those worries. They are attached directly to the grill to ensure your food is soggy ONLY from the sauce or marinade you've used on it.
- One of the best ways to increase the chances that your grill has a long life ahead of it is to use a grill cover. This will protect it from the elements and reduce the chances of exterior corrosion. Remember to always let the grill cool down before replacing the cover to minimize the chances of fire or damage to the cover.
- If your grill doesn't already have one built-in, a handy way to discover the inside temperature of a grill is to obtain a grill thermometer. The dial remains outside the casing of the grill, while the element is placed inside.
- There are various shelves and holders that allow you to safely place cooking supplies and tools within easy reach while keeping them out of your way. There are too many to mention here, so find the one(s) that suit you the best, dedicate a shelf near the back door, or have a special box to store your grilling supplies. There's nothing like a clutter-free cooking area.

THE 3 WORST THINGS TO DO...
WITH YOUR GRILL COVER

1 FORGET TO USE IT.

2 LET YOUR KIDS USE IT AS A TENT.

3 PLACE IT BACK ON THE GRILL WHILE THE GRILL IS STILL WARM.

THINGS YOU'LL NEED IN YOUR KITCHEN

There are some items I mention frequently that you'll need to have on hand to create the recipes in this book. I'll name a few, even though you'll probably already have most of them.

- A selection of glass bowls or casserole dishes of different sizes. These will be used mainly for marinades.
- Measuring cups and spoons—use these to measure the recipe ingredients precisely until you hone your "psychic cooking" abilities.
- Glass jars with lids to store any uncontaminated leftover marinades and sauces in the refrigerator.
- Large, heavy zip-closure plastic bags for marinating cuts of meat you'll need to turn often. These are handy because they allow you to "squeeze" the marinade around the food.

When you use a lot of glassware and utensils, the cleanup can seem to be an overwhelming task. It won't be if you prepare ahead of time and keep the *Lazy About* spirit. Chapter 5 will give you many tips on how simple "Minimizing the Mess" can be for you.

EASY TIPS ON EQUIPMENT SAFETY

Grilling is, and always should be, fun. However, there are some safety concerns you need to remember. If you keep the following things in mind, you can assure that your cookout will not only be enjoyable, but safe, too. Try to keep all long-remembered family memories of your cookouts happy ones.

- Don't place your grill underneath a tree in your yard. During the dry season this could be a fire in the making.
- Remember that you're using open flames to cook your food. Any time there are open flames, there's always a possibility of something going wrong. ALWAYS have a fire extinguisher handy when cooking on a grill. Keep your extinguisher a few feet away from the grill so you can get to it while avoiding any flames. And, as a backup, consider also getting the fifty-cent fire extinguisher I describe in Chapter 4.
- Always place your grill on a level surface. You don't want it tipping over or rolling away while you're cooking.
- Allow for some wind protection around your grill. High, wind-blown flames can either melt or set objects on fire around the grill.
- Keep extra bottles of fuel stored in a safe place. Always make sure the gas nozzle (the valve handle on top of the propane canister or the natural gas connection) is turned off when your grill is not in use.

- Get an old coffee can or something similar and put some sand in it, then get in the habit of throwing extinguished matches into it.
- Teach young children that a grill is not a toy and gets hot during use. You certainly don't want any burned fingers or worse.
- Unless you're using a grill specifically designed for the purpose, never grill indoors for any reason.
- Be sure to read all instuction manuals that come with your grill and its accessories. There may be model-specific safety concerns.

Following these tips and others in your manufacturer's documentation should ensure that you have happy grilling days ahead. Be sure to remember them, and that your friends and family know them, too. Remember to have your fire extinguisher checked yearly to ensure it's properly charged. If not, it may be useless to you when you need it most.

Chapter 3

Get a Grip on Grilling: Some of Us Gotta Have a Map

Many people swear by charcoal, insisting that the flavor it gives meat and poultry is far superior to that achieved when food is grilled over a gas flame. The thinking is that charcoal imparts a smoky flavor that you just can't get from a gas-generated flame.

Surprisingly (to many), taste tests prove that isn't always the case. Many can't discern between flavors when it comes to hamburgers, skinless and boneless poultry cuts, and other fast-grilling foods. Meats that take longer to grill are another story. It makes sense that the longer the food is on the grill, the longer it has to absorb the fiery flavor. However, a charcoal fire may take longer to coax than a gas one; you can decide for yourself whether or not it's time well spent.

To help you with that decision and others, in this chapter I'll provide advice on selecting charcoal and your grilling method (direct, indirect, or packet meals), and offer other steps to help you plan ahead.

I'm here to light a fire under you, so to speak, and get you started. Let's begin!

Gone Fishin'

To simplify the cleanup process, first line the firebox with aluminum foil. Then, once the coals have cooled, you can fold the foil up and over the ashes for easy disposal. Never douse the coals with water, or the extreme heat difference will warp the grill.

DON'T YOU HAVE ANYTHING IN A NICE PASTEL? CHOOSING THE CHARCOAL

Traditional charcoal briquettes are the most popular choice for grilling because their uniform shape and size help to distribute heat evenly during cooking. Others prefer the simplicity of flavored charcoal. Usually similar in size to standard briquettes, flavored briquettes contain ground mesquite or hickory wood added to the traditional material that imparts an authentic wood-smoke flavor to meat, poultry, and fish. Many combine the flavored ones with their regular briquettes for a more subtle smoky flavor.

Charcoal draws moisture, so it's often used to help prevent closets from becoming damp. However, soggy fuel is counterproductive for the grill. To keep "your powder dry," so to speak, when storing charcoal, consider dividing it in plastic buckets with tight-fitting lids.

Lump charcoal, or lump char as it is sometimes known, is actually charred wood which, due to its resulting nonuniform shape, tends to burn less evenly. It also burns hotter than regular briquettes, cools faster, and occasionally sparks. Because this charcoal is more difficult to control, it's best to only use it for fast-grilling items such as burgers. Keep in mind that because of the short time that food spends on the grill, most won't be able to distinguish any difference in its flavor over that prepared above a gas flame. Therefore, lump char is really only practical when you are using a hibachi and a fast flame and short-lived coals are your goals.

Once you've determined the type of charcoal you wish to use, you need to decide how much you actually need. There are several ways you can build your fire.

For direct grilling, you'll want to spread the coals in a single layer barely touching each other, extending two inches beyond where the

LAZY ABOUT GRILLING

food will cook. When it comes to indirect grilling, your coals will either surround a drip pan or be grouped on one side of the grill.

As you've probably surmised by this point, determining in advance the amount of charcoal you'll need is not an exact science. You must factor in the size of your grill, your cooking method, and your grilling time and temperature. Don't let this overwhelm you. Eventually you'll learn the science of your grill and someday get beyond the trial-and-error stages. To further help you with this learning process, be sure to see the information on lighting the fire, determining when the coals are ready, controlling the coals, using wood chips to add smoke flavor, and the other tips discussed in Chapter 4.

When you grill meat or poultry using the direct method, flip it over after it's lost its pink color on top—usually about three-fourths of the suggested grilling time. Then finish it off for a minute or two on the other side.

GRILLING METHODS FOR YOUR OUTDOOR COOKING MADNESS

When I travel, the direct route is usually the shortest distance between two points; the indirect one sometimes includes a few trips around the barn. I plan that itinerary according to the mode of transportation, time elements, and other factors.

So it is when I grill. As you'll discover in this section, sometimes the best path to a succulently grilled entrée is via a direct one; other times you can afford to be more subtle and use an indirect method.

Direct Grilling

The direct method is just what it sounds like—grilling your food directly over the flame or coals. Because it employs a hotter grilling temperature, you'll use this method for cuts of meat and other food-stuffs that cook quickly.

Indirect Grilling

The indirect method is most often used in a covered grill, or with the food grilled under an aluminum foil "tent." And as the name implies, the food does not sit directly over the flame.

If you're using a charcoal grill, employ the appropriate utensil (such as the long-handled tongs mentioned on pg. 17) to arrange medium coals around a drip pan into which you've poured water to a depth of one inch. Insert a meat thermometer (see pg.18) into the meat and place it fat side up over the drip pan. Lower the grill hood and cook for the suggested time, or until the meat thermometer registers the desired temperature.

On a gas grill, you'll keep the flame on one half of your grill and place your food on the other half. Depending on whether or not it's practical to rearrange the "lava rocks" on your gas grill or if it can accommodate a drip pan under the grill rack, you'll either follow the instructions similar to those given for the charcoal grill or simply place a pan of water on the rack over the flame. The latter is the method you'd use on an electric grill, too.

Special Effects

Unless you're using a smoker box as described in Chapter 2, the smoking method involves soaking wood chips for an hour and placing them directly on the hot coals. Most often, for this use of wood chips to be practical, you'll use the indirect grilling method. Plan on adding additional wood chips every 15 minutes throughout the grilling time. See Chapter 4 for some tips on prolonging the life of your wood chips.

Spit roasting is achieved with the use of a rotisserie and is probably the oldest open-flame roasting method. The cavemen probably used it to prepare a succulent leg of mammoth. Read your grill instructions. Some grills allow for a rotisserie attachment. (While some grills are designed to allow for even roasting, a rotisserie allows for even distribution of the meat juices throughout the cooking process.)

Grilling Terminology

Open grill is usually associated with backyard brick barbecues, hibachis, and inexpensive charcoal grills. However, for quick-grilling foods such as hamburgers, hot dogs, and thinner cuts of steak, you can achieve this grilling method by leaving the lid open. Simple enough.

Covered grill, as the name implies, is used for foods that take a longer grilling time, regardless of whether you're using the direct or indirect grilling method.

GRILLING CHARTS: HELPING YOU MAP YOUR METHODS

Once you've determined the best method to use for grilling your entrée, you can estimate the grilling time that's required by consulting the appropriate chart in this chapter. (See Chapter 13 for the recommended grilling times for vegetables.) These suggested grilling times are not chiseled in stone and are bound to vary with all the grilling quirks you must keep in mind. Weather conditions can influence cooking times, as lifting your grill lid on a cold and windy day will lower the temperature more than lifting the lid on a humid day.

> Don't give bacteria a chance to party on your steaks before you grill 'em. Wait until the last possible moment to remove them from the refrigerator. Sure, they grill faster if they're at room temperature. (But which room, which season?) As long as they're not frozen solid, you'll be fine.

Create a drip pan from an 18-inch-wide piece of heavy-duty aluminum foil. Tear off a length of foil about 6 inches long plus twice the length of the food the drip pan will sit under. Fold in half lengthwise. Fold all four sides in about 2 inches from the edge, flatten the folds, pull up the edges, and crimp together the corners to form the pan. The pan will resemble a fitted box lid when you're done.

Direct Grilling: Meat

Cut	Thickness (inches)	Grill Temperature	Doneness	Time (Minutes)
Beef				
Flank steak	¾	Medium	Medium	12 to 14
Steak	1	Medium	Rare	14 to 16
Chuck	1	Medium	Medium	18 to 20
Blade	1	Medium	Well-done	22 to 24
Top round	1	Medium	Rare	19 to 26
	1½	Medium	Medium	27 to 32
	1½	Medium	Well-done	33 to 38
Strip steak	1	Medium-hot	Rare	8 to 12
Top loin	1	Medium-hot	Medium	12 to 15
Tenderloin	1	Medium-hot	Well-done	16 to 20
T-Bone	1½	Medium-hot	Rare	14 to 18
Porterhouse	1½	Medium-hot	Medium	18 to 22
Sirloin, Rib, Rib eye	1½	Medium-hot	Well-done	24 to 28

Note: Flank steak, sometimes referred to as London broil, is a leaner cut of meat. But because it has less fat, it can also be somewhat tough unless you marinate it first.

Direct Grilling: Meat

Cut	Thickness (Inches)	Grill Temperature	Doneness	Time (Minutes)
Veal				
Chop	¾	Medium-hot	Well-done	10 to 12
Lamb				
Chop	1	Medium	Rare	10 to 14
	1	Medium	Medium	14 to 16
	1	Medium	Well-done	16 to 20
Pork				
Blade steak	½	Medium-hot	Well-done	10 to 12
Canadian-style bacon	¼	Medium-hot	Heated	3 to 5
Chop	¾	Medium-hot	Well-done	12 to 14
	1½	Medium	Well-done	35 to 45
Ham slice	1	Medium-hot	Heated	20 to 25
Miscellaneous				
Bratwurst		Medium-hot	Well-done	12 to 14
Hot dog		Medium-hot	Heated	3 to 5
Ground meat patties	¼ pound	Medium	Well-done	15 to 18

Indirect grilling, sometimes called the indirect method, is used for larger cuts of meats that require a longer cooking time. If you use a gas grill, preheat it until it reaches a temperature of 500°F to 550°F. For charcoal, count on a half hour of pregrilling prep time: You want your coals to be ash gray.

Note: Once the food is on the rack and the lid is shut, leave it closed until the food has been on the grill for at least the minimum amount of time given on the chart. Otherwise, each sneak peek can add an additional 15 minutes of cooking time.

Indirect Grilling: Meat

Cut	Weight (Pounds)	Doneness	Time (Hours)
Beef			
Rolled rump roast	4 to 6	150° to 170°	1¼ to 2½
Boneless sirloin roast	4 to 6	140° rare	1¾ to 2¼
		160° medium	2¼ to 2¾
		170° well-done	2½ to 3
Eye of the round roast	2 to 3	140° rare	1 to 1½
		160° medium	1½ to 2
		170° well-done	2 to 2¼
Rib eye roast	4 to 6	140° rare	1 to 1½
		160° medium	1½ to 2
		170° well-done	2 to 2¼
Rib roast	4 to 6	140° rare	2¼ to 2¾
		160° medium	2¾ to 3¼
		170° well-done	3¼ to 3¾
Tenderloin roast			
Half	2 to 3	140° rare	¾ to 1
Whole	4 to 6	140° rare	1¼ to 1½
Top round roast	4 to 6	140° to 170°	1 to 2

Indirect Grilling: Meat

Cut	Weight (Pounds)	Doneness	Time (Hours)
Veal			
Boneless rolled			
(breast or shoulder) roast	2 to 3	170° well-done	1¾ to 2
	3 to 5	170° well-done	2¼ to 2¾
Loin roast	3 to 5	170° well-done	2¼ to 2¾
Rib roast	3 to 5	170° well-done	2¼ to 2¾
Lamb			
Boneless leg roast	4 to 7	160° medium	2¼ to 2¾
Boneless rolled shoulder roast	2 to 3	160° medium	1¾ to 2¼
Rib crown roast	3 to 4	140° rare	¾ to 1
		160° medium	¾ to 1
		170° well-done	1 to 1¼
Whole leg roast	5 to 7	140° rare	1¾ to 2¼
		160° medium	2¼ to 2½
		170° well-done	2½ to 3
Pork			
Boneless top loin roast:			
Single loin	2 to 4	170° well-done	1½ to 2¼
Double loin, tied	3 to 5	170° well-done	1¾ to 3
Ribs, spareribs	2 to 4	Well-done	1 to 2
Loin blade or sirloin roast	3 to 4	170° well-done	1½ to 3
Rib crown roast	4 to 6	170° well-done	1¾ to 3
Tenderloin	¾ to 1	170° well-done	½ to ¾
Ham (fully cooked):			
Boneless, half	4 to 6	140° heated	1¼ to 2½
Boneless, portion	3 to 4	140° heated	1¼ to 2¼
Smoked picnic	5 to 8	140° heated	2 to 3

You'll ensure more even cooking if you truss your bird. Just wrap some presoaked kite string (so it doesn't get too hot and ignite) around the legs and body. Pretty doesn't matter, since you'll discard the string once the poultry comes off the grill.

As you'll discover when you see the number of such recipes throughout this book, chicken is one of my favorites for the grill. It's inexpensive, low in fat—if you follow my suggestions when you grill it—and it's delicious, too.

It's best to thaw chicken overnight in the refrigerator. When that isn't practical, either use a low setting (50 percent) according to the manufacturer's time recommendations (a setting too high will partially cook the meat and make it tough—ugh!) or run cold water over it in the sink.

Direct Grilling: Poultry

NOTE: White meat grills slightly faster than does dark meat.

Type of Poultry	Weight	Grill	Time (Minutes)
Broiler or fryer halves	1½ pounds	Medium	40 to 50
Chicken breasts, boneless, skinless	4 to 5 ounces	Medium	15 to 18
Chicken thighs, boneless, skinless	2 to 3 ounces	Medium	8 to 12
Cornish game hens, halves	¾ pound	Medium-hot	45 to 50
Turkey breast tenderloin steaks	4 to 6 ounces	Medium	12 to 15
Ground turkey or chicken, patties	¼ pound	Medium-hot	15 to 18

Indirect Grilling: Poultry

Type of Poultry	Weight	Time (Hours)
Chicken, whole broiler or fryer	2½ to 3 pounds	¾ to 1
	3½ to 4 pounds	1½ to 1¾
	4½ to 5 pounds	1¾ to 2
Chicken, whole roasting	5 to 6 pounds	1¾ to 2½
Cornish game hens	1 to 1½ pounds	¾ to 1
Pheasant	2 to 3 pounds	1 to 1½
Quail	4 to 6 ounces	about ½
Squab	12 to 14 ounces	¾ to 1
Turkey (Unstuffed)	6 to 8 pounds	1¾ to 2¼
	8 to 12 pounds	2½ to 3½
	12 to 16 pounds	3 to 4
Turkey, boneless whole	4 to 6 pounds	2¾ to 3½
Turkey breast, whole	4 to 6 pounds	1¾ to 2¼
	6 to 8 pounds	2¼ to 3½

THE 3 WORST THINGS TO DO...
WHEN DECIDING GRILLING TIMES

1 THINK THAT THE SUGGESTED GRILLING TIME ON THESE CHARTS ARE CHISELED IN STONE. THEY'RE CALLED "SUGGESTED" FOR A REASON.

2 FAIL TO REALIZE THAT IN ADDITION TO TAKING YOUR GRILL QUIRKS INTO CONSIDERATION, WEATHER CONDITIONS CAN ALSO BE A FACTOR IN DETERMINING THE AMOUNT OF COOKING TIME REQUIRED. LIFT THE GRILL LID ON A COLD, WINDY DAY AND YOU'LL LOWER THE TEMPERATURE MORE THAN YOU WOULD ON A HOT, HUMID ONE.

3 FORGET THAT IT OFTEN TAKES LONGER TO DESCRIBE THE PROCESS THAN IT TAKES TO DO IT. THE WRONGEST WRONG WAY IS TO NOT TRY GRILLING IN THE FIRST PLACE.

A Tisket, a Packet, a Special Foil-Made Basket

Throughout this book, you'll often see me refer to packet grilling. I include a special section on that method in Chapter 17, but it's also used in the preparation of many side dishes, such as those I tell you about in the vegetable chapter, Chapter 13. Regardless of the packet-making instructions given with the recipe, any method that serves the function of sealing up the food so it will cook and steam will work. The three most common packet styles are as follows:

WANT LOTS OF TIME TO LOUNGE IN THE HAMMOCK? USE PACKETS WHENEVER POSSIBLE. YOU KEEP YOUR GRILL CLEANER. YOU ELIMINATE DISHES, TOO, SINCE ONCE YOU REMOVE THE FOOD FROM THE FOIL, THE "PAN" GOES RIGHT INTO THE TRASH.

Rectangle Wrap: Place your food in an oblong piece of heavy-duty aluminum foil that's long enough for you to fold it at the top and sides. Bring the sides up and over the top of the food and fold it down, using a series of locked or crimped folds. Fold the short ends to finish sealing the packet.

Bundle Wrap: Place the food in the center of a piece of aluminum foil large enough to allow you to bring all four corners up and over the food. Twist the corners together to form what is also sometimes referred to as a "puff packet," and then fold the foil over at the twist to seal the top. This method will allow you to sometimes use a smaller piece of foil, but you must take special care to make certain it seals completely; you may need to crimp along the foil edges leading to twisted top to ensure a good seal.

Covered aluminum pie plate: This method works best for food you don't need to turn over during the grilling process. Place the food in an aluminum pie pan and, using a piece of aluminum foil, create a lid by placing the foil over the top of the pan and crimping it to the edges of the plate.

PLAN AHEAD

By now, you should appreciate that being *Lazy About Grilling* is truly the efficient way. In the same manner that a few minutes spent honing your to-do list and choosing your wardrobe the night before can save you countless time the next day, some advance planning eases your work around the grill, too. To help you do just that, see the next chapter for advice and shortcuts. You'll be well on your way to earning that Ph.G.—Doctor of Grillosophy—by the time you do.

LAZY ABOUT GRILLING

Chapter 4

Sanity-Saving Shortcuts and Tried 'n' True Tips

You've heard the phrase, "Plan your work, then work your plan." It certainly applies to grilling. Spend a little time to learn some planning tips and shortcuts. With a little bit of effort these practices will become habits, and soon you'll be grilling quickly and efficiently.

In this chapter, the valuable preplanning information includes how to build and maintain a proper fire, smoking hints, wood choice recommendations, grilling temperatures, and safety matters.

Gone Fishin'

If the bees are buzzing around your picnic table, give everyone a glass for their beverage instead of drinking from a can. The extra dishes or disposable cups are worth it if you help your guests avoid swallowing (or getting stung by) an insect.

The "Don't Panic" Planning Stage

Until you can intuit your next menu based on your knowledge of what lurks at the back of your refrigerator, these suggestions may help.

- Take baby steps at first. Don't feel obligated to use all new recipes for an entire meal. Pick one new one and serve tried-and-true family favorites to accompany it.

- Consider the food you have on hand when selecting a recipe to try. The task seems less daunting when you don't have to worry about stretching the grocery budget, too.

- When you have leftovers in the refrigerator, consider how they can be adapted for another meal. Some suggestions for how to do that are provided later on in this chapter.

- When you need to plan an entire meal, first select your main course. Once you've decided on that, it's much easier to plan what else you need to go with it.

- Whether you're considering a week's worth of menus or one meal, remember that diversity is important. You create interesting contrasts when you vary colors, flavors, textures, and temperatures.

- Adjust your menu according to the time of year. Serve cold soups (see Chapter 17) in the summer and heartier main dishes in the fall. Plan your vegetable and dessert courses based on the season, too.

- Be realistic about how much time you'll need to fix the meal you want, then plan accordingly. If your first choice is so complex that it requires more time than you can allot, adjust the menu. Food just doesn't taste as good if you lose your sanity in the process of preparing it.

THE QUEST FOR FIRE!

If you're using a gas grill, your task is a simple one. You only need to turn on the fuel supply and punch the automatic starter or, in primitive cases, strike a match. An electric grill is even simpler: Make sure it's plugged in, then turn it to ON.

If you plan to use charcoal, briquettes need a bit of coaxing to get them ready. You can use any of the following five methods to get them going.

Liquid Lighter Fluid: This is the most commonly used fire starter. Arrange the briquettes in a pyramid shape, then pour the fluid over them and let it soak in according to the directions on the label. Carefully ignite with a match.

THE THREE WORST THINGS TO DO... WITH LIGHTER FLUID

1 USE GASOLINE INSTEAD OF LIQUID LIGHTER FLUID INTENDED FOR CHARCOAL. THE IDEA IS TO IGNITE THE CHARCOAL, NOT THE NEIGHBORHOOD.

2 ADD LIQUID LIGHTER FLUID AFTER YOU'VE ALREADY STARTED YOUR FIRE. (SEE NO. 1 ABOVE FOR THE REASON WHY.)

3 FAIL TO ALLOW ENOUGH TIME FOR YOUR COALS TO GET READY. YOU NOT ONLY WANT TO BRING THE COALS TO TEMPERATURE, BUT ALSO YOU WANT TO BURN OFF ANY STARTER FLUID. PLAN ON SETTING THE FLAME TO THE CHARCOAL AT LEAST TWENTY MINUTES TO A HALF HOUR BEFORE YOU INTEND TO PLACE YOUR FOOD ON THE GRILL. (WHEN READY, THE CHARCOAL SHOULD APPEAR ASH GRAY IN DAYLIGHT OR IT SHOULD GLOW RED AT NIGHT.)

Cube Starters: These premeasured, solid starters free you from the guesswork of how much lighter fluid to use. Arrange the briquettes in a pyramid above the cube starter, leaving a corner of the cube exposed. Then carefully ignite the cube.

Quick Lighting Charcoal: This is charcoal that has been pretreated with lighter fluid. You simply arrange the briquettes into a pyramid shape and ignite them.

Chimney Lighter: This is a tall cylinder with a metal grate at the bottom for air circulation. To use, you first remove the grill rack, place the chimney lighter inside, and fill it with briquettes. There's no need to use lighter fluid. Instead, place pieces of crumpled newspaper under the chimney, then place the chimney on the charcoal grate. Use a long match to ignite the newspaper through the holes in the chimney. When the coals are ready, carefully pour them onto the charcoal grate, being certain to use fireproof gloves and the other necessary safety equipment recommended by the fire starter manufacturer.

Electric starter: This is an electrical element that is placed under the coals for a few minutes. Make sure to check the manufacturer's instructions before using. In most cases, you must remove the element within 10 minutes or risk damaging it.

NOW YOU'RE SMOKIN'

Just because you're using a grill doesn't mean you can't enhance the smoked flavor. (For full-force smoker suggestions, see the internal grill accessories section in Chapter 2.)

Even without a grill designed specifically to be used as a smoker or without a smoker accessory, you can still enjoy true wood-smoked flavor. To adapt your grill so that you can enjoy the smoky goodness heretofore only experienced by those who are willing to spend the entire day slaving over a barbecue pit, follow these steps:

1. Soak your choice of wood chips in water for 30 minutes to an hour.

2. Follow the indirect grilling directions for positioning your coals for your type of grill in Chapter 3, and place the wood chips on coals.

3. Place food on the cooking grate according to the instructions for your grill. On a charcoal grill, you'll want to close the vents most of the way. Regardless of your grill type, cook with the cover down and try not to lift it more often than necessary. To take full advantage of using the wood chips, it's best to grill over a lower temperature and to increase your grilling time.

4. Add additional wood chips every 15 minutes.

CONSERVE WOOD AND STILL ACHIEVE THAT DELICIOUS SMOKY FLAVOR. AFTER YOU SOAK YOUR WOOD PIECES IN WATER, WRAP EACH ONE IN A PIECE OF FOIL. USE A PIN TO PRICK HOLES AROUND THE FOIL-WRAPPED WOOD AND PLACE ON THE COALS ACCORDING TO THE SPECIFICATIONS FOR YOUR GRILL. THE WOOD WILL NOW LAST UP TO FOUR TIMES LONGER, OR UP TO AN HOUR.

Use this wood...	If you're cooking...
Alder	Seafood, vegetables; used in the Pacific Northwest for smoking salmon
Apple	Pork, beef, sausages
Cherry	Hamburger, turkey, chicken, lamb
Corncob	Chicken, turkey (combined with apple or cherry to impart a robust flavor)
Hickory	Beef, chicken, pork, ribs, sausage
Oak	Sausage (mixed with apple)
Maple	Cheese, ham, vegetables
Mesquite	Steak and other beef, lamb, chicken, turkey, other poultry
Peach	Salmon and other fish, beef, poultry
Pecan	Beef, chicken, game, lamb, sausage

JUST WHICH WOOD WOULD A WOOD SMOKE CHOOSE IF A WOOD SMOKE COULD CHOOSE WOOD?

The type of wood you choose to enhance the flavor is just as important as the decision to add smoke in the first place. Each wood type has its own special flavor. You want to select the one that will enhance your entrée's essence, not distract from it. In some cases, mixing woods works. Once you've learned which smoke flavors you prefer, you can experiment to develop your own unique blends. For now, I recommend that you use the following woods with the foods listed in the chart.

If you know a cabinetmaker or furniture craftsman who frequently uses your preferred choice of wood, such as cherry, ask him to save the sawdust for you. In addition to periodically tossing some sawdust directly on the coals, you can also soak some in water, form it into small blocks in a manner similar to making a mud pie, wrap that in foil, prick some holes in the foil, and then place the sawdust-filled foil packet on the coals. (Just make sure the sawdust isn't mixed with other "trash" from the shop floor, especially shavings from treated woods or particle board, for example.)

Many grill chefs like to add water-soaked herb sprigs such as rosemary, thyme, oregano, and basil directly to the hot coals. Also try using dried herb packets (they resemble tea bags), custom-blended to enhance the flavor of meats, poultry, or seafood and available commercially. You can use tea, too (see Chapter 11 for instructions on how to use Earl Grey tea in a special spicy tea-smoke blend).

To add smoked flavors to the food you grill, don't limit yourself to just wood. You can also soak herbs and use them to create smoke packets like the ones described for the sawdust.

HOT ENOUGH FOR YOU?

As I've stated, grilling is not an exact science. Still, you need to have an idea of your grill temperature in order to gauge how long to cook foods so that they will be the best that they can be.

WINE AND BEER AREN'T JUST FOR MARINADES, YOU KNOW. (NO, I'M NOT TALKING ABOUT DRINKING THEM. HOW PRIMITIVE!) USE ONE OR THE OTHER INSTEAD OF WATER TO SOAK YOUR WOOD CHIPS OR HERBS.

Some newer grills come with built-in temperature gauges. Otherwise, one way to judge the heat intensity of the coals is to carefully hold your hand, palm side down, about six inches above and over the area where you will grill the food. Start counting in a "one-one-thousand…" manner. When your hand feels too hot, withdraw it. The number of seconds you were able to hold your hand over the grilling area gives you a reasonably accurate idea about the coal temperature.

For example, direct cooking temperatures determined by this method would be:

Number of Seconds	Coal Temperature
2	High
3	Medium-high
4	Medium
5	Medium-low
6	Low

For the indirect cooking method described in Chapter 3, the coals must be one level hotter to obtain the correct temperature over the drip pan. In other words, you'll need coals that register as having high heat to get medium-high heat over the pan.

SHOWING YOUR COALS WHO'S BOSS!

If you need to control your coals to tone down the heat of your grill, try these cooling methods:

ᗷ Raise your grill rack.

ᗷ Cover or close the grill lid to prevent "breezes" from fueling the fire if it's a windy day.

ᗷ Space the hot coals farther apart using long-handled tongs.

ᗷ Close the air vents halfway to restrict airflow to the coals.

ᗷ On a gas or an electric grill, adjust the temperature setting.

If the coals aren't hot enough, try these techniques:

ᗷ Gently shake the grill or tap the coals with long-handled tongs to rid them of excess ash.

ᗷ Lower the grill rack.

- ⌣ Cover or close the lid to the grill (to save heat on a chilly day).
- ⌣ Nudge the coals closer together using long-handled tongs.
- ⌣ Add two or three briquettes to the hot coals.
- ⌣ Open the air vents so more air circulates.
- ⌣ On a gas or an electric grill, adjust the temperature setting.

MEATY MATTERS

A primary goal when preparing meat is to cook it to the correct temperature to ensure you destroy any potentially harmful bacteria. Proper cooking has the additional benefit that the meat is moist with better flavor. Keep the following in mind.

Flare-ups on the grill often occur when fat drips onto the coals. To prevent flare-ups before they start, select leaner cuts of meat or trim as much fat from the meat as possible.

Chicken is done when meat next to the bone is no longer pink. This will usually take 35–45 minutes if you're grilling chicken pieces; boneless, skinless chicken takes much less time to grill. Refer to the grilling charts in Chapter 3 to gauge the grilling time for whole chickens and other poultry.

Lean beef remains juiciest if you first sear the meat and then lower the heat and only grill it until it's medium, which will show as pink in the center and gray around the edges when you cut into the steak.

Pork can be tricky. It's okay to leave pork a little pink in the center. If you overcook pork, it gets tough and has less flavor.

Fish are thirsty. If you're preparing it on an open grill (instead of inside of a packet), baste fish every few minutes with reserved marinade to keep it moist. Allow four to six minutes grilling time for each ½-inch thickness. If fish is thicker than one inch, turn it once during cooking; otherwise, thinner pieces of less than an inch do not need to be turned.

Knowing in advance how meats and seafood are supposed to be cooked takes the guesswork out of grilling. With that knowledge, you can concentrate on preparing delicious meals, confident they'll be safe, healthy ones, too.

WHEN YOU HAVEN'T GOT ALL DAY

Employing a few shortcuts not only speeds up the grilling process, it lets you deposit the time saved back into your day's account to use for other tasks. Pacing yourself is good advice. Here are some ways to do just that.

Defrost meat in the microwave, if necessary, before you grill. Otherwise, the outside of frozen meat will char while the interior remains too cold to destroy bacteria. Just don't rush the defrosting process. Follow the instructions given for your microwave. Otherwise, if you use a temperature that's too high for too long, you run the risk of partially cooking the meat and making it tough. Because of the weird way that microwaves are more attracted to ice than they are to water, when you're in a hurry, it's often better to begin the process in the microwave and then finish defrosting the food by wrapping it and submerging it under cold water.

Precook foods such as poultry or ribs in the microwave or boil them the night before. Store them in the refrigerator until you are ready to grill, then use the grill briefly for that special "outdoors" flavor. You can also precook vegetables. For example, boil ears of corn in water with some sugar added (¼ cup for every 12 ears of corn) and then refrigerate the corn overnight. The next day, grill it until it's warm—a minute each side, or until your entrée is heated, too.

Marinades do the work for you. When preparing your marinade, don't panic if you're out of the type of sweetener called for in the recipe. Try substituting molasses, maple syrup, or honey.

Speaking of altering your "sugar" choices, let's take a look at my first recipe to give you an idea of what I mean.

Maple Teriyaki Chicken Quarters Backing

The amount of sugar you use in this marinade will depend on whether you use dry or sweet wine, or simply use mirin (a Japanese sweetened white wine) and omit the sugar. I named this one after my favorite way to prepare it for chicken. The maple imparts a subtle sweetness and distinct flavor change. Molasses instead of the maple syrup, on the other hand, makes this marinade more robust and adds gusto. Experiment and try it with a tablespoon of honey or brown sugar instead. The marinade will be a little sweeter if you use Bragg's Liquid Aminos instead of soy sauce. Be creative! There's no right or wrong way to create the sweet way.

Makes 8 servings

½ to 1 teaspoon sugar
2 tablespoons white wine
2 tablespoons soy sauce
1 tablespoon toasted sesame oil
1 tablespoon lemon juice
1 clove garlic
2 scallions
1 tablespoon maple syrup
Optional: 4 teaspoons sesame seeds

1 In a glass bowl, dissolve sugar into the wine. (Heat for a few seconds in the microwave if necessary.) Stir in the soy sauce, sesame oil, and lemon juice and mix well.

2 Add the crushed garlic, finely chopped scallions, and maple syrup or your choice of sweetener and stir again. Add sesame seeds if you choose.

3 This recipe makes enough for 8 boneless, skinless chicken thighs, or enough for 8 people if you serve each thigh over a generous portion of seasoned, fried rice. Otherwise, allow 2 thighs per person.

Substitute ¼ teaspoon each of roasted onion and sautéed garlic bases from Minor's for the crushed garlic and scallions. I've also used chicken base to create a sweetened broth instead of the wine. (see Sources for information on bases from Minor's and Redi-Base).

Now that you've decided what to cook, you need to determine how much to cook. I'll discuss alternative portion sizes in "Chapter 18: Healthier Food Fundamentals: Heart-Healthy Considerations." For hearty appetites, consult this table for help:

If you're grilling...	Allow...
Boneless cuts of meat	4 to 6 ounces per serving
Bone-in cuts of meat	6 to 8 ounces per serving
Vegetables	¾ cup (4 to 5 ounces) per serving

INFUSE AN OIL YOU CAN'T REFUSE

Instead of getting stuck in that same ol', same ol' butter-and-jelly rut for the dinner rolls, impress your friends by providing small bowls of honey or herb butters or containers of infused oil. Think of an infused oil as one in which something has been marinated to impart flavor. Infusing is the process. A resulting subtle, yet distinct, new flavor is the benefit.

To give you an idea of the possibilities, here is just one variety of infused oil. I use fresh herbs in this one; you'll notice throughout this book, that unless it states "fresh" in the recipe, I give the amounts for dried herbs—usually a third of what you'd use of the fresh. This one also makes an excellent basting sauce for grilled fish.

Makes 2 cups

2 cups olive oil
1 tablespoon lemon juice
Peel from ¼ of 1 lemon
3 cloves garlic
½ cup fresh basil
¼ cup fresh parsley

1 In a glass bowl or jar, combine the olive oil and lemon juice.

2 Grate the lemon peel and crush the garlic cloves. Chop the basil and parsley. Add to bowl.

3 Allow the mixture to stand at room temperature for 2 hours.

4 If you plan to store leftover oil, strain it through cheesecloth. The oil will keep for several days in the refrigerator. Place it on the table in a bottle or in dipping bowls. If used as a basting sauce, brush the fish with the oil when grilling.

Use the bases and concentrates in the Sources to create a wide variety of infused oils. In most cases, simply add ¼ teaspoon of base concentrate (such as ancho pepper) to ⅓ cup olive oil, 1 tablespoon of fresh lemon juice, and, if you want to stretch the infused oil to use it as a basting sauce, 1 tablespoon of water. For a dipping sauce, omit the water. Experiment until you get the taste you want. For a stronger infused oil, start with less oil. Continue to add oil until you arrive at the desired flavor.

SENSIBLE SUBSTITUTES

Once you learn to improvise (and go with the flow), you'll no longer panic when you discover you don't have a desired ingredient on hand. For example: Out of sour cream? Don't panic! Instead, you can mix together one of these substitutes:

- Blend 1 cup of cottage cheese with ⅓ cup of buttermilk or milk and 1 tablespoon lemon juice
- Blend equal parts cottage cheese and plain yogurt
- Blend 1 cup of cottage cheese with 2 tablespoons of lemon juice, 2 tablespoons of mayonnaise, and ¼ cup of buttermilk

SECOND TIME AROUND REBOUND

Serving leftovers in one of these ways will make your family think you intentionally cooked extra the night before, if they even notice they're getting reruns.

- Serve thinly-sliced chicken breast, pork, or other meat atop a bowl of Oriental noodles, sprinkled with chopped cilantro and green onion, and a dash or two of toasted sesame oil.
- Cut extra corn off of the cob and add it to salsa.
- Add grilled shrimp to almost any main dish salad.
- Thinly slice leftover grilled pork or beef and layer it on toasted French rolls along with roasted peppers and sautéed onion.
- Mix leftover meatloaf with some vegetables and cheese, roll everything up in a tortilla, and toast on the grill.

Suspect Grilling: Good Chop/Bad Chop

Last, but by no means least, in your quest to serve your friends and family (and yourself!) delicious meals, rest assured that you can do so and still make healthy food. Here are some recommendations to follow before you grill and while you are grilling.

Before You Step Up to the Grill

☾ If you use a bowl or pan to marinate foods instead of a plastic bag, be sure it's made of a noncorrosive material (glass, ceramic with a lead-free glaze, or stainless steel) that won't be affected by the acid in the marinade.

☾ To avoid contamination, never let the marinade in which you've soaked raw meat, fish, or poultry (or the dish it's been in) come in contact with cooked food you'll be eating. In other words, if you use a dish to carry raw meat to the grill, wash it before you use it as your serving platter. Also, play it safe and either discard the marinade after using it, or, if you do intend to use some as a sauce at the table, reserve some before marinating the meat. If you forget and all of the marinade has been contaminated, boil it to destroy the bacteria introduced by the raw meat.

☾ If a recipe calls for basting with marinade, in most cases don't baste during the last 10 minutes of grilling; that allows enough time for the marinade to cook through.

☾ Don't marinate meat, poultry, or seafood longer than 30 minutes at room temperature. If the recipe calls for longer marinating, place in the refrigerator.

☾ Remember: the more acidic the marinade—the greater the percentage of vinegar, lemon juice, or yogurt—the less time needed to marinate. Leaving meat or seafood in a highly acidic marinade for too long can alter the texture of the food and leave it unpleasantly mushy.

⌣ Marinades only penetrate about ½ inch (from all sides), so don't expect really thick cuts of meat to pick up flavor in the center unless you take additional preparation steps, such as using an injector (discussed in Chapter 20).

⌣ Unless you plan to slow-roast them on the grill, precook ribs, thick cuts of meat, and whole turkeys indoors before grilling. Then only sear them briefly over high heat, just long enough to caramelize the outside.

⌣ To prevent food poisoning, keep foods chilled until you're ready to grill or serve them.

THE 3 WORST THINGS TO DO...
BEFORE YOU GRILL MEAT

1 THAWING MEAT IN THE MICROWAVE ON HIGH. FOLLOW THE THAWING INSTRUCTIONS IN YOUR MICROWAVE OWNER'S MANUAL TO ENSURE THE BEST SETTING FOR YOUR APPLIANCE.

2 CONSIDER IT CHEATING TO USE THE MICROWAVE WHEN YOU'RE IN A HURRY.

3 SPEND SO MUCH TIME FRETTING ABOUT GETTING YOUR MEAL TO COME OUT PERFECTLY THAT GRILLING BECOMES A CHORE AND IS NO LONGER FUN.

At the Grill

Only use extremely high temperatures to sear the food. Charring meat can produce chemical substances that have been shown to cause cancer in some animal studies. And when meat is browned with intense heat over a direct flame and fat drips on the fire and coals, it creates smoke-containing carcinogens called polycyclic aromatic hydrocarbons. Following these suggestions will keep the grill from flaring up.

THE 3 WORST THINGS TO DO...
WHEN GRILLING MEAT

1 COOK QUICKLY AT A VERY HIGH HEAT.

2 LET TOO MUCH FAT DRIP ONTO THE COALS.

3 CHAR THE MEAT AND KEEP THE HEAT HIGH.

- If meat does char or burn, cut away the blackened portion.
- Raising the adjustable cooking racks to their highest position above the heat will help prevent charring.
- Brush barbecue sauces and glazes that haven't come into contact with raw meat on only during the last several minutes of grilling so they don't splatter and drip down on the flames; otherwise, the sugar in them can cause flare-ups and the wrong kind of smoke. Adding a glaze too early in the grilling process will also cause the

outside of the meat to burn before the meat is done.

- Skimping on fat isn't always a good thing. In order to prevent charring, it's okay to leave fat on the meat to help it absorb the good smoky flavor and tenderize the meat as it melts. (Most of it melts away and is burned off anyhow, so it doesn't end up on your plate or your hips!)

- Keep a squirt gun or bottle close by to put out unwanted grill flare-ups. Even when you take all of the precautions, unwanted flames can still occur.

- Lower the fat content of ground meats by mixing with rice, bread crumbs, crackers, or oatmeal before you shape it into patties. This suggestion also helps you stretch your main course when unexpected guests drop by. (Families and friends are like that!)

- In the event of a hard-to-control flame, invest in a fifty-cent fire extinguisher and keep it near the grill. Fifty-cent fire extinguisher? Yep—a box of baking soda! Be careful not to get any on the food, since it'll raise the sodium content and distort the food's intended flavor. Aside from that, it's the cheapest and best prevention you can have on hand when a cut of meat turns out to be fattier—and flame-ier—than you anticipated.

Before ending this chapter, I want to share what I believe is my most important suggestion: *Enlist family and friends to help. It's my opinion that martyrs don't have as much fun.*

You wear an apron to protect your clothes. Always remember to wear clothes that protect you. The grill area is not the place to wear shirts with long, loose sleeves or a flowing scarf around your neck. Wind and flare-ups are unpredictable. You don't want your clothes (or long hair you forgot to tie back, for that matter) to get caught in the crossfire, so to speak.

Chapter 5

Minimizing the Mess

Where is it written that you have to prepare your sauce, marinade, relish, salsa, or side dish at the exact same time you intend to serve or use it? The "frenzied, try to do everything at once" method certainly isn't the *Lazy About* way of doing things. In fact, the French even have a term for the *Lazy About* way of doing as much as possible ahead of time: *mise en place* (MEEZ ahn plahs)—getting all ingredients and equipment prepared and ready to begin cooking. There are benefits to advance preparation.

One, there's this synergy thing that occurs. After hanging around in the same mixture for a while, the ingredients all decide they're ready to cooperate and work together. I think they wrap their arms around each other's shoulders and maybe even choreograph some *Lazy About* way high kicks when your back is turned. Whatever it is they do, hours later or by the next day when you need 'em, they've melded into a working unit, all the more delicious for having done so.

Two, and best of all, while they're doing their thing, they're also indirectly making your cleanup tasks a bit easier. When it's convenient, any work done ahead of time—inside and close to the sink—means you can clean as you go instead of creating one huge mess to deal with later.

Only you and the circumstances regarding each outdoor cooking event can determine whether it's more efficient to do some of your

If you prepare your vegetables for the grill outside, you can toss those vegetable peelings directly onto your compost heap.

preparation steps inside near your stove and microwave or outside at the grill. Therein lies the first step in determining how to, as this chapter title suggests, minimize the mess.

Inside, as I've already indicated, you can keep dishwater ready for some cleanup details and, of course, the dishwasher is close by for other messes. Outside, it doesn't matter as much if you splatter a bit.

It's now time for you to decide which of the *Lazy About* tips will work best for you. In addition to those I mention throughout the book, I've rounded up some others and placed them here—somewhat grouped together by function, but by no means listed in any order of importance. You don't have to adapt them all at once. Just keep in mind that although you may now dread a new cleanup routine because you have to stop and think about it, it will become a habit before you know it!

As you'll soon discover, making cleanup a breeze doesn't mean you wait for the wind to blow away the debris.

THE 3 WORST THINGS TO DO... TO SAVE CLEANUP TIME

1 FORGET TO MAKE IT EASY FOR EVERYBODY TO RECYCLE. ALWAYS KEEP SEPARATE CONTAINERS FOR ALUMINUM CANS AND TRASH CLOSE BY.

2 FAIL TO USE RECYCLED PAPER PRODUCTS.

3 BECOME OVERWHELMED BY THE BEHAVIOR CHANGES I RECOMMEND.

GROOMING THE GRILL

Let the coals burn down or, for a gas or electric grill, leave the heat on for a few minutes after you finish cooking, then use a grill-grooming tool (a spatula-looking affair with wire rack–sized cutouts) or a wire grill brush to loosen stuck-on food particles.

For those times when the food left behind is stubborn and calls for more desperate measures, you can do one of the following:

IF YOU USE SUGGESTION 2 OR 3 TO CLEAN YOUR RACK, YOU CAN DO SO OUTSIDE. HOSE THE RACK DOWN WHEN YOU'RE DONE, RETURN IT TO THE GRILL, AND LET IT DRIP DRY. YOU DON'T HAVE TO WORRY ABOUT CHILDREN OR PETS COMING INTO CONTACT WITH THIS KIND OF CLEANER RESIDUE.

1. Spray the grill grate with oven cleaner and rinse thoroughly.

2. Wash with hot soapy water and rinse well.

3. Use my preferred method of applying a paste made from baking soda and water. This method takes a bit longer, but you don't have to hover over the rack during the entire process. Apply the paste and go do something else for a while. If you notice that the paste is drying out before you're ready to scrub it a bit with your wire brush, simply moisten it by spritzing on some of that water you keep close by in a spray bottle to control flare-ups. Another option is to keep a damp towel draped over the paste. Once you do scrub the rack, rinse thoroughly.

After you've cleaned your grill rack, remember that you need to "season" it before you use it again. This is best done after you've preheated the grill a bit, but if you do so, use appropriate safety measures to protect your hands and arms.

Brass bristles will scrape grime away without leaving a rusty residue. For porcelain enamel grill racks, use a nonabrasive porcelain cleaning brush.

Before you place food on the grill, rub the grid with vegetable oil or spray with nonstick cooking spray. This helps to prevent food from sticking, which means it'll be a long time before you have to wash and scrub the grid again.

You can line the grill box of your charcoal grill with aluminum foil for easy cleanup; fold the foil up and over the mess and dispose of it and voilà—you're ready to store the grill until its next use.

Packet meals also minimize the mess, because the food you're grilling is tucked away inside aluminum foil. See Chapter 3 for tips on how to prepare a packet; Chapter 17 includes packet meal suggestions.

Another way to minimize the mess inside your grill and save yourself some cleanup time is to use a disposable drip pan to catch juices from the food. This keeps your charcoal grill clean and, when you arrange the coals around the drip pan, it reduces flare-ups, too.

Some grilling accessories (such as grill-safe griddles and woks) and utensils are coated with nonstick material for easy cleanup. Be sure to follow the manufacturer's instructions when using such products. Most nonstick coated pans require that you use plastic utensils.

You'll also save cleanup time if you "season" your grill-safe pans and iron skillets, too. After each cleaning, and before you add your food, preheat the pan over the grill, then lightly rub in some oil or spray on some nonstick cooking spray.

OTHER WAYS TO SAVE TIME

That extra refrigerator you keep in the garage doesn't have to be limited to chilling your beer and soft drinks. Use it to store whatever condiments you plan to use with your grilled meals, too. That way the "fixin's" are always just a few steps away from the picnic table.

Scrape plates directly into the bag-lined trash containers you keep outside. Use appropriately sized buckets and rubber tubs to transport the dirty dishes from the picnic table to the dishwasher or sink. This way everyone in the family can assist during cleanup and you don't have to worry that juices remaining on the plates will drip onto your clean floors.

To clean the transporting containers, have the kids carry them back outside and hose them down. You can let them dry in the sun. Or, place them on their assigned shelf in the garage and forget about them until next time. The world won't end if the humidity goes directly back into the atmosphere instead of getting there via a dish towel–wielding middleman.

Marinate your food inside locking plastic bags. Simply add the marinade ingredients, then the meat, and zip to seal. Squish the bag all around so the marinade covers the meat. Then put the bag on a plate in the fridge and turn it occasionally to redistribute the marinade.

Why not sit in the sun while you clean those vegetables? Put the food in a colander and hose it down over your herb plants; this method washes the veggies and instantly recycles the water into the garden. Carry the colander back to the picnic table, put your feet up, and do your thing.

Create serving presentations that perform the dual duty of looking nice and reducing the amount of cleanup required. Whenever possible, mix salsa or relish in the serving dish. There's one less bowl to wash this way. In a basket or on a tray, nestle filled (and disposable) salsa containers in between multicolored paper napkins. At the end of the meal, just toss the contents of the basket or tray. The napkins serve the added function of catching drips and dribbles as your family or guests dip out their condiments. Sometimes having a few extra utensils to clean is worth it. Prevent anyone from dipping into a condiment for a second helping with the same tortilla chip by placing a spoon inside each dip container. This encourages people to spoon the condiments onto their plates.

And last but not least, that container of pop-up premoistened towelettes isn't just for the baby's diaper bag. Keep one at the picnic table and one next to the grill.

Following these tips and coming up with a few of your own will simplify the cleanup process.

Now that you know how to be *Lazy About* handling the messes, let's start making them! The recipe chapters are next.

Chapter 6

A Shiny New Coating

Many consider grilling to be an art unto itself. Others would disagree and call it a science. I tend to believe the former is more correct. Let's take a look and see if I can prove the point to you.

Artists use brushes; grill chefs do, too. Both dip their brushes into something and apply it to their "canvas." There is no scientific standard as to how a dish should taste. If you like it, then the dish has been created correctly. The same can be said for a painting. If you like what you see, the artist did a good job. See the similarities? No microscopes, beakers, or test tubes involved!

Take this into consideration while looking at this book's recipes. They are here simply to provide you with information on (modestly speaking) masterpieces I've created. You can take that masterpiece and make it your own, depending on your or your family's individual tastes.

This chapter deals with the "paints" you'll be using to create your own works of art. I'll show you various rubs, marinades, and sauces to get you acquainted with some of the ingredients commonly used. Chapters 7 through 16 will have many more for you to look over, but for now I'll give you three or four of each to get started. Try these and modify them if you wish. Remember, there's a da Vinci or Warhol hiding somewhere within you!

See Sources for information on ready-to-use broth bases that can substitute for the oil in a wet rub. They save you some time on those days when you need to closely budget every moment.

RUB-A-DUB-DUB, BUT NOT IN THE TUB

The rub is an easy and quick method of seasoning meat that's destined for the grill. There are two general types of rubs—dry and wet. Dry rubs are simply herb-and-spice mixtures that are spread thickly onto the meat and rubbed into the surface. Wet rubs are the same, except the herbs and spices are bound together with some sort of liquid, usually oil. Let's look at some recipes for use with various types of meat.

Deep-South Barbecue Rub

This is an excellent all-around beef rub. It can be used for pork, but it's much better on beef.

1 tablespoon brown sugar
1 tablespoon sugar
1 tablespoon chili powder
1 tablespoon ground cumin
2 tablespoons paprika
1 tablespoon kosher or sea salt
1 tablespoon freshly ground black pepper
1 teaspoon cayenne pepper

1 Mix all ingredients well.

2 Rub mixture into meat. Place meat in plastic bag and let sit for at least 2 hours.

3 Cook meat until done.

Firehouse Dry Rub

Can you say "hot"? Good. Have plenty of beverages handy while serving any dish using this rub. (And remember that this is a "dry" rub—the lemon juice goes directly on the meat, not in with the spices.)

½ cup lemon juice
5 ounces chili powder
½ tablespoon cayenne pepper
2 tablespoons garlic powder
1 tablespoon cracked black pepper

Place meat on top of a sheet of aluminum foil before you sprinkle on the dry rub. It will keep your counter clean and after you transfer the entrée to the grill, you can simply fold up the foil and throw it away.

1 Coat all surfaces of the meat with lemon juice.

2 Mix all dry ingredients in a glass container. Sprinkle generously over the meat and rub in well, making sure that the entire surface of the meat is covered thoroughly.

3 Leftover rub can be sealed in a glass container and stored in a cool, dry place or in the refrigerator.

Gone Fishin'

Everything But the Kitchen Sink Rub

Here's a rub with lots of ingredients, but trust me, it's well worth every one of them! Try this on beef, pork, and poultry.

While you're at it, go ahead and mix up a double batch of Everything But the Kitchen Sink Rub. You can store dry rub leftovers (that haven't come into contact with the meat) indefinitely in a covered glass jar.

2⅓ tablespoons chili powder
1⅓ tablespoon paprika
½ teaspoon cayenne pepper
2 teaspoons dried oregano
½ teaspoon black pepper
¼ teaspoon thyme
½ teaspoon sugar
¼ teaspoon tarragon
½ teaspoon dry mustard
¼ teaspoon kosher or sea salt
½ teaspoon ground cloves
½ teaspoon celery seed
2 crushed bay leaves
½ teaspoon garlic powder

1 Mix all ingredients well.

2 Sprinkle over meat and rub in well.

Chicken à la Rub

This wet rub is an absolute "must try." It goes so well with chicken, there's no reason to try it with anything else.

1 tablespoon dried minced onion
1 tablespoon onion powder
½ cup onion
¼ cup fresh chives
1 teaspoon coarse or cracked black pepper
¾ teaspoon cayenne pepper
2 teaspoons dried thyme
½ teaspoon kosher or sea salt
1 teaspoon ground allspice
4 tablespoons lime juice
¼ teaspoon ground nutmeg
2 teaspoons hot pepper sauce
¼ teaspoon ground cinnamon
2 teaspoons sugar
Optional: 1 tablespoon oil

1 In a blender or food processor, combine all ingredients. Blend to a thick paste. (For skinless chicken, add the oil to the paste.)

2 Rub the paste thoroughly over the chicken, cover, and refrigerate overnight.

3 Grill the chicken without removing the paste before cooking.

Gooey Garlic Rub

With or without the cayenne pepper, this rub is delicious on pork tenderloin.

5 cloves garlic
1 tablespoon fresh parsley
1 teaspoon cayenne pepper
¼ cup olive oil

1 In a sealable container, crush garlic and mix with parsley and cayenne pepper.

2 Add oil slowly while mixing.

3 Seal and store in refrigerator until ready to use.

Oh So Tangy Mustard Rub

Tangy and delicious describes any dish created with this rub. Try it with a roast or a London broil.

1 bunch fresh parsley
2 cups Dijon mustard
½ cup dried orange or lemon peel
½ cup rosemary leaves
¼ cup black pepper

1 Mince parsley to fill 1 cup.

2 In a sealable container, mix all ingredients.

3 Seal and refrigerate until ready to use.

MARINADES: IT WAS THE BASTE OF THYMES...

Marinades are liquids with seasonings added for flavor. They also usually contain an ingredient that is high in acidic content, which helps to tenderize the meat being marinated. Try some of the recipes below to discover some unique tastes you can create from some simple and not-so-simple ingredients sitting in your cupboard. At the end of this chapter there are some tips and a marinade time guide to help you along the way.

Ginger and Lemon Fish Marinade

This goes so well with fish, I decided to put it in the title! However, you can try it on pork chops, too.

4 tablespoons butter
½ cup lemon juice
2 teaspoons crushed garlic
2 teaspoons ginger paste
2 teaspoons Worcestershire sauce
4 shakes Tabasco sauce—or to taste

1 Melt butter in a small saucepan or in a microwave-safe container. Add remaining ingredients and combine.

2 Pour most of the mixture over fish or pork chops, reserving a portion for basting. Let sit, refrigerated, for 30 minutes.

3 While grilling, baste with sauce when you turn the meat.

YOU CAN EASILY CREATE YOUR OWN GINGER PASTE. BUY ½ POUND OF GINGER ROOT AND WASH THOROUGHLY. CHOP AND PLACE IN A BLENDER WITH A SMALL AMOUNT OF WATER AND COOKING OIL. BLEND UNTIL A PASTE FORMS. IF THE MIXTURE ISN'T SMOOTH, ADD EQUAL AMOUNTS OF WATER AND OIL UNTIL IT REACHES THE CONSISTENCY OF TOOTHPASTE. STORE LEFTOVER PASTE IN AN AIRTIGHT CONTAINER AND REFRIGERATE.

Jamaican Jerk Marinade

Whether you use it on chicken or pork, this marinade will impress everyone sitting around your table.

1 bunch scallions
Fresh gingerroot
1 onion
1 teaspoon salt
4 teaspoons Jamaican pimento or allspice
1 teaspoon nutmeg
1 teaspoon cinnamon
6 habanero chilies
1 teaspoon black pepper
4 garlic cloves
2 tablespoons lime juice
¼ cup olive oil
½ cup red wine vinegar
4 tablespoons soy sauce
4 tablespoons dark rum
2 tablespoons brown sugar
2 tablespoons fresh thyme

Save some time on cleanup by marinating food in a large, zip-closure plastic bag. These bags are great for large cuts of meat, pork chops, whole fish, etc. Remember to turn the bag occasionally to marinate each side evenly.

1 Chop scallions to fill 1 cup.

2 Grate gingerroot to make 2 tablespoons.

3 Liquefy all ingredients in a blender or food processor.

4 Marinate meat according to the guide at the end of this chapter.

All-Purpose Marinade

A marinade that goes well with anything. Got an old leather shoe handy?

2 cloves garlic
1½ cups salad oil
2 tablespoons dry mustard
¾ cup soy sauce
½ cup wine vinegar
¼ cup Worcestershire sauce
2¼ teaspoons salt
1 tablespoon black pepper
1½ teaspoons dried parsley flakes
⅓ cup lemon juice, fresh

1 Crush garlic and combine all ingredients in a glass container. Mix well.

2 Cover and refrigerate until ready to use.

IF YOUR MIXTURE DOESN'T COVER THE MEAT WHILE MARINATING, YOU MAY ADD UP TO 16 OUNCES OF WATER TO THE MARINADE MIXTURE. THIS WILL SAVE YOU TIME BECAUSE YOU WON'T HAVE TO TURN THE MEAT OVER AND YOU CAN WATCH YOUR FAVORITE SOAP OR SURF THE INTERNET.

Quick and Easy Marinade

Here's a fun one. Okay, what I'm going to do is tell you what's in it, but you decide how much, and what types of ingredients you want to add. I'll give you the first two amounts, then the rest is up to you!

16 ounces Italian salad dressing
¼ cup dried onions
2 different types of pepper (black, white, cayenne, other)
Fresh herbs of your choice (rosemary, thyme, cloves, other)

1 In a glass bowl, mix all ingredients well.

2 Pour over the meat and let sit a minimum of one hour, or longer, depending on the meat. (See the chart at the end of this chapter.)

Did you know that the reason so many recipes have you heat the skillet and then add the oil is that this "seasons" the pan and helps prevent food from sticking? Well, now you do!

Honey Dijon Herb Marinade

You must try this on beefsteaks or a small London broil. The mustard and honey give a unique taste to these meats!

1 cup dry white wine
⅛ cup white Worcestershire sauce
1 large clove garlic
1 bay leaf

1 pinch white pepper
⅛ cup honey
¼ cup Dijon mustard
1 teaspoon dried oregano
½ teaspoon dried basil

1 In a glass bowl, mix all ingredients.

2 Place meat in bowl, cover, and refrigerate according to the chart at the end of this chapter.

OH! YOU SAUCY THING!

If you open your refrigerator, you will most likely find an old bottle of barbecue sauce left over from holidays past. Why use the same store-bought sauce over and over? Make your own! It's fresh and tastes so much better. I've collected a few recipes for you to see what you've been missing. There are more recipes in the following chapters.

THE 3 WORST THINGS TO DO...
WITH HOT PEPPERS

1 RUB YOUR EYES WITHOUT WASHING YOUR HANDS THOROUGHLY.

2 POP A HANDFUL INTO YOUR MOUTH JUST FOR A TASTE.

3 FORGET TO WEAR GLOVES WHEN CUTTING THEM UP FOR A RECIPE.

Basic Beef Barbecue Sauce

A basic sauce for use with any beef cut. This is one you'll use often. Play around and change it to your taste if you want.

2 tablespoons olive oil
3 cloves garlic
4 tablespoons minced onion
14 ounces tomato sauce
1 small can tomato paste
1 teaspoon dry mustard
1 tablespoon brown sugar
2 tablespoons vinegar
1 tablespoon Worcestershire sauce
2 teaspoons cayenne pepper
1 teaspoon ground pepper

1 In a saucepan, heat oil. Crush garlic and add to pan with onion. Cook until slightly brown.

2 Stir in all other ingredients.

3 Bring to a boil and reduce heat. Allow to simmer until it becomes thick.

4 Use on ribs or steaks.

Florida Citrus Barbecue Sauce

How about this? The citrus juices make this sauce wonderful! Try this sauce on beef, pork, or poultry for a taste of the Sunshine State's best.

If you wish, substitute bottled citrus juice in this sauce to save yourself some time. Fresh is better, of course, but you don't always have time to spare.

1 tablespoon vegetable oil
1 large onion
1 tablespoon ground red chilies
¼ teaspoon ground red pepper
1 ancho chili
1 cup orange juice, fresh
½ cup lime juice, fresh
2 tablespoons sugar
2 tablespoons lemon juice, fresh
Cilantro
1 teaspoon salt

1 Heat oil in a saucepan. Chop onion and add to pan with ground red chilies and ground red pepper.

2 Seed and finely chop ancho chili and add to saucepan. Stir frequently, until onion is tender, 5 minutes.

3 Dice cilantro to make 1 tablespoon and add along with remaining ingredients.

4 Bring to a boil and reduce heat to low. Simmer uncovered 10 minutes, stirring occasionally.

Southwest-Style Barbecue Sauce

Ready for a different taste (assuming you don't live in Arizona or New Mexico)? The ancho and pasilla chili powders give this sauce a nice "change of pace" taste. This sauce freezes well, too. Make up a double batch and ice some away to have on hand when you need it.

2 tablespoons unsalted butter
½ medium red onion
1 clove garlic
6 plum tomatoes
1 tablespoon ancho chili powder
1 teaspoon pasilla chili powder
¼ cup ketchup
2 tablespoons Dijon mustard
2 tablespoons dark brown sugar
1 tablespoon honey
1 teaspoon cayenne pepper
1 tablespoon Worcestershire sauce

1 In a medium saucepan over medium heat, heat the butter. Dice the onion and garlic and add to pan. Sauté until translucent.

2 Coarsely chop the tomatoes and add to saucepan.

3 Simmer for 15 minutes. Add all other ingredients and simmer for an additional 20 minutes.

4 Purée the mixture in a food processor, pour into a bowl, and allow to cool at room temperature.

5 Use immediately, or cover and refrigerate.

Jamaican Barbecue Sauce

I just can't stay out of the Caribbean, huh? The islands have some of the most wonderful barbecue sauces. Here's another. Don't worry about the rum in this sauce; remember, alcohol burns off while cooking.

½ cup ketchup
3 tablespoons soy sauce
2 tablespoons dark brown sugar
2 tablespoons distilled or white wine vinegar
1 piece fresh ginger
1 clove garlic
2 scallions
1 tablespoon dark rum

1 In a small saucepan, combine the ketchup, soy sauce, brown sugar, and vinegar.

2 Mince ginger to make 1 tablespoon and add. Mince garlic and scallions and add.

3 Bring to a boil. Simmer over low heat until thick, 10 minutes.

4 Stir in the rum during the last 2 minutes.

HELPFUL MARINADE TIPS

Being *Lazy About Grilling* never involves cutting corners when it comes to taste, convenience, or safety. You've probably heard the line: "Support bacteria; it's the only culture some people have." While humor has its place, when you are talking about safe and healthful cooking practices, it is time to be serious. You certainly don't want cross-contaminations of foodstuffs to turn your marinade storage container into some sort of biohazardous petri dish. If you follow my suggestions you can prevent that from happening—and you can create some awesome-tasting dishes, too.

☾ Marinades have a high acidic level. Therefore, always use a noncorrosive dish like a glass, ceramic, or stainless-steel container in which to marinate your meats. NEVER use aluminum!

☾ A marinade should completely cover the meat. If it doesn't, turn the meat approximately every two hours to ensure that it marinates evenly.

☾ Always cover and refrigerate foods while marinating. Leaving marinating food at room temperature could allow the growth of bacteria in the marinade mixture, or on the meat itself.

☾ Beef roasts and other large cuts of meat are best if marinated for up to two days. The extra time allows the flavor to work its way into the center of the meat and to tenderize it in the process.

☾ Scraping the surface of large cuts of meat with a fork will help marinades penetrate the meat more easily.

☾ Thin or tender cuts can marinate according to a balance between the recipe instructions and your tastes, i.e., how much of the flavor you wish to impart to the meat.

☾ You can serve leftover marinade over cooked meats, but be sure

to boil it for 5 minutes before using in this manner. This will kill any bacteria that may have formed in the liquid.

- NEVER baste food, while cooking, with marinade that hasn't been boiled as stated in the item above.

MARINATING TIME GUIDE

When in doubt, get a second opinion. That's why I've put this Marinating Time Guide here for you. Bookmark this page; you'll probably want to refer to it often.

Place in marinade...	Keep in marinade...
Beef – Steaks	2 hours to overnight
Beef – Roasts	Up to 2 days
Fish Fillets	Up to 30 minutes
Fish Steaks	Up to 1 hour
Whole Fish	Up to overnight
Shrimp	Up to 30 minutes
Pork – Chops	2 hours to overnight
Pork – Roasts	Overnight
Poultry – Breasts	1 hour to overnight
Poultry – Whole	Overnight

Chapter 7

A Chicken on the Grill Is Worth Two in the Yard

I know, I know: Everything tastes like chicken! Why strap on the ol' hunting boots and the camouflage gear to drive across town to the exotic meats store for something that "tastes like chicken"? Why not eat the real thing? Besides, it's chicken season year-round everywhere! No license (or ammo) required.

It's up to you as to what kind of chicken you slap on your grill. You can purchase it fresh from the supermarket. Or, if you insist that your entrée first observed a fitness routine of running laps around the barnyard, check out the free-range varieties available at specialty markets or direct from the farmer. (If you only have a generic one on hand, yet still want to feel closer to nature, you could flex the chicken's legs into some stretching exercises before you cut it up.) Your call. I love 'em all!

In this chapter, you'll discover chicken recipes that are simple, tasty, and unforgettable. Ready that spatula or two-pronged fork and let's get on with it.

Oriental Grilled Sesame Chicken

Grilled Sesame Chicken goes well with wild rice and salad and has a certain Asian quality. Another option is to serve it over a ribbon pasta, like fettuccine, covering it with leftover marinade and reserved to avoid cross-contamination. For a change of pace, have a Peking picnic party. Get out those chopsticks and serve Oriental Grilled Sesame Chicken with fried rice, stir-fried vegetable salad, and fortune cookies for dessert.

Makes 4 to 6 servings

2 tablespoons sesame seeds	⅛ teaspoon ground red pepper
1 tablespoon sugar	1 white onion
½ cup soy sauce	2 cloves garlic
¼ cup water	4 chicken quarters or 6
½ cup vegetable or olive oil	chicken breasts
1 teaspoon ground ginger	

1 In large, nonmetallic container, mix together sesame seeds, sugar, soy sauce, water, oil, ginger, and red pepper. Chop onion to make ¼ cup and add.

2 Mince the garlic and add to the above mixture.

3 Add chicken, cover tightly, and refrigerate at least 12 hours, turning occasionally.

4 Remove chicken from marinade and reserve liquid. (Boil the reserved marinade for 5 minutes and use to baste the chicken as you grill.)

5 Grill 4 to 5 inches from medium-hot coals, turning and basting with reserved marinade frequently, for about 15 minutes total.

Hawaiian Grilled Chicken Salad

This is a good all-purpose meal that is relatively quick to create and is diverse enough to impress friends and family alike. No grass skirts required here, so have fun with this one.

Makes 6 servings

2 tablespoons prepared mustard
⅔ cup unsweetened pineapple juice
3 tablespoons soy sauce
2 tablespoons red wine vinegar
1 tablespoon honey
1½ pounds of chicken tenders
1 bunch leaf lettuce
One 14-ounce can pineapple tidbits
3 Anaheim (mild) peppers
1 small onion
½ cup almonds
¼ cup sesame seeds

1 In saucepan, add mustard, then slowly stir in the pineapple juice to prevent lumping.

2 Add soy sauce, vinegar, and honey; place over high heat and bring to a boil.

3 Pour the warm sauce over chicken. Cover and refrigerate at least 1 hour.

4 Remove chicken from marinade. Place marinade in small saucepan and boil 5 minutes.

5 Place chicken on prepared grill about 6 inches from heat.

6 Grill, turning and basting with boiled marinade, about 6 minutes or until fork can be inserted in chicken with ease.

YOU CAN ADD A LITTLE VARIETY TO YOUR SALAD BY EXPERIMENTING WITH DIFFERENT PEPPERS. OTHER PEPPERS IN THE SAME "HOTNESS" RANGE INCLUDE CHERRY, GUAJILO, AND POBLANO VARIETIES. IF YOU THINK YOU CAN STAND THE HEAT, TRY AN ANCHO OR CHIPOTLE TYPE.

7 To assemble salad, arrange lettuce on a plate, then add pineapple.

8 Clean peppers and onion; slice into rings and arrange on lettuce.

9 Toast the almonds and sesame seeds. Slice almonds and sprinkle with sesame seeds over salad.

10 Top with grilled chicken tenders and spoon remaining marinade over all.

Never use the same dish that held the raw chicken as your serving platter without washing it first. Also, don't let any of the utensils that came in contact with the raw chicken touch the finished meat. Think "food safety first" at all times.

wOOhOO Worcestershire Chicken

This recipe is especially good if you allow the flames to flare up during cooking. The lightly charred chicken skin adds a distinct flavor, as does the smoke from the chicken fat that melts away and drips onto the coals.

Makes 4 servings

1 tablespoon cider vinegar
⅛ cup Worcestershire sauce
⅛ cup water
2 tablespoons butter
2 tablespoons honey
1 chicken, quartered

1 In a glass bowl, combine cider vinegar, Worcestershire sauce, water, butter, and honey, and heat over low flame or in the microwave until butter melts.

2 Place chicken on grill and baste often with the sauce.

3 Grill for 7 to 8 minutes per side or until juices from chicken run clear.

To save preparation time, substitute commercial honey-mustard salad dressing.

Grilled Honey-Mustard Chicken

Is it sweet because of the honey, or tangy because of the mustard? Hmmm. Kind of remind you of a beer commercial? You decide with this one! I know one thing for sure—it is absolutely delicious. Your mouth will thank you afterward. Serve over long-grain wild rice, with vegetable side dishes. Grilled Honey-Mustard Chicken is also delicious tossed with pasta, as a green salad topped with honey-mustard dressing, or as a cool main dish.

Makes 4 servings

Honey-Mustard Dressing

⅓ cup mayonnaise
¾ cup sour cream
⅓ cup prepared mustard
⅓ cup honey
1 tablespoon lemon juice, fresh
Salt and pepper to taste

Honey-Mustard Chicken

¼ cup Honey-Mustard Dressing
3 heaping tablespoons stone-ground Dijon mustard
2 tablespoons lemon juice, fresh
1 tablespoon honey
Salt and freshly ground black pepper, to taste
4 boneless, skinless chicken breasts (about 4 ounces each)

1 To make dressing, mix mayonnaise, sour cream, and mustard with wire whisk. Add honey, lemon juice, salt, and pepper, stirring until well combined.

2 In a large bowl, whisk ¼ cup of the Honey-Mustard dressing with the Dijon mustard, lemon juice, honey, salt, and black pepper.

3 Coat chicken halves in mixture. Cover and marinate 1 hour or overnight. Scrape excess marinade from chicken. Place chicken about 6 inches above medium-hot coals.

4 Grill chicken, turning occasionally, for 3 to 5 minutes per side until juices run clear.

THE 3 WORST THINGS TO DO...
WITH SALT

1 ADD SALT TO ANY OF THE RECIPES USING SOY OR WORCESTERSHIRE SAUCE. THE SODIUM CONTENT IN THOSE SAUCES IS SUFFICIENT TO ACT AS A FLAVOR ENHANCER.

2 USE GARLIC SALT AS A SUBSTITUTE FOR MINCED GARLIC. YOU'LL END UP WITH A RECIPE FAR TOO HIGH IN SODIUM. THE FLAVOR WILL SUFFER, TOO.

3 FORGET TO THROW SOME OVER YOUR SHOULDER FOR GOOD LUCK IF YOU SPILL ANY.

An easy way to add flavor to dishes and save yourself some work is to keep a glass jar of minced garlic in olive oil tucked away in the refrigerator. You can prepare your own, but keep in mind that it'll only keep for a week.

To Live for Chicken Marinade

Name brands are given in this recipe because each offers its own distinct flavor. Combining the variety of sauces is what gives my original recipe its wonderful taste. Leftover chicken is delicious served smothered in cheddar cheese, wrapped in a tortilla shell, and heated in the microwave for 15 to 20 seconds, or until the cheese melts.

Makes 8 servings

1 clove garlic
1 tablespoon butter
1 tablespoon honey
⅛ cup La Choy soy sauce
⅛ cup Kikkoman soy sauce
⅛ cup French's Worcestershire sauce
⅛ cup Lea & Perrins Worcestershire sauce
8 boneless, skinless chicken thighs

1 Mince garlic and add it with the butter to a microwave-safe bowl. Microwave on high for 15 to 30 seconds. Add remaining ingredients and whisk until thoroughly combined.

2 Coat chicken thighs with the marinade.

3 Grill over high heat with a flame. Once flame has seared the meat (which caramelizes the sugars in the sauce), lower heat to medium and grill for an additional 3 to 5 minutes, or until juices run clear.

Optional: Fresh rosemary complements the flavors in this marinade. For a change of pace, sprinkle some on the chicken while you grill it. You'll love the added aroma, too.

Trust Me on the Vinegar Chicken

This recipe brings back memories of childhood cookouts with chickens split in half, slowly sizzling on a huge grill that Dad had made out of a burn barrel. This sauce is best if used to baste the chicken often. The original recipe calls for pints of the ingredients; I've cut it down to home grill-sized proportions.

Makes 4 servings

⅛ cup cider vinegar
⅛ cup water
2 tablespoons butter
1 tablespoon Worcestershire sauce
1 whole chicken, quartered

1 In a glass dish, combine the cider vinegar, water, butter, and Worcestershire sauce and heat over a low flame or in the microwave until butter melts.

2 Place chicken on the grill and baste with the sauce. Turn the chicken and baste often.

3 Grill chicken for about 10 to 15 minutes per side; it's done when juices run clear.

For an enhanced flavor, marinate the chicken for an hour in the refrigerator in half of the Trust Me on the Vinegar sauce. Use the reserved marinade to baste the chicken during grilling.

Caribbean Thyme Chicken

You ever have one of those days where you feel like grabbing a fistful of the seasonings you have on hand and seeing what you can come up with? No? Well, I do. I recall creating this recipe during one of my Ohio midwinter treks back and forth through the snow to use the gas grill. A trip to the islands sounded good about then.

Makes 6 to 8 servings

Most supermarkets now carry flash-frozen boneless, skinless chicken breasts and thighs. When you factor in the time you save skinning and deboning the meat, the price per pound is reasonable indeed.

Dry Rub Seasoning Mix

½ teaspoon ground allspice
½ teaspoon ground nutmeg
¼ teaspoon ground cinnamon
½ teaspoon ground cloves
1 teaspoon ground thyme
⅛ teaspoon ground cayenne pepper
¼ teaspoon kosher or sea salt
½ teaspoon ground garlic powder

KEEP IN MIND THAT BONELESS CHICKEN TAKES LESS GRILLING TIME. IF YOU BUY BONELESS CHICKEN, YOU WON'T HAVE TO GET YOUR HANDS ICKY DEBONING IT AND YOU WILL HAVE MORE TIME TO CHOOSE ANOTHER RECIPE TO TRY!

To Make Caribbean Thyme Chicken

5 pounds skinned chicken pieces
Walnut or olive oil to coat

1 Combine ingredients for the dry rub.

2 Wash chicken and pat dry with paper towels. Lightly coat chicken pieces with walnut or olive oil.

3 Rub seasoning mixture into chicken pieces.

4 Grill over medium flame for 10 to 15 minutes per side. Chicken is done when juices run clear.

Orange You Glad You Made This Chicken

You'll need to grill this dish a little further away from the flame and watch it closely so it doesn't scorch, but it's worth the extra effort. You'll savor this sweet and salty, succulent and stimulating taste sensation.

Makes 4 servings

¼ garlic clove
⅛ cup orange marmalade
1 tablespoon sherry
1 teaspoon red wine vinegar
2 teaspoons soy sauce
2 teaspoons honey
Four boneless, 4-ounce, skinless chicken breasts or thighs

1 Mince the garlic enough to make ¼ teaspoon for use in the recipe. In a glass bowl, combine the garlic, orange marmalade, sherry, red wine vinegar, soy sauce, and honey, and mix well.

2 Coat chicken with mixture.

3 Grill over medium heat for 3 to 5 minutes each side or until juices run clear.

Tasty Tahini Chicken

This recipe has a slightly nutty flavor. If you prefer something a bit stronger or want to please the kids, substitute peanut butter for the tahini. Prepared either way, it's sure to become a family favorite.

Makes 4 servings

1 clove garlic
1 teaspoon roasted tahini paste
¼ teaspoon toasted sesame oil
1 teaspoon candied ginger
1 teaspoon honey
1 teaspoon soy sauce
1 teaspoon Worcestershire sauce
Four 4-ounce boneless, skinless chicken breasts or thighs

1 Mince garlic and add to tahini paste and sesame oil in a glass bowl. Sauté in the microwave on high for 15 seconds.

2 Combine the above mixture with the chopped candied ginger, honey, soy sauce, and Worcestershire sauce.

3 Coat chicken and grill over medium to low heat, about 6 inches above the coals. (Watch chicken closely because it will scorch.) Grill chicken 3 to 5 minutes on each side or until juices run clear.

Before you mix the ingredients for Tasty Tahini Chicken:

1. *Mix up a double batch of the Tasty Tahini Chicken sauce.*

2. *Wash 4 potatoes, pierce them, and microwave on high for 5 minutes.*

3. *Slice the potatoes and coat with half of the sauce.*

4. *Grill the potatoes along with the chicken.*

To avoid contaminating any reserved marinade, try my two-fisted basting method:

1. Place dish of reserved marinade within easy reach on your grill shelf.

2. With one hand, use a spoon to drizzle on the marinade as you baste with the brush in your other hand.

3. When not basting, it's okay to leave the spoon in the marinade, but place the brush (which has touched the raw chicken) in a separate container.

4. When the chicken is almost done and you baste for the last time, use the back of the spoon to spread the marinade instead of the contaminated brush.

Chapter 8

Where's the Beef Here?

What's the first thing that pops into mind when you think "barbecue"? (Say "beef" here.) That's right! Beef! There's probably more recipes for beef than there are ways for a politician to get into trouble. However, here are a few to get you started.

You don't have to follow these exactly. The recipes in this chapter are "tried and true," so to speak. Try adding or removing ingredients according to your tastes. After all, a recipe isn't created in a day.

Get to know the man or woman in the white apron behind the meat counter at your local market. That way, whenever you have a question about whether or not you can substitute one cut of beef for another, you have somebody whose opinion you know you can trust. While pretty much any cut of beef can be prepared on the grill, special cuts often need special consideration. Some are too tender to marinate for very long; others are too tough to grill without some advance preparation. I give you some suggestions throughout this chapter. Your "butcher" can give you instant advice. Following the advice of the friendly person in the nice white apron can save you the hassle of somebody having to summon those friendly guys in the nice white coats to calm you down because you've ruined another meal.

Gulf Coast Hurricane Hamburgers

My Pensacola friend, Keith Giddeon, created these burgers after one of two hurricanes in 1995. Lack of electrical power made cooking on the grill a necessity. In a maddening rush to salvage his frozen food, he quickly became an experimental chef, soon to be hailed from all corners of…his yard. This was the best of the dishes.

Makes 8 servings

4 pounds ground beef, round or chuck
2 teaspoons garlic powder
1 tablespoon parsley, dried flakes or fresh
2 teaspoons Tony Chachere's Cajun Creole Seasoning
½ teaspoon pepper
1½ cups of mesquite barbecue sauce
1 medium white onion

1 In a large bowl, mix ground beef, garlic powder, parsley, Creole seasoning, and pepper. Form eight 1-inch-thick patties.

2 Grill patties over medium-high heat for 2 minutes, turn. Repeat. Add barbecue sauce in desired amount to patties and continue to grill the patties until done, 16 to 20 minutes, turning once or twice.

3 Slice peeled onions into ½-inch slices. Break into rings. Grill the rings on grill top for 5 minutes, turning once.

4 Serve on buns with choice of condiments and toppings.

To establish your reputation as a gourmet griller, try these burger toppings and listen to the ooohs and ahhhs:

- *Ranch dressing substituted for mayonnaise*

- *A slice of bacon, or two*

- *Black olives*

- *A combination of all of the above*

Not-so-London(ish) Broil

There is more than one delicious way to do things. To prove my point, I'll show you three different techniques to get these ingredients ready for the grill. The first two methods require that you marinate the meat; the third gets the meat ready for the grill immediately.

Makes 6 to 8 servings

One 3- to 4-pound London broil (1½ to 2 inches thick)
⅔ cup dry red wine
½ cup orange juice, fresh
⅓ cup lime juice, fresh
½ cup honey
¼ cup cider vinegar
¼ cup soy sauce
2 tablespoons olive oil
1½ teaspoons minced garlic

1 teaspoon finely grated orange zest
⅛–1 teaspoon Tabasco peppersauce
½ teaspoon ground cumin
½ teaspoon dried thyme, crumbled
¼ teaspoon freshly ground black pepper
2 teaspoons butter

Black pepper, to taste

Technique #1:

1 In measuring cup with a spout, mix together the red wine, orange and lime juices, honey, vinegar, soy sauce, olive oil, garlic, orange zest, Tabasco to taste, cumin, thyme, and pepper.

2 With a sharp knife, make a deep, blade-width cut into the side of the meat, being careful not to cut all the way through. Keeping the cut as narrow as possible, slice the meat to create a pocket.

3 Pour seasoning mixture into meat pocket. Refrigerate for at least 2 hours, or overnight.

4 Spread butter over top of meat. Add pepper, to taste. Place in aluminum foil or grilling bag. Even though this London broil is delicious as is, you can add other ingredients on top of the meat before closing the foil or bag to enhance the flavor, like sliced mushrooms, onions, or barbecue sauce. Seal tightly.

5 Place on grill and cook for 30 minutes. Turn, and cook until done. Slice into ¼- to ½-inch-thick pieces to serve. Season with additional freshly ground black pepper, if desired.

Technique #2:

1 In glass dish or heavy-duty zip-closure plastic bag large enough to hold the meat, mix together the red wine, orange and lime juices, honey, vinegar, soy sauce, olive oil, garlic, orange zest, Tabasco to taste, cumin, thyme, and pepper.

2 Add the meat to the marinade, turning it to coat it completely.

3 Refrigerate for at least 2 hours, or overnight.

4 Spread butter over both sides of the meat. Add additional pepper, to taste, if desired. Bring meat to room temperature.

5 Place on hot grill about 4 inches above the heat and cook for 5 minutes on each side to sear the meat. Reduce temperature of grill to medium. Continue to cook meat until it reaches desired doneness. Remove meat from the grill to a serving platter and let it "rest" for 5 minutes, then slice into ¼- to ½-inch-thick pieces to serve. If desired, boil remaining marinade for 5 minutes and serve it as a sauce for the meat.

Technique #3:

1. In measuring cup, mix together the red wine, orange and lime juices, honey, vinegar, soy sauce, olive oil, garlic, orange zest, and Tabasco to taste.

2. Ready a meat injector (like the one from Cajun Injector described in Chapter 20) by attaching the needle and turning it clockwise until it's snug, but not overly tight.

3. Make sure the marinade is well-mixed. Draw it into the injector. Insert needle of injector as far as it will go into the side of the meat. Push plunger down slowly while pulling the injector out of the meat. Repeat, spacing the insertion points about an inch apart until you've "circled" the meat, refilling the injector with more well-mixed marinade as needed. If any marinade remains, inject the needle into the top of the meat until it almost goes through the meat but doesn't break the skin on the other side. Push plunger down slowly while pulling the injector out of the meat, repeating the process across the top of the meat until all of the marinade is used.

4. Mix cumin, thyme, and pepper into the butter and spread the mixture over both sides of the meat.

5. Place on hot grill about 4 inches above the heat and cook for 5 minutes on each side to sear the meat. Reduce temperature of grill to medium. Continue to cook meat until it reaches desired doneness. Remove meat from the grill to a serving platter and let it rest for 5 minutes, then slice into ¼- to ½-inch-thick pieces to serve. Season with freshly ground black pepper, if desired.

Gone Fishin'

Marinate cheaper cuts overnight or even longer. (Pierce really tough cuts of meat with a fork first.) The vinegar will tenderize the meat.

Pucker Up Grilled Steak

Is it the steak, the cook, or the diners that pucker up from this recipe? I was never able to decide which until I tried it. Try it and find out for yourself. (Hint: If you want the pucker less pronounced, consider pouring red wine or beer into your marinade instead of the red wine vinegar.)

Makes 4 servings

1 clove garlic
1 tablespoon butter
⅛ cup soy sauce
⅛ cup red wine vinegar
⅛ cup ketchup
2 tablespoons honey
Four 8-ounce tender steaks of choice

1 Mince garlic and add to butter in microwave-safe container. Microwave for 30 seconds, or until butter is melted.

2 Add soy sauce, red wine vinegar, ketchup, and honey. Mix well.

3 Place steaks in shallow glass dish and pour marinade over the steaks. Refrigerate for 4 to 6 hours, covered.

4 Grill steaks over medium-high heat until cooked to desired doneness, or about 20 minutes, turning once.

Grill-Roasted Beef and Pepper Dinner

If you like everything cooking in front of you at once, here's your answer. Your grill will sag from the weight of this great recipe.

Makes 4 servings

2 teaspoons ground black pepper
2 teaspoons garlic powder
1 teaspoon cornstarch
½ teaspoon salt
Pinch each of ground thyme, white pepper, and cayenne pepper
1½ to 2 pounds beef shoulder roast
4 medium baking or sweet potatoes
4 ears corn on the cob, unshucked
1 red bell pepper
1 green bell pepper

1 In a bowl, mix together black pepper, garlic powder, cornstarch, salt, thyme, white pepper, and cayenne to make a rub. Press mixture into both sides of roast.

2 For conventional grills, build wood or charcoal fire to one side. Use enough fuel to sustain heat for 1 hour. For gas grills, preheat one side; turn to low.

3 Wash potatoes, pierce with a fork, and brush with oil.

4 Place beef, potatoes, and corn on cool side of grill. Cover and cook 50 to 60 minutes; maintain grill temperature of 300°F.

An easy way to build your fire on one side of a charcoal grill is to use two bricks in the middle—placed end-on-end—to halve the cooking area.

De-seed and quarter peppers, add to hot side of grill, and cook covered during last 10 minutes.

5 Remove when thermometer reads 140°F for medium-rare or 155°F for medium. Let stand 10 minutes before carving, which allows the juices to redistribute throughout the meat. Slice thinly across the grain. Serve with peppers, potatoes, and corn. Use leftover sauce if desired. To serve corn, peel back husks.

Cutting beef is one of the times you do want to go "against the grain." Slice it with the grain and you end up with a stringy and tough mess. Yuck! Portion it against the grain and you get pieces that are more tender and less chewy.

Calypso Caribbean Steak

Bring the taste of the islands to your table with this wonderful steak creation. (If you have a "tender" mouth, substitute a milder pepper.) Undo the top button on the ol' trousers and listen to the steel drums playing softly in the background as you eat. Do you hear them?

Makes 4 to 6 servings

1 small onion
1 or 2 jalapeño peppers
3 cloves garlic
¼ cup soy sauce
¼ cup honey
¼ cup lime juice
10 to 20 thin slices peeled fresh ginger
1 teaspoon whole brown mustard seeds, optional
½ teaspoon allspice
½ teaspoon paprika
½ teaspoon thyme
1½ pounds top round or top sirloin steak, 1 inch thick

1 Cut onion into chunks. Remove stems and seeds from jalapeños and cut in half. Peel garlic cloves.

2 Blend onion, soy sauce, honey, lime juice, ginger, jalapeño, garlic, mustard, allspice, paprika, and thyme in a blender or food processor until mixed well.

3 Place steak in a zip-closure plastic bag or shallow glass dish and pour marinade over steak. Seal well and refrigerate 20 minutes to 6 hours, turning bag, or steaks, occasionally. Remove meat and reserve marinade.

Don't give bacteria a chance to party on your steaks before you grill them. Wait until the last possible moment to remove them from the refrigerator. Sure, they'll grill faster if they're at room temperature, but which room, what season? As long as they're not frozen solid, you'll be fine.

4 Grill steak 4 to 6 inches from medium coals for about 16 to 20 minutes, turning once, until done. Remove steak to carving board and let stand 10 minutes.

5 Bring reserved marinade to a boil in a saucepan over medium-high heat. Reduce heat and simmer 5 minutes.

6 Carve steak into thin slices, diagonally. Place on a platter and cover with heated sauce.

Use rubber gloves when cutting hot peppers. Be careful not to rub your face, especially around the eyes, before removing the gloves.

Louisiana Stuffed Roast Beef

No, Louisiana isn't an ingredient here. But the flavor of the great state sure is! Leftover alert! Lock some of this away in a vault for sandwiches on French bread the next day! Make some of your guests go hungry, if necessary.

Makes 6 servings

1 onion	¾ teaspoon black pepper
2 stalks celery	¾ teaspoon minced garlic
1 bell pepper	½ teaspoon dry mustard
2 tablespoons unsalted butter	½ teaspoon ground cayenne
1 teaspoon kosher or sea salt	4 pounds boneless sirloin
1 teaspoon white pepper	roast

1 Very finely, chop onions, celery, and bell pepper to make one cup of each.

2 In a bowl, mix together onions, celery, bell pepper, butter, salt, white pepper, black pepper, garlic, mustard, and cayenne.

3 Place roast in a large pan, fat side up. Using a large knife, make 5 to 10 deep slits in the meat, forming pockets, down to a depth of about ½ inch from the bottom; do not cut all the way through. Fill the pockets completely with the vegetable mixture, reserving a small amount of the vegetables to rub over the top of the roast.

4 Grill, covered, until a meat thermometer reads 160ºF for medium doneness. For a rarer roast, only grill until thermometer reads 140ºF. Allow meat to rest for 10 minutes before you carve and serve.

Kooky Caraway Burgers

Caraway seeds, with their pleasant wintergreen-like scent, go well with many dishes. You'll find them to be fantastic on burgers as well.

Makes 6 servings

1 onion
1½ pounds ground beef, chuck or round
1 teaspoon kosher or sea salt
1 teaspoon caraway seeds
1 teaspoon Worcestershire sauce
¼ teaspoon pepper
Optional: 1 cup beer, any American brand

1   Finely chop onion to make ½ cup and, in a bowl, mix together with ground beef, salt, caraway seeds, Worcestershire sauce, and pepper.

2   Shape mixture into 6 patties, each about 1 inch thick.

3   Place the patties in a shallow dish. Pour beer over the patties. Cover and refrigerate 3 to 4 hours. (The patties may turn gray—this is okay.)

4   Remove patties from the marinade and grill 4 inches from heat, turning once, to the desired doneness, 15 to 20 minutes.

Remember—Be adventurous! Occasionally try something different. For example, on those days it's so hot outside you know you're going to want to drink all of the beer you have on hand, pour red wine over your Kooky Caraway Burgers instead. In the fall, use cider.

Florida Barbecued Spareribs

Florida, you say? Yep...there's cows in that thar state! And they know how to grow 'em, too. Who knows, maybe better than that "little" state on the western side of the Gulf of Mexico. See what you think.

Makes 6 servings

2 cups butter
1 cup cider vinegar
1 cup ketchup
One 6-ounce jar prepared
   horseradish
6 lemons, for juice

1 teaspoon kosher or sea salt
1 tablespoon Worcestershire
   sauce
1 teaspoon hot pepper sauce
5 pounds spareribs

Keep a spray bottle filled with water handy for this recipe. The butter in this sauce causes it to flame up when it hits the coals. If not, you might end up with "Charcoal Ribs" instead.

1 In a medium-sized saucepan, melt butter over medium heat. Add vinegar, ketchup, horseradish, the juice of the 6 lemons, salt, and Worcestershire and pepper sauces. (If you're feeling extra adventurous, add the zest from one of the lemons, too.) Simmer, uncovered, 20 to 25 minutes to blend flavors. Use as basting sauce for spareribs.

2 Place ribs on grill 6 inches above hot coals. Brush with sauce and cook until brown on one side. Turn, brush once more with sauce, and brown the other side.

3 Turn and baste every 10 minutes until ribs are done, about 1 hour. Cut near bone in a center section of ribs; when juices run clear or golden, the ribs are done.

4 Place ribs on a platter and cut into sections of one to three ribs. Serve with any remaining uncontaminated sauce.

Gunny's Mediterranean Stuffed Steak

Quick and easy describes this steak. Oh, did I mention it tastes great? The black olives are the secret to this one. Mmmmm…

Makes 4 servings

1 clove garlic
¼ cup sweet cream butter
½ teaspoon chives
½ teaspoon basil
Four 6- to 8-ounce sirloin steaks (at least 1 inch thick)
2 cups mushrooms
2 cups black olives

1 Mince garlic. Place butter, chives, basil, and garlic in microwave-safe container. Microwave for 15 seconds, or until butter is partially melted.

2 With a very sharp knife (be careful, please, no finger-stuffed steaks here!), slit steaks along one edge, deeply enough to create a large, pita-like pocket.

3 Coat both sides of the pocket with butter and spice mixture.

4 Slice mushrooms and black olives thinly, and layer inside the steak; close pocket with a skewer.

5 Grill over medium-high heat, turning once, 10 to 12 minutes total.

Optional: Gunny says that before he places the steaks directly on the grill, he first "salt sears 'em" to enhance the flavor and seal in the juices. To add this step, put a cast-iron skillet over hot coals and once it's very hot, sprinkle ¼ teaspoon of kosher or sea salt in the skillet and one by one, slap in a steak. Flash-sear each side of the steaks for 15 to 30 seconds. Then grill according to Step 5.

Beefy Caesar Salad

Want something quick and light as a snack, or even a side dish? A Caesar salad is always a good solution.

Makes 4 servings

1 tablespoon white wine vinegar
1 teaspoon Worcestershire sauce
1 pound sirloin stir-fry strips
Parmesan cheese
One 10-ounce bag prepared romaine lettuce salad mix
1 cup croutons, Caesar flavored
1 tablespoon Dijon mustard
⅓ cup low-fat Caesar salad dressing

1 Mix vinegar with the Worcestershire sauce and pour over sirloin strips. Marinate for 30 to 40 minutes.

2 Heat cast-iron skillet on a hot grill and sear beef 1 minute per side. Thread strips onto skewers and grill 4 to 6 minutes.

3 Grate ½ cup cheese.

4 Place salad mix, croutons, and cheese into a large serving bowl. Add grilled strips of beef, cut to desired length.

5 Mix mustard with Caesar dressing and pour over salad. Toss and serve immediately.

To avoid burning your fingers while you thread seared beef strips onto skewers or dropping the strips into the coals, place a piece of heavy-duty foil over the grilling area. Puncture the foil with a fork several times to allow the flavor of the smoke to penetrate through to the meat.

Chapter 9

High-on-the-Hog Grill Fills

Everyone likes pork. Well, almost everyone. If you're a fan of my curly tailed friend, please read on. Treats await you within the next few pages.

Pork isn't just the other white meat. Sure, I can choose between pork chops, pork steaks, pork tenderloin, pork roasts, or pork ribs. I'll leave the pork bellies to the commodities speculators. But even so, that still leaves pork sausage, bacon, and ham, too. How many tummies just growled? Raise your hands!

This chapter has more pork than the annual budget of the United States of America! But don't worry, you'll need no political maneuvering, or votes in Congress, to reap the rewards of these fantastic recipes.

So, with an oink, oink here, and an oink, oink there, let's break out the humble grillingware—we're off to hog heaven.

You can speed up the marinating process if you allow your entrée to marinate outside of the refrigerator. However, for safety's sake, don't let it sit at room temperature for longer than 30 minutes.

Pleasing Peachy Pork Steaks

Here's one that'll even make my friends down in Georgia yell for more. Try this one out on the mother-in-law. You're sure to gain a few points with her after she tastes this pork with its peachy side dish.

Makes 4 servings

4 boneless pork chops/steaks (1 inch thick)
1 tablespoon lime or lemon juice
2 tablespoons unsweetened peach juice
1 tablespoon vegetable or olive oil
1 teaspoon ground cumin
Pinch cayenne pepper
Pinch black pepper

1 Arrange steaks side by side in shallow glass dish.

2 Stir together lime or lemon juice, peach juice, oil, cumin, and cayenne and black peppers.

3 Pour mixture over steaks; cover and marinate 30 minutes at room temperature or up to 4 hours in refrigerator. (If refrigerated, let steaks sit at room temperature for 30 minutes before grilling.)

4 Place steaks on grill over medium heat and reserve marinade.

5 Cook 6 to 8 minutes per side, brushing often with marinade. Do not overcook.

6 Serve with Peach Salad (recipe opposite).

Peach Salad

Don't get stuck in the "it's pork so I've gotta serve it with apple-sauce" rut. Peaches please persnickety pork pundits, too. Try this recipe and see what I mean. Be forewarned, however. The citrus juice makes this dressing somewhat tart. You may want to add it gradually to arrive at the taste you want; otherwise, you can cut the tartness by adding some peanut, canola, or extra-virgin olive oil to it.

Makes 4 servings

2 ripe peaches
2 stalks green onion
Cilantro
½ teaspoon red pepper flakes
½ teaspoon cumin
2 tablespoons lime or lemon juice
Salt and pepper to taste

1 Peel and dice peaches.

2 Chop onion finely to make 2 tablespoons and mince cilantro to make 1 tablespoon.

3 Mix together peaches, onion, cilantro, red pepper flakes, cumin, lime or lemon juice, salt, and pepper.

4 Allow to sit 30 minutes before serving beside pork chops or steaks.

Try using canned peaches for the Peach Salad. This will save you 5 to 10 minutes in preparation time. However, make sure you use peaches packed in natural juices, not syrup. The syrup is too sweet and will cover the taste of the spices in the recipe. You want your salad to pack its full punch!

Keep a paperback book tucked inside one of your apron pockets. You'll have time to read a few pages while your roast does its own thing on the grill—at least 20 minutes per side.

Quick 'n' Easy Pork Roast

This is a great roast recipe that goes well with potato side dishes. If you're lucky, there'll be plenty remaining afterward, because the leftovers are better than the original!

Makes 4 servings

4 tablespoons brown mustard
3 pounds boneless pork roast
¼ cup tamari or soy sauce
¼ teaspoon Tabasco pepper sauce

1 Mix mustard, tamari or soy sauce, and Tabasco pepper sauce and apply liberally on both sides of pork.

2 Marinate roast in mixture 1 to 2 hours. (Turn once or twice.)

3 Place roast on hot grill and sear each side for 1 to 2 minutes.

4 Lower temperature and grill 20 minutes on each side or until done to your taste. Adjust time for larger or smaller roasts. The meat will taste best if not overcooked and still juicy. Allow meat to rest for 10 minutes before you carve and serve it.

112   **LAZY ABOUT GRILLING**

Arizona Pork Tenderloin

Strap your grilling tools onto your belt six-shooter style to add to the feeling you're in the old Southwest while making these tenderloins. Just be careful where you point those things.

Makes 6 servings

5 garlic cloves
5 teaspoons chili powder
1½ teaspoons dried oregano
¾ teaspoon ground cumin
1 tablespoon vegetable oil
5 pounds pork tenderloin

For those times you need crushed garlic and don't have a base or a garlic press handy, you can place the peeled garlic cloves between pieces of waxed paper and whack 'em a few times with a hammer.

1 Crush garlic cloves.

IF YOUR TASTE BUDS ARE MORE CONSERVATIVE, REDUCE THE AMOUNT OF CHILI POWDER TO FIT YOUR INDIVIDUAL PREFERENCE.

2 In a small bowl, mix the chili powder, oregano, cumin, garlic, and vegetable oil.

3 Rub mixture over all surfaces of tenderloin.

4 Cover and refrigerate 2 to 24 hours.

5 Grill over medium heat 15 to 20 minutes, turning occasionally. Allow tenderloin to rest for 5 to 10 minutes, then slice and serve.

Spicy Jerk Pork Chops

Jerk seasoning is a Jamaican original that has spread in popularity out of the Caribbean to become a favorite pork and poultry seasoning. Get ready, mon, these chops will have you listening to Bob Marley and the Wailers all night long!

Makes 2 to 4 servings

You can save time by buying bottled (Jamaican) jerk sauce, as it is readily available in supermarket condiment aisles. Simply marinate pork chops in sauce and cook as directed.

½ cup yellow onion
Whole nutmeg
5 teaspoons dried thyme
5 teaspoons sugar
1 teaspoon salt
1 teaspoon ground allspice

1 teaspoon black pepper
½ teaspoon cayenne pepper
¼ teaspoon cinnamon
Four ½-inch-thick rib pork
    chops (each about
    4 ounces)

1 Mince the onion.

2 Grate ¼ teaspoon nutmeg.

3 Add thyme, sugar, salt, allspice, black pepper, cayenne, and cinnamon and grind into a coarse paste.

4 Pat pork chops dry and rub both sides with the jerk paste.

5 Oil grill rack with vegetable oil.

6 Grill for 4 minutes on each side, or until just cooked through.

Orange-Glazed Baby Back Ribs

What makes oranges and pork go well together? I don't know, but I'm glad they do because they are a match made in heaven!

Makes 4 to 8 servings

⅔ cup honey
½ cup fresh orange juice
2 tablespoons Worcestershire sauce
2 tablespoons minced orange peel ("zest" or orange part only)
1 tablespoon minced garlic
1 tablespoon soy sauce
4 to 5 pounds baby back pork ribs

1 In large container, mix together honey, orange juice, Worcestershire sauce, orange peel, garlic, and soy sauce.

2 Pierce meaty areas of ribs with a fork and place in container with marinade. Cover and refrigerate for 6 to 24 hours.

3 Grill over medium to high heat until cooked through, turning occasionally. Grilling time will be approximately 25 minutes, depending on the heat of the grill, cut of the ribs, and distance from coals.

Gone Fishin'

Florida Sunshine Pork Steaks

Here's a great recipe that tends to drive everyone within smelling distance crazy while it's cooking. You'll be so anxious to taste this one, you'll want to take it off the grill before it's time, but trust me, you'll be glad you waited.

Makes 4 to 6 servings

2 pounds ¾-inch-thick pork steaks

Marinade

½ cup orange juice, fresh or packaged
3 tablespoons brown sugar
3 tablespoons cider vinegar
¼ teaspoon kosher or sea salt
½ teaspoon dry mustard
¼ teaspoon ground ginger
2 tablespoons ketchup

1 In a shallow glass dish, mix all marinade ingredients. Add pork steaks. Cover dish with plastic wrap or foil. Refrigerate 6 to 24 hours.

2 Allow steaks to sit at room temperature for 30 minutes before grilling.

3 Place steaks on grill over medium heat and reserve marinade.

4 Grill 4 to 6 minutes per side, basting the steaks often with the marinade.

Garlic and Honey Pork Chops

Serve these chops with stir-fried vegetables and you get the chance to improve on perfection. (Sprinkle some toasted almonds or sesame seeds over the veggies and you'll actually swoon while you eat!)

Makes 4 servings

2 cloves garlic
2 tablespoons soy sauce
¼ cup honey
¼ cup lemon juice
1 tablespoon cooking sherry
Four 1- to 1½-inch boneless pork chops

1 Chop and mince garlic.

2 In a nonmetallic container, mix garlic, soy sauce, honey, lemon juice, and sherry.

3 Pour mixture over chops in a shallow glass dish. Cover and refrigerate overnight.

4 Secure aluminum foil on grill 15 minutes before cooking.

5 Remove chops from dish, allowing marinade to drip away.

Pour your liquid ingredients (the honey and lemon juice in the Garlic and Honey Pork Chop recipe) into a glass measuring cup first; then add the other ingredients that either require you use a measuring spoon (soy sauce, sherry) or whose amounts can vary slightly (garlic cloves). You get an accurate amount and you'll save yourself from dirtying a mixing bowl in the process—you can stir it all up in the cup.

6 Reserve leftover marinade.

7 Place chops on foil. Raise grill to medium height or reduce heat to medium if using a gas grill.

8 Cook for 16 to 18 minutes, turning occasionally until done

9 Boil reserved marinade for 5 minutes. Serve over chops.

THE 3 WORST THINGS YOU CAN DO... WITH SPICES

1 STORE THEM SO LONG THEY LOSE THEIR POTENCY. (MOST COOKS AGREE NO MORE THAN A YEAR, BUT SOME SAY REPLACE THEM EVERY THREE MONTHS.)

2 ADD SO MUCH THAT THEY OVERPOWER THE FOOD INSTEAD OF COMPLE-MENTING THE FLAVOR.

3 FAIL TO USE THEM AT ALL.

Tangy Citrus Pork Chops

Baked potatoes topped with butter and a couple pinches of rosemary make these chops irresistible. For an extra treat, sprinkle garlic and a few drops of Worcestershire sauce on bread and toast on the grill. It's great!

Makes 3 to 6 servings

Bunch of fresh parsley

2 cloves garlic

2 tablespoons olive oil

1 tablespoon fresh rosemary, chopped

1 tablespoon grated orange peel

1 tablespoon grated lemon peel

1 teaspoon sugar

½ teaspoon dry oregano

½ teaspoon salt

½ teaspoon black pepper

Six ½-inch-thick pork chops

1 Chop parsley and mince garlic.

2 In a bowl, mix together parsley, garlic, oil, rosemary, orange and lemon peels, sugar, oregano, salt, and pepper.

3 Spread mixture over each chop. Cover and refrigerate overnight.

4 Scrape away as much of the marinade as possible and grill for 2 to 3 minutes on each side.

Guests stop by unexpectedly. While you preheat the grill, thaw some pork chops or steaks. For each 4 chops, sauté 1 minced clove of garlic in 1 tablespoon of olive oil, or do a quickie-fake sauté by putting the garlic and oil in the microwave on high for 20 seconds. Rub the oil on both sides of each chop and grill several minutes on each side, depending on the thickness of the chops. No other seasoning is needed. Serve with a salad.

Deep South Pork Roast

The weather isn't the only thing they like hot in the South. And, as you'll discover in this recipe, they don't just add a touch of "shugah" to their voices. Y'all will like the sweet 'n' tangy mergin' in this dish, darlin'.

Makes 10 to 20 servings

3 cloves garlic
1 teaspoon parsley
1 large onion
2 tablespoons steak sauce (Lea & Perrins)
1 to 2 teaspoons seasoned salt (dry rub)
½ cup Tiger Sauce (brand name sweetened hot sauce)
½ cup Worcestershire sauce
2½ tablespoons dry mustard
10 pounds boneless pork roast
One 6-ounce can of tomato paste
3 tablespoons brown sugar

1 Chop garlic, parsley, and onion.

2 In a small bowl, mix together the garlic, parsley, steak sauce, onion, Tiger Sauce, Worcestershire sauce, and dry mustard.

3 Use the seasoned salt to rub the entire outside of the roast, pressing the salt into the meat as you go.

4 Make several deep slits into the roast, being careful not to puncture the opposite side. Fill slits with sauce and rub over the outside of the roast well.

5 Place roast in container, cover, and refrigerate for 6 hours or overnight.

6 In another small bowl, mix tomato paste and brown sugar well. Set aside.

7 Grill roast with lid closed until internal temperature reaches 170°F.

8 Brush with tomato paste and brown sugar mixture. Allow meat to rest for 10 minutes before you carve and serve.

You can employ some of the optional grilling equipment covered in Chapters 2 and 20 to help make a good Deep South Pork Roast great if you:

- Use a basting syringe to place sauce into the slits in the roast.
- Have a meat thermometer handy while cooking the roast. Since meat sizes differ, exact cooking times for roasts are difficult to determine.

Be-a-Pepper Pork Ribs

Sometimes it's best not to question why something works—just accept that it does. These great ribs are tender, tasty, and delicious any time of the year. The best part is the Dr. Pepper—it tenderizes the meat and provides a different flavor from the usual rib recipes. The good folks at Dr. Pepper may know exactly why their drink tenderizes meat, but I don't. I'm just certain that you'll appreciate the new flavor dimension Dr. Pepper adds to the Be-a-Pepper Pork Ribs. This one is a "must taste." (I'm still trying to create a Mountain Dew recipe!)

Makes 8 to 12 servings

1½ cups ketchup
¾ cup brown sugar
⅜ cup honey
4 tablespoons soy sauce
One 12-ounce can of Dr. Pepper
4 to 6 pounds baby back pork ribs
Pepper to taste

1 Mix together ketchup, brown sugar, honey, soy sauce, and Dr. Pepper in a large container.

2 Pierce meaty areas of ribs with a fork and place in container with marinade. Cover and refrigerate for 6 to 24 hours.

3 Place ribs on grill over medium to high heat, and lightly add pepper to taste.

4 Grill until cooked through, turning occasionally, 25 minutes total.

Chapter 10

Seafood–And They Will, And They Will, Sizzle Right on the Grill

It's time now for some recipes for which you'll fall hook, line, and sinker. They're all keepers. You won't be tempted to throw a single one back.

Those familiar with P. G. Wodehouse's novels know that his character Bertie Wooster is convinced that his butler Jeeves is so smart because of all of the fish he eats. Whether or not seafood is brain food is open to speculation. What is known is that fish does have definite benefits. Not only is it our leanest source of meat protein, it's heart healthy in other ways, too.

The omega-3 essential fatty acids found in fish help lower triglycerides—the bad blood fat that increases the risk of coronary artery disease. Because they alter the ability of platelets to stick together, omega-3 fatty acids also act as a natural anticoagulant, which reduces the chances of dangerous blood clotting. And, as if that isn't enough, studies show that omega-3 fatty acids also appear to lower blood pressure.

So, now that you're home from the seafood market, take off those waders and get ready to jump right in!

It's Gingery Grilled Grouper Steak Lime

Ginger may have left the Spice Girls, but ginger will never leave my spice rack. Once you taste this recipe, you'll know why.

This Gingery Grilled Grouper Steak Lime works with any type of firm fish steak. Just keep in mind that if your steaks are thinner than 1 inch, you'll need to reduce the cooking time slightly. Of course, if they are thicker, you'll want to increase the cooking time accordingly.

Makes 6 servings

Fresh gingerroot
¼ cup lime juice, fresh (2 to 3 limes)
2 tablespoons olive oil
1 clove garlic
1 tablespoon soy sauce

1 teaspoon Dijon-style mustard
¼ teaspoon kosher or sea salt
¼ teaspoon freshly ground black pepper
6 grouper steaks (about 1 inch thick)

1 Grate gingerroot to make 1 teaspoon.

2 In a small bowl, mix together the lime juice, olive oil, finely chopped garlic, soy sauce, ginger, Dijon mustard, and salt and pepper.

3 Divide the marinade into two portions, using half to brush the grouper. Reserve the remaining marinade in a separate small bowl.

4 Place fish on a medium grill and cook until the steaks are golden on the outside and done to taste inside, 5–7 minutes per side.

5 Remove the fish steaks from the grill and place them on a serving platter or onto each individual plate. Drizzle some of the reserved lime mixture over each steak.

Keep in mind you can always adjust recipes to your own tastes or to accommodate the ingredients you have on hand. For example, at times I've used ground ginger and candied ginger instead of the grated fresh ginger called for in this recipe.

A Fine Fenneled Swordfish

The fennel seeds give this recipe a distinctive flavor. For a change, you can substitute butter for olive oil; just keep in mind that if you do, you'll need to watch it a bit more closely so the steaks don't burn.

Makes 4 servings

Fresh parsley
3 tablespoons fresh lemon juice
4 tablespoons olive oil
2 tablespoons fennel seeds
½ teaspoon kosher or sea salt
2 garlic cloves
Four ½-pound swordfish steaks

1 Chop parsley finely to make 2 tablespoons.

2 In a small bowl, mix the lemon juice, olive oil, fennel seeds, salt, finely chopped garlic, and parsley. Pour over the fish and marinate it in the refrigerator, covered, for 4 to 6 hours.

3 Grill the steaks over white-hot coals for 5 minutes on each side.

Guests' Favorite Garlic Grilled Shrimp

You can omit the water chestnuts and serve the shrimp in this recipe on crusty bakery rolls as gourmet po-boys (Louisiana's version of the sandwich known as a hero to some, a submarine to others). However you serve it, it's the tarragon that does the trick in making this one special.

Makes 12 servings

½ cup butter
2 teaspoons garlic powder
⅛ teaspoon red pepper sauce
One 8-oz. can sliced water
   chestnuts
1 large green pepper

1 slice onion, chopped
½ teaspoon kosher or sea salt
½ teaspoon dried tarragon
   leaves
3 pounds cleaned raw shrimp

1 Form a pan, 11 x 11 x ½ inch, from double-thickness, heavy-duty aluminum foil. Place butter, garlic powder, and red pepper sauce in pan.

2 Place pan on grill 4 to 6 inches from medium coals until butter is melted. Remove pan from grill and add the drained water chestnuts, green pepper rings, chopped onion, salt, and tarragon. Mix well, being careful not to tear the foil pan. Clean the shrimp and add it to the pan, tossing them with the seasoning mixture.

3 Cover the pan with a piece of heavy-duty aluminum foil, sealing edges well. Grill until shrimp are done, 20 to 30 minutes. Season with additional salt and freshly ground black pepper to taste.

Love That Lemon Shrimp

Seafood is a bit more economical in the neck o' the woods where there's a coastline, so those nearer to a fresh supply sometimes serve these on sandwiches, too. Despite sometimes saying that "I live on the 'west coast' of Ohio," in actuality, I am from the Midwest, where the motto seems to be: "We'll let you buy seafood, but we're gonna make you pay big time if you do." Therefore, I like to present the shrimp directly on each serving plate, so my guests can get a good look at (read: appreciate) each and every one of them!

Makes 4 servings

Keep moustache scissors cleaned and ready in your kitchen. They come in handy for snipping the shells, as called for in Love That Lemon Shrimp.

2 pounds large shrimp
Parsley
3 cloves garlic
1 medium-sized onion
1 teaspoon dry mustard
1 teaspoon kosher or sea salt
½ cup olive oil
3 tablespoons fresh lemon juice

1 Rinse the shrimp, then snip the shells down the back, being careful that the shells remain on. Place the shrimp in a bowl large enough to hold them and the marinade.

2 Chop parsley finely to make ½ cup. Chop garlic and onion finely.

3 In a small bowl, combine the finely chopped garlic and onion, dry mustard, salt, olive oil, lemon juice, and parsley. Pour the mixture over the shrimp.

4 Cover and marinate the shrimp in the refrigerator for 10 to 30 minutes. (If you plan to use bamboo skewers to grill the shrimp, now is the time to soak them in water so they'll be ready when the shrimp is.)

5 Place the shrimp on a grill rack over hot coals. Cook the shrimp for 5 to 8 minutes, turning them once. The shrimp will turn pink when they're done. Serve them in their shells.

We'll Have a Hot Time on the Ol' Shrimp Tonight!

Tempted to make your guests laugh with that "jumbo shrimp" oxymoron joke one more time? Keep your head in the game and remember, man doesn't live by mild alone. Sometimes he just feels the need for something to add some sizzle in his life. Here's a painless, palate-pleasing way to do just that.

Makes 6 servings

Parsley
4 tablespoons olive oil
1 teaspoon salt
½ teaspoon pepper
½ teaspoon garlic powder
6 tablespoons chili sauce
6 tablespoons vinegar
2 tablespoons Worcestershire sauce
⅛ teaspoon hot pepper sauce
2 tablespoons melted butter
2 pounds large shrimp

1 Chop parsley finely to make ½ cup.

2 In a small bowl, mix the olive oil, salt, pepper, garlic powder, chili sauce, vinegar, Worcestershire sauce, hot pepper sauce, parsley, and melted butter. Pour over shelled and deveined shrimp; cover and refrigerate for up to 1 hour.

3 Remove shrimp from marinade. (You can reserve the leftover portion of the mixture to serve alongside the shrimp if you remember to first boil it to destroy any bacteria introduced by the raw shrimp.) Either thread shrimp onto skewers or put them on a pan made of two pieces of greased heavy-duty aluminum foil. If using skewers, be sure to grease the grill rack or spray it with nonstick cooking spray. Grill the shrimp about 4 to 6 inches above a bed of low-glowing coals.

4 Cook for 4 minutes on each side or until shrimp turn pink, turning them at least once. Baste with the reserved (boiled) marinade, if you wish.

How to Eat a Lobster

Although it can seem intimidating at first, it's easy! Just follow these steps:

1 Twist off the large claws and crack open. (Some like to suck the meat out of the claws.)

2 Break off the tail and remove the flippers. Using a lobster fork, push the tail meat out in one piece. (Remove and discard the black vein.)

3 Crack open the body.

4 Break off each of the small walking legs attached to the body. (You'll want to suck the meat out of these, too.)

5 Make sure you eat every succulent morsel of your lobster.

Grilled Whole Lobster

Lobster is so sweet and delicious, it needs little embellishment. I like to add some fresh lemon juice to the butter. That choice is yours, as is adding the salt, pepper, or tarragon—or other seasonings, for that matter. The nice thing about eating this outside is that you can forget the lobster bib. Just hose yourself down when you're done!

Per lobster

½ cup butter
¼ cup lemon juice
1 whole lobster

Optional:
Sea salt
Pepper
⅛ teaspoon dried whole
   tarragon

Prefer steamed lobster? Then substitute water for the butter and lemon juice. Grill according to the instructions for Grilled Whole Lobster. Serve with melted butter and a lemon wedge.

1 In a small bowl, melt the butter in the microwave, then add the lemon juice. (If you insist, you can add salt, pepper, and the tarragon to the mixture now, too.)

2 Place each lobster on its back (belly up) and split it from head to tail. Remove all internal tracks, including the sac. Create a foil packet large enough to generously hold the lobster (shell side down) out of two sheets of heavy-duty aluminum foil. Bring the foil up and over the lobster, crimping and folding it on the sides to create a container. Pour the melted butter and lemon juice mixture in through the top opening, crimp and seal one layer of foil, then do the same with the next layer to create a double seal.

3 Place packet on grill so that the shell side is facing down. Grill over a medium heat for 5 minutes. Turn the packet and cook for another 6 to 8 minutes.

No bones about it, sometimes even a fish fillet isn't free of them. But don't let that slight risk keep you from serving seafood. Break fish into bite-sized pieces so you can check for bones when you serve it to small children. Many people swear by keeping bread at the table to help a bone go down, if need be.

Grilled Snapper Fillets with Lime-Orange Marinade

Great! There's that tarragon again! No, I'm not in some sort of wicked herbalist-induced tarragon trance. Tarragon complements seafood; therefore, it is our friend!

Makes 4 servings

Bunch shallots or scallions
¼ cup lime juice
¼ cup orange juice
1 tablespoon olive oil
2 tablespoons fresh tarragon

⅛ teaspoon ground nutmeg
1¼ pounds red snapper fillets
1 lime
1 orange

1 Mince shallot or scallions to make 2 tablespoons.

2 In a shallow bowl large enough to hold the fillets and marinade, combine lime juice, orange juice, oil, shallots or scallions, tarragon, and nutmeg. Place red snapper fillets in bowl, turning to coat evenly with marinade. Marinate, skin side up, covered, in the refrigerator for 1 hour.

3 Cook fillets on a hot grill, skin side up, for 3 minutes. Turn fillets over, baste with marinade, and grill for another 3 to 6 minutes.

4 Slice lime and orange into ½-inch slices. Place on grill and baste with marinade, turning once. Serve the fruit with the fish fillets.

Grilled Oysters Au Gratin

I bake an escalloped oyster dish every Christmas. Sometimes the oyster craving hits during the summer, so I prepare them this way instead. For those times I'm in a hurry, I beat an egg into the reserved oyster liquid, mix all of the remaining ingredients together, and put them in a foil-covered aluminum pan to bake over indirect heat for about 45 minutes while I grill the rest of the meal.

Makes 6 to 8 servings

2 cups fine cracker crumbs
1 teaspoon sea salt
1 quart shucked oysters
½ pound butter, melted

1 In a shallow dish, mix the cracker crumbs with the salt. Roll the oysters well in a clean napkin to make them as dry as possible. Thrust a fork through the tough muscle of each oyster.

2 Next, dip each oyster into the crumbs, then into the butter, then into the crumbs again.

3 Arrange the oysters in a hinged wire grill basket and broil them over hot coals for 3 minutes, turning the wire grill every 5 or 10 seconds to prevent the cracker coating from burning.

4 When the oysters are plump and the juices run clear, they are done. Serve immediately.

It's easy to make changes to the Grilled Oysters Au Gratin recipe. Simply use a different type of cracker. And remember this simple recipe the next time you need to prepare some appetizers.

Shellfish Grill

Neat! Now you can enjoy your own seafood smorgasbord!

Makes 4 servings

40 clams
20 medium-sized oysters
¼ cup butter

1 Scrub the clams and oysters. Place butter in a grill-safe pan on outer edge of grill to melt and keep warm.

ALWAYS BE SURE TO CLEAN THE SHELLFISH WELL WHEN YOU'RE COOKING THEM IN THE SHELL. THIS WILL ASSURE THAT NO SAND, SEDIMENT, OR OTHER UNTASTY MORSELS GET ONTO YOUR PLATE LATER.

2 Set clams and oysters on the grill 4 to 6 inches above a solid bed of glowing coals. After 4 minutes or when clams and oysters begin to open, turn them over and continue to cook until they pop wide open, 3 to 4 minutes.

3 Hold clams and oysters over butter pan to drain juices into butter. Pluck out meat with a fork, dip in butter, and eat.

I was tempted, but I omitted adding pork to the Shellfish Grill smorgasbord…so, you'll find no "serve the oysters before the chops, casting pearls before swine" jokes here.

Grilled Tuna Steaks

12 servings? Not to worry! If you don't need to serve an army, simply divide the recipe accordingly. Just plan on getting your tuna fork ready to set the pitch for anyone who's fortunate enough to eat this dish.

Makes 12 servings

Twelve 1-inch-thick tuna steaks
1 cup lemon juice
½ cup soy sauce
2 bay leaves
½ teaspoon dried whole thyme

1 Place steaks in a large, shallow container. Combine lemon juice, soy sauce, bay leaves, and thyme in a small bowl, stir well, then pour the mixture over fish. Cover and refrigerate 1 hour, turning fish frequently.

2 Remove fish from marinade. Place remaining marinade in a grill-safe pan at the back of the grill to bring it to a boil to destroy any bacteria introduced by the fish.

3 Place tuna steaks in greased wire grilling baskets. Grill over hot coals 20 minutes or until fish flakes easily with a fork. Turn and baste occasionally with marinade.

Aloha-Sesame Albacore

Get out that grass skirt and get ready to wiggle your way to a mighty fine meal. Just be careful not to overcook it; albacore tends to dry out quickly. This sauce is great on other firm white fish or chicken breasts, too.

Makes 4 servings

Fresh gingerroot
⅓ cup soy sauce
¼ cup dry white wine
4 tablespoons butter
2 tablespoons sugar
1 clove garlic, crushed
Four ½-pound albacore steaks
8 slices bacon
8 tablespoons butter
6 tablespoons lemon juice
¼ cup dry sherry
¼ cup sesame seeds
1 lemon wedge

1 Grate ginger to make ¾ tablespoon.

2 In a small bowl, combine the soy sauce, dry white wine, melted butter, sugar, ginger, and garlic and mix well to make a marinade. Place the albacore steaks in a shallow dish, pour in ½ cup of the marinade, cover, and refrigerate for one hour.

3 Remove steaks from marinade, wrap each piece of fish with two bacon slices, and fasten the bacon with wooden picks (that you've soaked in water).

4 In a small grill-safe pan, melt the 8 tablespoons of butter and remove from heat. Stir in the remaining marinade, the lemon juice, and sherry.

5 Arrange the tuna on an oiled grill rack over medium-hot coals, then brush with a generous amount of the butter mixture.

6 When the steaks are done on one side (after 8 to 10 minutes), sprinkle them with sesame seeds, turn them over, and cook them until the other side is brown. Baste the fish again with the butter mixture and sprinkle them with the remaining sesame seeds.

7 Before serving, turn the steaks over once more to toast all the seeds. Total cooking time should be 15 minutes. Serve with a lemon wedge on each plate.

Seafood dishes are often so rich and wonderful that it's enough to limit your menu to a main seafood course and a simple salad. I often place a crusty loaf of French bread in a basket or on a cutting board with a knife so it's there for those who want it; you can also set out some butter pats floating in a bowl of ice chips if you wish. (Pluck a flower blossom from your garden to place in the middle of that bowl for an impressive touch.) I've given you the map; it's up to you as to which route you take to make the journey. Happy travels!

Easy as ABC: Add Balsamic Cod

I recommend you mix up an extra batch of this marinade using extra-virgin olive oil, divide it in half, and call the extra "vinaigrette." (Depending on your taste, you want to add a little extra oil to the vinaigrette "half." The ratio in salad dressing is usually 3 parts oil to 1 part vinegar; however, the mustard cuts some of the tartness so you may not need a ratio quite that high.) It's delicious drizzled over the greens and veggies in your side dish salad. This marinade is delicious with shrimp and scallops, too.

Makes 4 servings

¼ cup olive oil
⅛ cup balsamic vinegar
1 shallot
1½ teaspoon Dijon mustard
½ teaspoon thyme or fennel seeds
1 tablespoon white wine vinegar
Four ½-pound cod fillets

Pour a batch of the Easy as ABC: Add Balsamic Cod marinade (a.k.a. vinaigrette) over a can of drained artichoke hearts. Whether you let the artichokes "marinate" overnight in a covered glass dish or immediately toss them with your salad greens and veggies, you'll love the results!

1 In a glass dish large enough to hold cod fillets, mix together the olive oil, balsamic vinegar, finely chopped shallot, Dijon mustard, thyme, or fennel seeds (according to your taste preferences), and the white wine vinegar.

2 Add the cod fillets and allow to marinate for 30 minutes at room temperature, or cover the dish with plastic wrap and marinate in the refrigerator overnight.

3 Grill on an oiled rack over hot coals for 4 to 5 minutes per side.

Chapter 11

Meats That Prove Variety Is the Nice of Life

If it looks like a duck, walks like a duck, and quacks like a duck…it's not dressed and ready for the grill. Otherwise, assuming that your main course can't still get up and walk away, my goal in this chapter is to give you suggestions on how to prepare it.

As you read the recipes in this chapter, I remind you that the serving suggestions are just that—suggestions. Some appetites are, shall I say, healthier than others. Plus, the amount of meat after grilling time can vary dramatically. A 5-pound free-range duck can probably be quartered for four servings; a wild duck of the same size—if you can find one that large—oftentimes will barely serve two. When in doubt, ask your butcher. Unless you're on a diet, just remember to look in his eyes so you can concentrate on what he says; avoid glances at his apron.

Wild game does often have a richer flavor, so you may want to counter that taste with subtler side dishes. Fruit dishes are always a good choice: all-natural blueberry preserves on crusty bread, for example. Or raspberry vinaigrette dressing on a spinach salad. Or a baked potato and fresh fruit or a sorbet for dessert. Is your mouth watering yet?

All It's Quacked Up to Be Roast Duck

Choose your red wine for this recipe according to your tastes. Burgundy or port are fine, or use a sweet, fruity wine. Some grill chefs like to flambé the duck as their final step in preparing this dish.

Makes 2 servings

One 5-pound duck
Salt
Pepper
1 small orange
Duck liver
½ cup butter
½ cup red wine

1 Wash the duck, pat dry, prick the skin with a fork, and rub with salt and pepper. Cut the orange in half and place it and the duck liver inside the cavity. (Some cooks truss the bird at this point.)

2 In a small saucepan, melt the butter and stir in red wine. Remove from the heat and keep close by so you can baste this dish frequently throughout the roasting process.

3 Brush the duck with the butter-wine mixture and place it breast side up on a hot grill, close the grill lid, and grill for 15 minutes.

4 Reduce grill setting to low. Continue grilling the duck, 20 minutes per pound, basting frequently with the butter and wine sauce.

For a successful flambé, preheat the liqueur. That way, it'll ignite instantly when you touch the flame to it. Also, choose a liqueur that complements the dish, such as Triple Sec for à la orange dishes.

5 Remove from the grill, place on a platter, and let rest for 10 minutes. To serve, cut the duck into two halves.

To keep the meat moist and the skin crispy, place a pan of water inside your closed grill while you roast the duck. If you can move the coals, place them around a drip pan filled with water. Using the indirect method on your gas grill, set a pan of water over the warmer portion of the grill.

Mousse and Squirrel

Okay, indulge me. I'll admit I included this one just so I could use the recipe name. You'll find the recipe for Who Goosed the Mousse? in Chapter 15 on desserts. This is just one more example of how you can use The Swiss Army Knife Equivalent of Barbecue Sauces (on the following page).

Makes 2 servings

1 squirrel
1 cup of the Swiss Army Knife Equivalent of Barbecue Sauces

1 Split or cut the squirrel into two halves lengthwise and place cut side down in a rectangular glass baking dish.

2 Pour the cup of sauce over the squirrel. Cover the dish with plastic wrap and refrigerate from 1 to 24 hours.

3 Grill over medium-hot coals for 20 to 25 minutes, turning once.

The Swiss Army Knife Equivalent of Barbecue Sauces

Some people swear that this sauce stores well at room temperature. I prefer to keep it in the refrigerator in quart jars. The ketchup imparts a subtle tomato flavor. The vinegar will tenderize about any meat, which makes this sauce perfect for wild game. In fact, I've simmered "gamy" cuts overnight, covering them with water to which I've added ⅓ to 1 cup of cider vinegar. The next morning, I pour off that water and replace it with the Swiss Army Knife Sauce. You can use this as a basting sauce for more tender cuts of meat. Others insist it gives a mean kick to a glass of tomato juice. I'm sure you'll find lots of uses for it, too, so I'm including a recipe for a huge batch.

Makes 12 cups (or 3 quarts)

½ cup brown sugar
½ cup Worcestershire sauce
½ cup Dijon mustard
1⅓ cup ketchup
⅛ cup black pepper
1 tablespoon red pepper flakes
1 quart (4 cups) red wine vinegar
2⅔ cups water
1⅓ cups white wine
½ cup salt

This recipe is best made in advance on your stovetop.

1 Pour all ingredients into a large stainless-steel pot and bring to a boil. Reduce the heat and simmer for 30 minutes, covered. Allow to cool and measure into quart jars to store in the refrigerator.

Bratwurst and Beer

Presto! Chango! To turn these from good sandwiches to great ones, spread stone-ground mustard on some deli buns and toast them on the grill.

Makes 4 servings

4 bratwurst
1 bag sauerkraut
One 12-ounce can of beer
1 tablespoon dried minced onion

1 Place bratwurst on the rack over medium-hot coals and grill them while you prepare the sauerkraut, turning them often to keep them from burning. This step allows the bratwurst to absorb some delicious smoke flavor created when the fat drips off of them—plus there's the added bonus of reducing some of the fat content.

2 If you want to remove some of the "kick" from the sauerkraut, first place it in a colander and rinse well. Put a heavy iron skillet on the grill, add the sauerkraut, pour in the can of beer, and add the minced onion. Bring to a boil and then move skillet to a cooler portion of the grill. Add the bratwurst to the skillet and cover. Once you have your bratwurst simmering, take a break. Go ahead and indulge; no need for that brat to drink alone! Have a beer or a lemonade. You've got 30 minutes to an hour for the simmer cycle. When time is up, put a bratwurst and a generous amount of sauerkraut on a toasted bun and enjoy.

Saucy Horseradish Leg of Lamb

Just 'cause it's lamb doesn't mean it has to be served with mint. And horseradish isn't just for roast beef (although this seasoning is great on a beef roast as well). Dare to be different!

Makes 6 to 8 servings

½ cup prepared horseradish
½ teaspoon ground black pepper
1 teaspoon finely shredded lemon peel
4 teaspoons lemon juice
½ cup butter, melted
One 6-pound leg of lamb

1 In a small mixing bowl, combine horseradish, pepper, lemon peel, and lemon juice. Stir melted butter into horseradish mixture. Spoon desired portion of rub into a small bowl and brush it onto meat before grilling. This recipe makes about 1 cup or enough for 4 to 6 pounds meat. (Leftovers can be stored up to 2 weeks in the refrigerator. Reheat to melt butter before using.)

2 Rub the horseradish sauce into the meat. Use the indirect method to grill the leg of lamb for 1½ hours or until the temperature on the meat thermometer reaches 160°F for medium. Brush with additional Saucy Horseradish mixture several times during the grilling process.

For those times you're in a hurry, season butterflied lamb chops with Saucy Horseradish. Rub and grill those instead of a leg of lamb.

Gobble 'Em Turkey Burgers

These go well with your standard condiments. Or try providing some chutney or salsa instead. Put them on buns or alongside a salad. They'll disappear quickly, no matter how you serve 'em.

Makes 8 servings

1 Vidalia onion
1 yellow or red bell pepper
1 cup fresh mushrooms, chopped
2 teaspoons garlic, finely minced
1 teaspoon olive oil
1 tomato
1 carrot
2 pounds ground turkey
1 egg
½ cup fresh bread crumbs
1 tablespoon Maggi seasoning
Sea salt
Freshly ground pepper to taste

1 Chop onion, then seed and chop pepper. Chop mushrooms and mince garlic.

2 Place a grill-safe sauté pan on the rack and heat the pan. Pour 1 teaspoon of olive oil into the pan, and when it begins to sizzle, sauté onions, transferring them to a large bowl to cool slightly while you sauté the pepper. Transfer the pepper to the bowl and sauté the mushrooms, then the garlic. Add scant amounts of additional olive oil as needed.

3 Seed, peel, and chop tomato. Peel and finely grate carrots. Sauté.

4 Add the ground turkey, egg, bread crumbs, and Maggi seasoning to the vegetables. Mix well.

5 Form mixture into 8 burger patties. Lightly spray patties with olive oil spray and place on grill. Grill burgers for 5 to 6 minutes on each side, until they are browned and firm to the touch.

6 Season with salt and pepper to taste. Serve immediately.

LET'S TALK TURKEY

I'm about to share three different methods for grilling a turkey. **Note:** Please be safe and DO NOT STUFF your turkey with dressing. You can still fix your dressing on the grill. Just mix up your favorite recipe and either wrap it in foil or put it into an aluminum tray that you cover with foil. Your dressing will be done in 30 minutes, so you can prepare it while your turkey starts to cook.

Grilled Turkey

Don't be tempted to peek at the turkey during the first hour to hour and a half. Lifting the lid causes heat to escape and can add another 15 minutes to the time it will take the turkey to get done. It's more fun checking during the last half (while you baste it), anyhow; the aroma just keeps getting better and better.

One 9- to 12-pound turkey
Salt
Cooking oil
Butter

1 Rinse turkey and pat dry with paper towels. Sprinkle some salt inside of the cavity. Skewer neck skin to the back, tie the legs to the tail, and twist wing tips under back. Rub the entire turkey with cooking oil. Insert a meat thermometer into the center of the inside thigh muscle, not touching the bone.

2 In a covered charcoal grill, arrange preheated coals around a large drip pan. (Use the indirect method on a gas grill.) You'll use a medium heat. Pour 1 inch of water into the drip pan.

Place unstuffed bird, breast side up, on the grill rack above the drip pan but not over the coals.

3 Lower lid and grill for 2 to 3 hours or until a meat thermometer registers 180°F to 185°F, brushing occasionally with butter during the last half of the cooking time. If you're using a charcoal grill, add additional coals, if necessary; in most cases, the coals will last for 3 hours. Add water to the drip pan every 20 to 30 minutes or as necessary.

Don't be tempted to taste your turkey too soon. After you take it off the grill, wait 15 minutes before you carve it. It'll be juicier if you do.

THE 3 WORST THINGS YOU CAN DO... WITH TURKEY

1 BUY A TURKEY THAT'S TOO LARGE FOR YOUR GRILL (YOU'LL NEED TO BE ABLE TO CLOSE THE GRILL LID).

2 FORGET TO ALLOW SUFFICIENT TIME FOR FROZEN TURKEY TO THAW.

3 ONLY SERVE TURKEY ON THANKSGIVING.

Type-A Behavior Turkey

Don't want to wait 3 hours for your turkey to get done? Then follow these microwave precooking directions.

1 Follow the preceding instructions for Grilled Turkey through Step 1.

2 Place the turkey, breast side down, in a microwave-safe dish. Cover the wing tips and legs with small pieces of foil if you can use foil in your microwave. Then cover the entire turkey with a tent of waxed paper and microwave on high for 1½ minutes. Turn the dish a half turn and microwave on high for another 1½ minutes.

3 Turn the turkey breast side up and brush with more cooking oil. Microwave on high for 1½ minutes per pound, turning the dish halfway through the cooking time.

4 Insert a meat thermometer and continue to microwave on high until the temperature registers 140°F.

5 Transfer the turkey to the grill, breast side up, and grill according to Step 3 for the Grilled Turkey instructions, except that it should only take about an hour for the turkey to reach the desired temperature of 185°F.

Make skillet cranberries during the last half of your turkey's grilling time. Pour 1 pound fresh cranberries in a cast-iron or grill-safe skillet. Sprinkle with 2 cups white or brown sugar. Cover and set on the coolest part of grill. After an hour, remove the lid and add 2 cups rum. The alcohol evaporates within 15 minutes and you'll have a marvelous, sweet side dish.

Wood-Smoked Turkey

Again, it's your call. Choose the type of wood you prefer: hickory, cherry, alder, or mesquite. Any of them will give your turkey a wonderful smoky taste and a bird grilled to a rich mahogany color.

1 Follow the instructions given previously for Grilled Turkey through Step 1.

2 In a charcoal grill, such as the high-domed one from Weber or Char-Broil, place a drip pan in the center under the rack. Place a generous amount of coals around the drip pan. Light the fire, and once the embers are thoroughly gray, put the wood chips you've first soaked in water for several minutes directly on top of the coals.

3 Fill the drip tray three-quarters full of water. (This is what helps keep the meat moist, so don't skip this step.) Place the turkey in the center of the rack, breast side up. Cover the grill with the lid, with all of the vents open. Smoke the turkey for 3 to 3½ hours, checking periodically to baste with butter and move the bird around enough so that it browns evenly. Add additional coals, if necessary, and be sure you don't let the drip pan go dry. Make sure it always has water.

4 The preferred serving method for smoked turkey is to let it cool and then refrigerate it until you're ready to enjoy your meal.

Chapter 12

Take Another Pizza My Heart!

While I certainly don't believe cooking is an exact science—after all, I've yet to meet the recipe I can't...er, in my humble opinion...improve—nowhere is that more evident than when it comes to grilling pizza. This does take some experimentation. You'll need to know the quirks...er, individual personality...of your grill and then adjust your cooking times accordingly. However, once you and your grill start talking in the same language, you'll be amazed that you ever even considered baking your creations, which now seem so perfectly suited for the grill.

The easiest way to accomplish that task is to first understand a few pizza creation options. After that, simply pick the one that seems easiest (think: lazy equals efficient) and chances are that's what will work best for you. The possibilities are limited only by your pantry and your imagination.

A PERFECT FOUNDATION IS A CRUST

The wise man built his house upon the rock. Consider your pizza crust your Gibraltar, and let the construction begin!

YOU CAN EXPAND THE "SHELF LIFE" OF YEAST BY STORING IT IN THE REFRIGERATOR.

The Dough

Makes four 8- to 10-inch pizza rounds

1 cup lukewarm water (105°F to 115°F)
1 tablespoon sugar
1 envelope dry yeast
3 tablespoons olive oil
3 cups (or more) all-purpose flour (bread flour is okay, too)
1½ teaspoons kosher or sea salt

1 (a) **Food Processor Method** In processor, combine water and sugar. Sprinkle with yeast and let stand until foamy, about 10 minutes. Add oil, then 3 cups of flour and salt. Process until dough comes together, about 1 minute. Knead dough for 2 minutes or until it is smooth and elastic, adding more flour by the tablespoon if dough is sticky. (Note: Newer food processors like the Cuisinart PowerPrep Plus have a "dough" setting and knead dough in less time. Consult the instructions that come with the model you use.)

If you recall how to do the baby bottle test, you can check the water temperature before adding your yeast. Drip a bit on your inside wrist. It should feel slightly warmer than body temperature. If you flinch, the water's too hot! To see the trick I use to cool the water to the proper temperature, consult the instructions for the "Pam's Breaking All of the Rules But It Works Pizza Crust" recipe later in this chapter.

SOME PIZZA GOURMETS SWEAR BY USING KOSHER SALT IN THEIR DOUGH. KOSHER SALT DOESN'T HAVE THE CHEMICAL PRESERVATIVES AND ADDITIVES IN SOME TYPES. SEA SALT IS ANOTHER POPULAR CHOICE. THE CHOICE IS YOURS. (I NEVER USE "TABLE" SALT; I'VE FOUND IT TAKES LESS KOSHER OR SEA SALT TO SEASON FOODS.)

(b) **Breadmaker Method** Add all ingredients to breadmaker in order, according to the manufacturer's user's manual. Set breadmaker on dough setting.

(c) **Mixer Method** In the bowl of a stand mixer fitted with a dough hook, mix the water, sugar, and yeast. Let this stand until yeast is foamy. Add the oil to the bowl and mix well. With the mixer on low speed, add the flour and salt to the bowl and mix until all the flour is absorbed and the dough pulls away from the side of the bowl, adding additional flour a tablespoon at a time, if necessary.

(d) **Mix by Hand Method** In a large bowl, stir together water, yeast, and sugar and let stand until foamy. Stir in remaining ingredients and blend until mixture forms a dough. Knead dough on a floured surface for 5 to 10 minutes, until it is smooth and elastic. Sprinkle the dough with additional flour a tablespoon at a time as necessary to prevent dough from sticking during the kneading process.

2 Lightly oil large bowl, add dough, and turn it to coat with oil. Cover bowl with plastic wrap or a towel. Let stand in warm, draft-free area until dough doubles, about 1 hour.

3 Punch down and then knead the dough in the bowl until smooth, about 2 minutes.

4 Next, divide it into 4 equal portions, shaping each into a ball. Place each dough round onto an oiled baking pan, or dust bottom portion with flour and leave near your floured crust-rolling area.

5 Brush the tops lightly with olive oil and cover with plastic wrap, or dust them with flour and cover with a lightweight towel. (After portioning, you can store the dough for 1 day in the refrigerator, but you must let it sit at room temperature for 1 hour before using.)

Once your dough rounds have risen again for up to an hour, you're ready to roll them out for grilling. On a lightly floured surface, roll out a ball of dough until it is about ⅛ inch thick or up to 10 inches in diameter. Now you're again faced with several options, which are:

1. If you're making your crust in advance of when you intend to grill your pizza, brush off the excess flour, transfer dough with your hands to an oiled baking sheet, and cover surface completely with plastic wrap or waxed paper. Repeat procedure with remaining dough balls and plastic wrap in same manner, stacking rolled-out pieces on top of one another on baking sheet. Wrap baking sheet with more plastic wrap to ensure that dough is completely covered. Chill dough until firm, about 1 hour, or freeze until needed.

2. If you're ready to fix your pizza now, you can either transfer a 10-inch round of dough to an oiled pan or, if the dough is firm enough—meaning it won't ooze its way onto your coals, flavor bar, or lava rock—place it directly on the oiled grid to your grill. Grill for 1 to 3 minutes and then flip over and add your toppings to the grilled side. (Grilling time will depend on the amount of toppings you intend to use. Thicker layers of toppings require longer grilling times during this step, so you'll grill for a shorter amount of time before you flip over the crust. Refer to the pizza varieties later in this chapter for more information on grilling times.)

3. If you prefer to grill your crust directly on the grid but you're concerned that the dough may not be firm enough to do so, you can transfer it to an oiled pan and place it in the freezer for 15 minutes. Then place the crust directly on the grid and follow the steps explained in Step 2.

THE 3 WORST THINGS TO DO...
WHEN MAKING PIZZA

1 OMIT SALT FROM YOUR CRUST RECIPE. INCLUDE AT LEAST A PINCH FOR FLAVOR ENHANCEMENT.

2 USE WATER THAT IS TOO HOT; IT WILL KILL THE YEAST. (YOU CAN COOL OVERHOT WATER BY RAPIDLY STIRRING IN THE SUGAR UNTIL IT DISSOLVES.)

3 NOT LET THE CHILDREN PARTICIPATE. (IF YOU DON'T HAVE ANY OF YOUR OWN HANDY, INVITE THAT KID RIDING BY ON HER BICYCLE!)

GETTING THINGS ALL FIRED UP: READYING THE GRILL

Regardless of the fuel you use, you'll get the best results using a covered grill. If your grill doesn't have a cover on hinges, don't despair. You can achieve similar results by creating an aluminum foil tent and using it to "shelter" your pizza.

Experienced pizza grilling gourmets swear by an assembly line-type of process possible on a larger grilling surface. Using that method, you crisp one side of your crust over hot coals (direct method) and then flip the crust over to the other unlit side of the grill to warm the toppings and melt the cheeses (indirect method).

Other grilling options:

- To cook pizzas on a charcoal grill, build a medium-hot fire in one half of the grill. Two bricks can be placed end-to-end to serve as a divider.
- For a gas grill with two burners, preheat one burner on high and leave the other burner unlit.
- For a single-burner gas grill, first preheat on high, then lower the flame to medium and then to low to cook the second side of the pizza. (You can experiment with this. If your grill allows for your shelf to be at least 4 to 6 inches from your lava rock or flavor bars, you should be able to do all of your pizza grilling on medium.)
- Those of you who can afford a three- or four-burner gas grill should alternate between the direct and indirect grilling methods, according to your personal preferences.

INTERROGATION TECHNIQUES: GRILLING OPTIONS FOR CRUSTS

Variety is the spice of life. And nowhere is that more evident than when it comes to the number of ways you can use a crust.

1. Place a dough round you've first pricked with a fork directly on the preheated and oiled grid. Grill over medium heat until the top of the dough puffs and the underside is crisp, about 3 minutes. Flip and either grill for another minute or transfer to a baking sheet, well-grilled side up, and add your toppings. Repeat with remaining dough rounds.

2. When complete, form crusts on pizza pans, cover, and let rise again. Prick dough with a fork so that air can escape during grilling. Grill 2 to 3 minutes per side until light brown.

If you don't intend to use the crusts right away, allow them to cool. Then wrap them tightly in foil and freeze until you get the pizza urge. These are handy for easy last-minute dinners or when unexpected guests arrive at your door. Push those guests out the back door and seat them at the picnic table (and outside of your messy...er, lived-in...house) until you're ready to serve the meal. If you want to go all out and be an exceptional host, you might offer them something to drink while they wait. This, of course, depends on how long you want them to stick around. Serve a salty anchovy pizza and they'll soon leave in search of something to satisfy their thirst.

The Price is Rice Pizza

Don't limit your pizza crust options to those made from dough or French bread. Here's one way to use up that leftover rice and serve pizza in the process.

3 cups cooked rice (brown or white)
2 eggs
1 cup mozzarella cheese, grated
Dash salt and pepper
½ teaspoon dry mustard
1½ tablespoons butter
3 tablespoons flour*
1½ cups milk
1 chicken bouillon cube, crushed, or ½ teaspoon of chicken soup base (Minor's or Redi-Base)
½ teaspoon oregano
½ teaspoon basil
¼ teaspoon garlic powder
2 cups leftover cooked vegetables, such as broccoli or 1 cup cooked chicken and 1 cup vegetables
1 cup grated cheddar cheese

1 In a glass bowl, mix rice, eggs, mozzarella cheese, salt, pepper, and dry mustard together thoroughly. Spread the mixture onto an oiled 15 x 10-inch cookie sheet. Grill on low for 10 minutes or until eggs are set. Remove from grill until sauce is ready.

2 To prepare the sauce, place a cast-iron skillet over medium to high heat and melt the butter. Mix in the flour with a whisk or a fork. Add milk and stir until thickened and smooth. You'll need to bring the milk-roux mixture to a boil and then simmer it to thicken it and remove the starchy taste. Mix in the crushed

chicken bouillon cube or the chicken soup base. Next add the oregano, basil, and garlic powder. Remove from heat and spoon over crust.

3 Spread the vegetables or chicken and vegetables on the sauce and top with the grated cheddar cheese.

4 Grill over low heat or indirect heat for 15 to 25 minutes, or until cheese topping is melted and bubbling.

*Note: An alternative is to use Ener-G potato flour or instant mashed potatoes to thicken the sauce; it's quicker and you don't have to worry about ridding the sauce of that unwanted starchy taste.

Use leftover gravy in place of pizza sauce. Or perhaps top the rice crust with pizza sauce, pepperoni, and mozzarella cheese. Onion and green pepper taste great, too—sauté first or add them raw so they stay a bit crunchy. Consider serving with Tabasco pepper sauce for extra zing! For a quick crust, spread leftover mashed potatoes onto an oiled pizza pan. Add sauce or leftover gravy and your choice of toppings and grill.

In a hurry? Consider using dried minced garlic and onion in your sauce and simmer until they're tender.

HITTING THE SAUCE

Your sauce choices are as varied as the toppings you can layer on your pizza. With all of the recipes listed below, serving amounts depend on how much sauce you prefer on each pizza.

Now, get ready to think versatility!

The Kind Everybody Recognizes Pizza Sauce

This sauce works for either thick- or thin-crust pizza. If you prefer a thicker, zestier sauce, add more tomato paste. (Buying the kind in the tube comes in handy for just that sort of thing.) An alternative is to sauté the tomato paste in the oil before you add the tomatoes; this caramelizes the sugar in the paste and adds another depth of flavor.

1 tablespoon olive oil	1¼ teaspoons basil
One 28-ounce can plum tomatoes, crushed	¼ teaspoon kosher or sea salt
	¼ teaspoon black pepper
2 tablespoons tomato paste	½ teaspoon sugar
2 cloves garlic	½ teaspoon oregano
1 small onion	¼ teaspoon red pepper flakes

1 Place a heavy saucepan on the grill. Once it's heated a bit, add the olive oil and be certain it coats the entire bottom of the pan.

2 If you desire a milder sauce, mince the garlic and chop the onion and sauté them in the olive oil before adding the other ingredients. Otherwise, mix the plum tomatoes, tomato paste, minced or crushed garlic, chopped onion, basil, salt, black pepper, sugar, oregano, and red pepper flakes in the saucepan and simmer until sauce reduces to desired consistency.

"Who Is Alfredo and Why Is He Sauced?" Alfredo Sauce

Nowhere is it written that pizza sauce always has to be red. Give it a chance and this pasta classic will soon become one of your pizza favorites, too.

3 tablespoons butter
2 cloves garlic
2 heaping tablespoons flour
1 pint half-and-half or heavy whipping cream

Bunch fresh parsley
⅓ cup grated Parmesan cheese

1. In a heavy saucepan or cast-iron skillet, melt butter over medium-low heat. Mince the garlic and sauté in the butter for 2 to 3 minutes. Stir in flour to create a roux and then gradually add half-and-half, stirring constantly. (See the note for The Price is Rice Pizza for suggestions on how to use Ener-G potato flour or instant mashed potatoes to thicken the sauce.)

2. Coarsely chop parsley to make ¼ cup.

3. Once the sauce is heated through and thickened, add the Parmesan cheese and parsley.

For a lower-fat Alfredo sauce, substitute nonfat cottage cheese for the half-and-half or cream. Purée the cottage cheese in a blender or food processor before adding to the Alfredo sauce. Should the sauce separate while you're heating it, add Ener-G potato flour, cornstarch, instant mashed potatoes, or arrowroot in ½-teaspoon increments until the sauce thickens.

Why not make your own "special" Alfredo sauce by adding some secret ingredients to impress your guests. (Forget trying to impress your family!) Consider trying alternatives, such as deglazing the pan with a splash of white wine (after you've sautéed the garlic) or adding some cayenne pepper or onion powder.

Another Alfredo (But No Relation) Sauce

Choices are good. There's more than one way to get sauced. And there's more than one Alfredo, too. Feel free to substitute cottage cheese for the ricotta; you don't even have to drain it first because the cornstarch or Ener-G potato flour will keep it from going watery.

1 clove garlic
1 tablespoon butter
¼ cup part-skim ricotta cheese
¼ cup nonfat plain yogurt
¼ cup grated Parmesan cheese

Optional: ½ to 1 teaspoon cornstarch or Ener-G potato flour
Optional: ¼ teaspoon white pepper
Optional: ¼ teaspoon oregano
Optional: ¼ teaspoon basil
Optional: ¼ teaspoon parsley flakes

1 In a heavy saucepan or cast-iron skillet, melt butter over medium-low heat. Mince the garlic and sauté in the butter for 2 to 3 minutes. Stir in the ricotta cheese, yogurt, and Parmesan cheese.

2 Some yogurts can separate during the heating process. If so, stir in enough cornstarch or Ener-G potato flour to thicken the sauce and stir until well-blended.

3 After sauce is heated through, add the white pepper and other optional herbs if you wish.

Some fireside chefs prefer to sauté the garlic in olive oil instead of butter. Another way to add a change-of-pace taste to your sauce is to sauté the garlic a bit longer than usual, until it has a nutty aroma and is golden brown.

Pep Up Your Pizza Red Pepper Sauce

Roasted red peppers are truly one of life's food pleasures. You'll please your palate with this recipe.

1 clove garlic
¼ teaspoon kosher or sea salt
6 ounces roasted red peppers (No time to roast red peppers? Drain and rinse a jar of red peppers instead.)
1 tablespoon tomato paste
Freshly ground black pepper to taste

1 In a bowl, use the back of a spoon to mash garlic and salt into a paste.

2 Move the garlic and salt paste to a blender or food processor and then add roasted red peppers (See Chapter 13 for instructions on how to roast red peppers) and tomato paste. Add black pepper to taste. Purée until smooth.

Serving suggestion: Use this sauce on a pizza that you top with one 6½-ounce can solid white tuna in water, drained and flaked, 2 tablespoons drained capers, 2 red onions sliced into ¼-inch-thick rings and grilled, and another 6 ounces of chopped roasted red peppers that have been tossed in 1½ tablespoons of extra-virgin olive oil, 3 tablespoons fresh lemon juice, ½ teaspoon thyme, ¼ teaspoon salt, and 1 crushed clove garlic. Top with your choice of cheese.

SOME ASSEMBLY REQUIRED: PIZZA POSSIBILITIES

The choice is yours. You can stick with topping your pizza with the same ol', same ol' available from the local pizzeria. Or you can choose the quick and efficient way to impress your friends by trying these suggested combinations:

Lemon-Pepper Pleaser

Add 2 teaspoons of lemon zest and 1 teaspoon of cracked black pepper to your crust recipe. This makes a crust ideal for eggplant caviar or a seafood topping.

Color Cascade Pizza

Layer the pizza in this order: pizza sauce, finely grated mozzarella cheese, spinach, chopped red bell peppers, fresh mushrooms, and (optional) feta cheese.

Roasted Garlic and Rosemary Razzmatazz

Add 6 diced cloves of roasted garlic and 2 teaspoons of fresh rosemary (or ⅔ teaspoon of dried rosemary, first soaked in some water for an hour, then drained and patted dry) to your crust recipe. This one is perfect for a pizza made using Alfredo sauce and topped with grilled chicken, black olives, sliced fresh mushrooms, steamed broccoli, and grated romano, parmesan, and mozzarella cheeses.

Pizza Carbonara

Some claim that carbonara sauce was invented by charcoal workers to sustain them while working on the slopes of the Apennines. Others say that the generous layer of black pepper sprinkled over the pasta dish looks like charcoal dust, and hence the name. Regardless of its origins, you can create a carbonara–style pizza by adding a beaten egg to each pizza-sized portion of the cottage cheese-style Alfredo sauce. Top your pizza with crispy pieces of bacon, onion, mozzarella cheese, and, of course, freshly ground or cracked black pepper.

Stuffed Crust Special

When it comes to what you use to stuff the crust, the choice is yours: cheese, meat, veggies, or a combination of all three. To make certain that your crust "bakes" completely on the grill, think omelette…sort of.

Generously coat a cookie sheet with olive oil. Combine two pizza rounds and roll that amount of dough out until it's not only very thin, but so that it's a rectangle that fits the cookie sheet, too. Dust off extra flour and place on the cookie sheet. Prick the dough with a fork. Grill for about 3 minutes, or until some air bubbles form on the upper crust. The crust will need to be firm enough for you to flip it over on the cookie sheet.

After you've done that, add your "stuffings" to half of the crust, keeping them close to the center. Fold the crust over and secure edges by pressing with a fork. Grill for another 3 minutes. Flip the crust over again. Add your toppings and return to the grill until the cheese melts and bubbles.

Instead of Pizza Sauce

Don't get stuck in a rut! Who says pizza always needs a red sauce? Open up your world using one of these suggestions:

- ✑ Think about substituting a generous layer of garlic butter instead.
- ✑ Another tasty possibility is using one of your favorite vinaigrette dressings, such as ⅛ cup of extra-virgin olive oil, 1 tablespoon of balsamic vinegar, 1 clove of crushed garlic, and ⅛ teaspoon rosemary.
- ✑ You can even use a homemade or commercial salad dressing, such as ranch or Italian, to complement the appropriate toppings.
- ✑ I'm still not done! Grab your favorite barbecue sauce and spread some across the crust. This makes a great complement for a ham-and-pineapple pizza.

Very Veggie-tarian Varieties

Just as there's more than one type of sauce for your pizza, there are also other mushroom varieties besides the standard white button type. I'm including a recipe for portabello mushrooms to showcase one alternative.

Variations on this theme present a sure-fire way to get your kids to eat their veggies. When you serve them pizza-style, they probably won't even notice that they're eating healthy.

Grilled Portabello Mushroom and Eggplant Feast

Mix 1 crushed clove garlic together with a tablespoon of olive oil and use to coat 4 sliced portabello mushrooms and 20 eggplant slices; grill the vegetables for 2 minutes each side. Brush the crust with the remaining garlic and olive oil. Top with 2 cups of grated mozzarella cheese and the mushroom and eggplant slices, followed by ½ cup of grated Parmesan, and grill until cheeses melt.

Use That Extra Crust Salad Pizza

The next time you fix pizza, grill an extra crust until done. Refrigerate and before serving, top with a thin layer of mayonnaise and 4 to 8 ounces of softened cream cheese. You can either add a layer of chopped raw vegetables and 1 cup of grated cheddar cheese or top with raw or roasted vegetables that have been marinated overnight in balsamic vinegar and extra-virgin olive oil, or lemon juice and extra-virgin olive oil.

Deep dish and other styles of pan pizza

To ensure your topping will warm completely, grill, cook the pizza in two steps. Cover your pizza with half the toppings. Grill 3 to 5 minutes or until the cheeses melt. Add remaining ingredients and repeat. The thicker your crust, the longer you'll need to "prebake" your topping side of the crust before you pile on the goodies and cheeses.

Dessert Pizza

I include even more pizza recipes elsewhere in this book. Check out Chapter 15 for some dessert pizza creations.

Pam's Breaking All of the Rules But It Works Pizza Crust

One time, when a friend asked for my pizza recipe, I used "some" as the measurement for most of the ingredients. (When I mentioned the amount of sugar, I told the friend "not as much some of this 'some'" so she'd be sure to use a higher ratio of flour.) I believe it's important to keep in mind that this is another one of those situations where you first have to know the rules before you can break them. This started out as my means to make homemade crusts whenever I only had enough time to do so in a hurry. With practice, the "wet" method crust evolved to where I intuitively knew the amounts of flour to use by the "feel" of the dough. It's now my family's preferred method for making crusts. Keep in mind that this method makes a crust you'll definitely need to either grill on a pan or prefreeze to make it firm enough to place directly on the grid.

Makes four 8- to 10-inch pizza rounds

1 cup hot water
¼ cup (4 tablespoons) sugar
2¼ teaspoons dry yeast powder
1 teaspoon sea salt
1 tablespoon olive oil
2 cups flour (plus up to 1 additional cup)

1 Here's the method I use to get the water temperature to the perfect bubble-up-the-yeast state: Run water at the faucet until it reaches its hottest temperature and measure out a cup. Slowly pour that water into a glass or plastic bowl large enough to hold all of the ingredients. Add the sugar and stir until the

sugar dissolves. Add the dry yeast powder and stir enough to dampen the yeast. Let the mixture sit for 5 to 15 minutes so the yeast begins to form a foam on top. (Waiting for that "foam" to form is called "proofing" the yeast.)

2. Once the yeast and sugar water mixture begins to bubble (and not before), add the olive oil. Dump in the entire 2 cups of flour and salt, and use a fork to mix, going against all you've been told about making yeast bread recipes and being careful not to overmix the ingredients. At this point, you should be able to pull the mixture from the sides of the bowl so that it forms a large ball. If it is too moist to do this, dust over-moist areas with a tablespoon of flour, moving the dough ball around in the bowl enough to coat the mixture with the flour.

3. Dump ½ cup of flour onto your table or rolling area and spread it around until it's the circumference of your dough. Dump the ball of dough out of the bowl and into the middle of that flour. Pour a tablespoon of flour into the palm of one hand and then rub your hands together over the dough so that the flour dusts the top of the dough and coats your hands. (Remember, this mixture is a bit more moist than you're probably used to working with, so you'll need to be careful until you get the hang of it and feel your way around at first.)

4. Pour 4 tablespoons of flour onto the table in 4 even piles; this is where you're going to put your dough rounds. Carefully roll the dough in the flour on the table until it's coated and then pinch off a fourth of the dough, again coating it with flour if it seems too moist, and form it into a ball and set it in one of the

tablespoon-sized mounds of flour. Repeat 3 more times until you have 4 equal sections of dough.

5 Depending on the warmth of your room, you only need to let the 4 dough rounds rise for 5 to 15 minutes! They won't double in that time, of course; they'll just feel a bit, shall I say, punchier. (That's the official term!) Pick up the punchiest dough round first and move it back to the original floured area. Dust the top with flour. Press it down into a flat round and then, using a rolling pin (with a very light touch! Press too hard and it'll stick to the table), roll the dough until you have an 8- to 10-inch pizza dough about $\frac{1}{8}$ inch thick. (If the dough refuses to roll out to that size, wait a minute and then complete rolling it out. Allowing the dough to rest for a bit is usually sufficient to complete the process.)

6 Brush off excess flour and move the dough to a baking sheet that will fit on your grill. Use a fork to punch a few holes in the crust. Grill for 2 to 3 minutes per side and move to a rack while you prebake the remaining crusts. Once you prebake the crusts, they can be placed directly on the grill when you add your choice of toppings. (Then you'll grill anywhere from 3 to 10 minutes, depending on the amount of toppings.)

A Crustimonial: It really does take longer to describe how to prepare this crust than it takes to actually make it. Once you get the hang of it, you'll love it. I tried an experiment to confirm just how easy it is to make these crusts come out right. When my granddaughter Taylor was 3 years, 2 months, and 17 days old, I had her measure (with 3-year-old accuracy), add, and then stir all of the ingredients. "Gramma" then divided the dough into the 4 segments, but Taylor coated them with flour and made the rounds, repeatedly counted to 10 until it was time to roll them out, and then rolled out the crusts herself. Gramma just had to dust off the extra flour and move the crusts to the pan to grill them. Keep in mind that it's now a tradition at my house to tear off chunks of the first crust and eat them with butter, so plan accordingly. (Taylor is now older and her three-year-old brother Charlie participates in this ritual now, too. We've made a game of the first crust tradition: Gramma says "oops" as I "accidently" tear off the first chunk as I remove the crust from the pan.)

Pam's Sweet As She (Modestly) Is Pizza Sauce

This makes enough sauce for a bunch of pizzas! Of course, the number in your bunch will depend on whether or not you like as much sauce on your pizza as I do. This sauce only keeps for about two weeks in the refrigerator, so freeze the extra.

Makes 4½ cups

1 tablespoon olive oil
One 29-ounce can of tomato
   purée (I prefer Contadina)
1 cup water
¼ cup plus 1 tablespoon sugar
1½ to 2 teaspoons sea salt

1 tablespoon garlic powder
1 tablespoon dried onion
   flakes or minced onion
2 teaspoons oregano

1 Heat a heavy saucepan on the burner until warm and add the olive oil, turning the pan to coat the bottom. (This "seasons" the pan and helps keep the sauce from sticking.) Add the tomato purée, then dump water into that can, swoosh it a bit to rinse out the rest of the purée, and pour it into the saucepan. Once the purée is heated through, reduce heat to low and add sugar, salt, garlic, onion, and oregano.

2 Simmer over low heat for an hour, stirring occasionally to verify the sauce isn't sticking to the bottom of the pan or scorching. Spoon onto the pizza crust and add toppings.

Congratulations! By now you have enough sauce and crusts on hand to be ready to feed any hungry horde. If you want even more, see the suggestions for the fresh tomato and other pizza recipes in Chapter 18.

Chapter 13

A Lucky Number for Vegetable Grilling Details

While you can still use your grill to satisfy your plebian tastes for a generic cookout of hamburgers and hot dogs, if I've taught you nothing else in this book, it should be that if you stop there, you're missing out on a lot.

I'll cover some cast-iron skillet vegetable grilling options during a discussion of kabobs in Chapter 14 and in Chapter 16, "The Whole Shebang—Preparing Entire Meals on the Grill." In this chapter, I'm primarily concerned with the following two vegetable grilling options: foil-wrapped packets and slices large enough to grill directly on the grid.

Soon you'll have everyone thinking that veggies are our friends. Because whichever method you use to prepare them, I'm convinced you'll find that grilling not only retains the nutritional value, but it makes already great vegetable flavors taste even better.

Vegetable Grilling Methods

A wide variety of vegetables taste delicious grilled. I recommend grilling these vegetables in foil:

Beets	Peppers
Cabbage	Potatoes
Carrots	Rutabagas
Cucumbers	Summer squash
Eggplant	Tomatoes
Fennel	Turnips
Onions	Winter squash
Parsnips	

Of course, eggplant, fennel, onions, peppers, summer squash, and tomatoes can hold their own directly on the grill (see Grate Grid Method on pg. 176).

TO FOIL OR NOT TO FOIL, PLEASE USE DISCRETION

Some grilling purists consider using foil packets as "simply steaming" food and don't appreciate the all-around ease of that method—less cleanup involved, no worries of smaller veggies falling through the rack, etc. True, vegetables grilled directly on the rack will absorb more of that smoky, rich, outdoor-cooking flavor. But I'll give you some foil packet hints that let you combine the best of both worlds.

Cooking Times

Foil-wrapped Vegetables	Amount	Estimated Cooking Time
Beans, green and wax (whole)	1 cup	30 to 35 minutes
Beets, small whole	1½ cups	30 to 60 minutes
Broccoli florets	1 cup	15 to 18 minutes
Brussels sprouts	1½ cups	18 to 20 minutes
Cabbage	1½ cups	20 to 25 minutes
Carrots (½-inch slices)	1½ cups	15 to 20 minutes
Cauliflower florets	2 cups	20 to 25 minutes
Corn on the cob	4 medium ears	25 to 35 minutes
Eggplant	(1-inch slices) 1 small	20 to 25 minutes
Kohlrabi (julienne strips)	1½ cups	25 to 30 minutes
Mushrooms (whole or sliced)	1½ cups	8 to 12 minutes
Peppers (1-inch strips), sweet red, green, or yellow	1½ cups	15 to 20 minutes
Potatoes (foil-wrapped)	4 medium	50 to 60 minutes
Yellow summer squash	1½ cups	6 to 10 minutes
Zucchini (½-inch slices)	1½ cups	6 to 10 minutes

Foil Packet Grilling Directions

Cut an 18-inch square of heavy-duty aluminum foil. Place vegetables in center of the foil. Season to taste with salt and pepper. Dot with butter, coat with an infused olive oil (see Chapter 4, "Sanity-Saving Shortcuts"), or add 1 tablespoon water or broth. Bring up the two opposite edges of foil, leaving some space for expansion of steam. Roll the foil to tightly seal the top of the packet and then seal each end in the same way. Place the foil packet on cooking grate. Cook over indirect heat for the time given in the chart, turning packet over once halfway through grilling time. The times given are for crisp-tender vegetables, but if you prefer tender vegetables, just cook longer.

Wrap unpeeled beets in foil and roast on the grill. You can easily slip off the skin once the beets are cool and avoid messy purple-stained fingers in the process.

Speed up the cooking time for brussels sprouts by cutting a small "X" into the bottom of each one.

Potato Possibilities

Now that you have your potatoes sliced, diced, or quartered, before you seal up that foil packet, consider one of the following seasoning suggestions:

  ☾ Add butter and sliced shallots. The subtle garlic and onion distinction created from the shallots turns your ho-hum, humdrum potatoes into a dish that will convince your friends you truly are a gourmet chef!

  ☾ Add butter and sprinkle the potatoes with dill. Another pleasant, yet different, taste treat.

  ☾ Add olive oil and grill. Toss with a bit of extra-virgin olive oil and sprinkle some balsamic vinegar or lemon juice over the potatoes before serving. Truly wonderful!

THE GRATE GRID METHOD

Large vegetables can be grilled directly on the cooking grate. Brush with oil and season with salt and pepper before placing them on the grill. Halve large tomatoes horizontally; slice squash lengthwise. Turn once during grilling.

Corn on the Grill

At least once a year, I make a meal of nothing but sweet corn and crusty chunks of homemade bread with butter. Roll the corn on the bread and then salt to taste. Delicious.

Servings vary

Sweet corn in the husk
Water

1 For each ear of corn, peel back the husks enough to be able to remove the silk, then pull the husks back up and over the ear.

2 In a pan or bucket large enough to completely cover the corn with cold water, soak the ears for 20 minutes to an hour. (Some people swear by adding a little sugar to the water at this step. Use 1 cup of sugar for a dozen ears of corn.)

3 Grill the corn in the husks on the upper shelf over medium heat, turning every 5 minutes. Grill 20 minutes or until the corn is dark yellow in color and the husks are light to medium brown. If the husks dry out too much during this time and either look like they'll start burning or do ignite, sprinkle them with more water.

An earful of suggestions:

1. If you'd rather not turn the ears by hand during grilling, consider placing them in a vegetable holder.

2. Why settle for plain old butter when you can add minced garlic, chives, or other favorite herbs to make a hearty herbed butter that'll add distinct flavor to your corn?

3. Substitute an infused oil for butter.

You MUST try this to believe it! Use lime juice and freshly grated black pepper on corn on the cob instead of butter. This heart-healthy suggestion gives corn a unique flavor that will make you wonder why you ever served it with butter.

Balsamic Eggplant

This recipe teaches you the secret to good eggplant. Whether you plan to use this marinade or simply intend to brush the eggplant with olive oil, always salt it first according to the directions in Step 1 below.

Makes 4 servings

1 large eggplant
1 cup balsamic vinegar
½ cup sugar
1 teaspoon parsley
1 teaspoon chives
1 teaspoon salt
½ teaspoon ground black pepper
½ cup light olive oil

1 Skin and slice the eggplant into ¼-inch-lengthwise slices. Salt and drain in a colander for a half hour. Rinse and pat dry.

2 In a glass bowl large enough to hold the marinade and the eggplant, combine the remaining ingredients. Marinate 4 hours or overnight.

3 Grill over medium heat for 5 minutes each side. The eggplant will appear dark brown and lightly crisp on the outside and will be soft in the center.

Roasted Garlic

Roasted garlic takes on a mild, nutty taste that is wonderful when spread onto crusty bread by itself or first mixed with some butter. (Plan on using an entire head of roasted or grilled garlic for each stick of butter.) You'll love both of these easy methods:

Option 1. Wrap unpeeled heads of garlic in heavy-duty foil and place on upper shelf of grill. Roast for 35 minutes. Allow to cool and then squeeze the cloves out of the skin and into a small glass bowl. Mash the garlic and it's ready to serve or to add to butter.

Option 2. For each head of garlic, peel off the loose layers of skin, but don't expose the delicate flesh of the cloves. Shape heavy aluminum foil into a muffin-sized cup, one for each head of garlic. Put the garlic heads in the foil cups. Drizzle with a tablespoon of olive oil. SPRINKLE WITH SALT, PEPPER, THYME OR ROSEMARY. PLACE THE CUPS ON THE OUTER EDGE OF THE COOKING GRID. CLOSE GRILL LID AND COOK OVER LOW HEAT FOR ABOUT AN HOUR, DRIZZLING TWICE MORE WITH OLIVE OIL. (IF USING AN OPEN GRILL, CREATE A COVER FOR EACH CUP WITH A SMALL PIECE OF ALUMINUM FOIL. THE CLOVES WILL FEEL QUITE MUSHY WHEN READY.

Storing roasted garlic: Roasted garlic will keep for a week or more in the refrigerator if you put it in a sealed glass container and add enough olive oil to cover all of the roasted garlic cloves. The olive oil somewhat solidifies when cool, so it's easy to spread on toasted bread—with or without some of the roasted garlic, depending on your tastes. If you use extra-virgin olive oil, add it to a vinaigrette to impart a subtle garlic taste. "Gourmetlicious" and scrumptious!

Storing garlic: A garlic braid, available in many produce departments, is the easiest way to store garlic. As long as you remember to hang it out of direct sunlight and away from moisture (such as steam from the stove or sink), you can snip off as much as you need, when you need it.

To make a garlic braid, either select choice bulbs from your garden or visit your favorite produce stand in late summer or early fall and buy at least 12 softneck bulbs with stems that are still flexible. Leave about a half inch of the roots on the bulbs, then lay three bulbs on a flat surface and braid the stems together several times. Work in each additional bulb by holding a new stem together with one of the other stems and continue to braid. Once you add the last bulb, braid until you have at least 6 inches from which to make a hanging loop.

Fiery Sweet Mushrooms

Perk up an ordinary meal with this extraordinary mushroom dish.

Makes 4 to 6 servings

1 pound fresh small button mushrooms
1 clove garlic
1 small green onion
Fresh gingerroot
⅓ cup honey
¼ cup white wine vinegar
¼ cup dry white wine or vegetable broth
1 tablespoon soy sauce
1 teaspoon sesame oil
½ teaspoon grated orange peel
¼ teaspoon ground red pepper

1 Clean the mushrooms, pat dry with paper towels, put into a glass bowl, and set aside.

2 Place a cast-iron skillet on the grill rack. Mince the garlic and chop the onion. Grate the ginger to make 1 teaspoon, and add to skillet along with the garlic, onion, honey, wine vinegar, white wine or broth, soy sauce, orange peel, and red pepper. Continue to cook until mixture is hot.

3 Pour mixture over the mushrooms, stirring to coat all. Serve warm or refrigerate, covered, for 3 hours or longer to serve cold.

Optional: Use parsley springs and orange wedges for garnish.

Glorious Grilled Onions

One method for grilling onions is to peel them, cut 'em in half, brush 'em with oil, and grill 'em until they're charred on each side. That takes around 15 to 20 minutes. (Lightly scrape off the charred stuff before you serve them.) This is another alternative.

1 tablespoon balsamic or red wine vinegar
1 tablespoon water
1 tablespoon brown sugar
Dash of pepper
2 tablespoons vegetable oil
6 medium Bermuda or large yellow onions

The easiest way to peel onions is to delegate. However, for those times when there isn't anyone else handy (or willing) to do it, cut the onion into quarters, then cut off the tiny portion at both ends of the resulting four pieces, and voilà! The peel now slides off easily.

1 Combine vinegar, water, brown sugar, pepper, and oil in a bowl and mix well.

2 Halve unpeeled onions, cutting an "X" into the flat portion. Cut a large enough section from each of the unpeeled ends so that the onions will sit upright once they're grilled. Brush cut surfaces with the marinade.

3 Arrange onions, larger cut side down, on oiled grill and cook 5 to 6 inches above hot coals for 10 minutes. Turn over and brush again with the dressing. Continue to grill until the onions are crisp-tender and browned, or about another 10 to 15 minutes.

4 Stand onions upright with smaller cut side down to serve, opening them by pushing against the "X" cut so that they have an opened flower appearance.

Roasted Peppers

If I had to pick a favorite grilled vegetable, it would have to be roasted red peppers. They're colorfully attractive and delicious. However, these instructions work for any peppers you have on hand, from run-of-the-mill green ones to the hot, hot varieties. (Just remember to wear rubber gloves and practice "never touch your eyes" precautions when roasting habanero and other zesty varieties.)

1 Wash peppers.

2 Using a long-handled fork, char peppers over an open flame, turning them until skins are blackened, 2 to 8 minutes. Alternatively, grill whole peppers directly on the rack, turning them every 5 minutes, until skins are blistered and charred, 15 to 25 minutes.

3 Transfer peppers to a bowl and let stand, covered, until cool enough to handle. Or place peppers in a brown paper bag and seal the bag top, setting aside until peppers are cool.

4 Keeping peppers whole, peel them, starting at blossom end. Cut off tops and discard seeds and ribs. (Wear rubber gloves when handling chilies; be careful not to touch your face, especially around the eyes.)

Once you're hooked, you'll never run out of uses for roasted red peppers. They're great in pasta and pizza sauce (see Chapter 12) or added to a sandwich or salad. It's a taste sensation you have to experience to believe!

Storing roasted red peppers: You can store roasted red peppers indefinitely in the refrigerator if you use the "place in a sealed container and cover with extra-virgin olive oil" method described for roasted garlic. You'll create a delicious infused oil in the process— one that is also good in salad dressing or drizzled over freshly grilled vegetables or pizza.

THE 3 WORST THINGS TO DO...
WITH GRILLED VEGETABLES

1. PARBOIL VEGETABLES BEFORE GRILLING, WHICH ROBS THEM OF FLAVOR. IF YOU'RE SHORT ON TIME, PRECOOK THEM IN A COVERED DISH IN THE MICROWAVE.

2. LIMIT YOURSELF TO ADDING ONLY OIL, BUTTER, OR WATER TO YOUR FOIL PACKETS. FOR EXAMPLE, MARSALA WINE CREATES AN INTERESTING GLAZE FOR CARROTS; THE ALCOHOL COOKS AWAY AND YOU'RE LEFT WITH THE DELICATE FLAVOR ENHANCEMENT.

3. ADD TOO MUCH OF A GOOD THING. WHEN IN DOUBT, START OUT USING SMALLER AMOUNTS OF AN HERB THAN THE RECIPE CALLS FOR SO YOU DON'T OVERPOWER THE DISH. YOU KNOW YOUR OWN TASTES, SO TRUST YOUR JUDGMENT.

Seasoned Simmering Summersations

This mixed vegetable combination is delicious served warm as a side dish or when chilled in the marinade for at least 4 hours and served with greens as a salad. Use any combination of vegetables you have on hand or those fresh from your garden. This dish lends itself to the type of fun meal preparation where the family can gather around the picnic table and help slice vegetables while the marinade simmers on the grill.

Makes 2 cups of marinade, 4 to 8 servings

Marinade

2 tablespoons olive oil
1 clove garlic
¼ cup dry white wine
1 cup chicken stock
¼ cup water
2 tablespoons lemon juice
⅛ teaspoon thyme
¼ teaspoon parsley
¼ teaspoon ground celery
  seed
¼ teaspoon salt
4 peppercorns

Vegetables

Broccoli florets
Brussels sprouts
Carrots
Cauliflower florets
Celery or fennel hearts or strips
Cucumbers
Green beans
Pearl onions
Red potatoes, small
Sweet onion
Sugar snap peas
Summer squash (crookneck
  yellow, zucchini, etc.)
Turnips
Winter squash (acorn,
  butternut, etc.)

For a pucker-up pleasing, out-of-the-ordinary side dish, season grilled squash with some extra-virgin olive oil and raspberry or strawberry wine vinegar. If guests drop by and you need a way to stretch a meal, toss the mixture with pasta and top with some freshly grated Parmesan cheese.

1 Place a deep cast-iron or other heavy skillet or Dutch oven over a medium grill. Once pan is heated, add the olive oil and allow time for the oil to come up to temperature, making certain it coats the entire bottom of the skillet. Add minced garlic and allow it to sauté for a minute or two.

2 Stir in the white wine (and then pause for a moment to savor the aroma as the wine deglazes the pan), chicken stock, water, and lemon juice. Add the thyme, parsley, ground celery seed, salt, and peppercorns. Simmer for 30 to 45 minutes, adjusting the grill temperature as necessary. (You do not want to boil this marinade…yet.)

KEEP BAGS OF FROZEN VEGETABLES ON HAND. ADD THEM IN PLACE OF FRESH VEGGIES AND SAVE YOURSELF SOME CHOPPING. YOU CAN ALSO GET 100 PERCENT LEMON JUICE IN YOUR FREEZER CASE. I USE THE KIND THAT COMES IN THE NEAT YELLOW SQUIRT BOTTLE AND I'VE YET TO GET A TICKET FROM THE COOKING PRECISION POLICE!

3 NOW! After 30 to 45 minutes, increase the temperature of the grill or, if using charcoal, move the skillet to the area directly over the coals and bring marinade to a boil. Add your vegetables and simmer or poach until crisp-tender (almost tender). Keep in mind that some veggies cook faster than others. Add the slower-cooking ones first. Because you don't want to overcook any of your choices, you may need to fish some out with a slotted spoon and put them in your serving dish until the other veggies are done.

Gone Fishin'

Tomato and basil are a match made in heaven. So, by all means, if you have basil growing in your herb garden, use it fresh. Use a half to a full teaspoon of chopped basil on each tomato half. Place some on the plate or serving platter as garnish, too. Cheesy Herbed Tomato Grill is another dish you can serve with pasta. Place a grilled tomato half over each serving of pasta and drizzle with a little extra-virgin olive oil. Sprinkle with more freshly grated Parmesan cheese, if desired.

Slightly Skewered

I cover kabobs in Chapter 14, so check out those pages for even more ways to grill vegetables.

Cheesy Herbed Tomato Grill

Fresh tomatoes, cheese, and your grill. Sheer delight. All this and heaven, too!

Makes 6 servings

3 large firm, ripe tomatoes
2 tablespoons olive oil
Salt and pepper to taste
1 teaspoon dried basil
1 tablespoon grated Parmesan cheese or more to taste

1 Wash tomatoes and cut them in half. Brush the six tomato sections with olive oil. Place them on the oiled grill, cut side down, 4 to 5 inches over hot fire, and grill 4 to 5 minutes.

2 Turn tomatoes using a wide spatula and sprinkle with salt, pepper, and basil.

3 Grate 1 tablespoon cheese and sprinkle on tomatoes.

4 Cook 4 to 5 minutes longer or until tomatoes are tender but still hold their shape. Remove from grill and serve hot or warm.

Chapter 14

Stab 'Em and Grab 'Em Finger Foods

When Mongol nomads took a break from their marauding and pillaging, they'd often spend time on the steppes of Asia Minor, roasting horse meat over their campfires. (Hey! Don't complain to me. I didn't pick out their main course!) The Turks called this meal *sis kebabi*, which literally means "sword meat." They threaded the horse meat onto their sabers. Since there aren't many opportunities in the marauding and swashbuckling departments anymore, most of us no longer carry a sword and we have to improvise.

Any shish kabob (sometimes spelled shish kebab) is made up of three components: the marinade, the meat, and the skewer. In an ideal world, the meat should be cut in uniformly sized pieces. This ensures even cooking. This is also not the time to skimp on the fat; it's what absorbs the smoky flavor from the coals and it tenderizes the meat as it melts.

Of course, kabobs aren't always used as appetizers. The first recipe below can serve as a main course. However, because food prepared that way lends itself so well to what I think of as "pick-it-up-with-a-toothpick-or-my-fingers" food, I decided to include kabobs in the appetizers chapter. I'll start out with a kabob recipe, follow that up with some kabobbin' good suggestions, and then wrap up this chapter with lots of other appetizer ideas. En garde!

Tempting Teriyaki Kabobs

The addition of the green onions in this recipe not only adds flavor, it adds character to this appetizer's presentation.

1 pound beef sirloin steak or beef round steak, 1¼ inches thick
2 bunches green onions

Marinade

¼ cup soy sauce
¼ cup red wine vinegar
¼ cup water
2 tablespoons honey
¼ teaspoon garlic powder
¼ teaspoon ground allspice
⅛ teaspoon ground ginger

1 Cut the meat into 1-inch strips. Then cut each strip into ¼-inch pieces and cut an "X" in the center of each piece. (The "X" will make the meat easier to thread onto the onion, part of Step 3.)

2 In a glass bowl large enough to hold all of the meat, mix the marinade. Add beef pieces and refrigerate 24 to 48 hours, using the longer marinating time for cheaper cuts of beef.

3 When ready to prepare for the grill, wash the green onions and trim away tops and roots. Thread an onion onto each of your skewers. Then carefully thread the meat over the onion, leaving some space between each piece of meat.

4 Grill over hot coals, about 10 to 15 minutes, turning frequently.

The Tempting Teriyaki Kabobs marinade can be used with chicken pieces if you omit the wine vinegar (or use a much smaller amount, if you prefer to retain some to enhance the flavor).

Metal skewers retain the heat for a long period of time after they're removed from the grill. Use appropriate caution so nobody gets burned.

SLIGHTLY SKEWERED

Your succulent kabobs will be an even bigger success if you remember these few tips:

- Soak wooden or bamboo skewers as suggested on next page. The only thing that should go up in smoke are your coals, and it will keep things juicy.
- That heat will also continue to cook the meat, so if you're not serving the kabobs immediately, remove them from the grill a bit earlier so the meat doesn't get overly done.
- Leave spaces between the pieces of food when you thread them on skewers. Food will cook faster and more evenly when you do this.
- If you're using thin bamboo skewers, consider threading the food onto two of them. This prevents the food from rotating and better ensures an even cooking exposure.
- Threading zucchini and squash through their skin side gives the vegetables more stability on skewers.
- If your grilled ingredients will get mixed together (like in a grilled vegetable salad), chop 'em before you grill 'em and string like varieties on each skewer. Put 'em on the grill according to each veggie's required grilling time. (See Chapter 13.)
- To grill small stuff when a skewer won't do, use heavy-duty

Add self-basting foods to your skewers. For example, thread bacon between chicken livers or pineapple chunks between some ham. The trick is to use foods that either require a similar grilling time or those, such as fruits, that are flexible enough to adapt to the time required by their skewer mates.

aluminum foil. Punch a few holes in it so the smoke can get through to flavor the food it holds.

- So that they can handle the heat from the grill, ALWAYS soak combustible (wooden or bamboo, for example) skewers in water for at least a half hour to an hour before you intend to use them.
- Don't discard those twiggy stems when you cut back your herbs. Soak thyme or rosemary sprigs and use them as your skewers to impart additional flavor.

KABOB COMBINATIONS

As you can tell by my title for Chapter 11, I believe that "variety is the nice of life." Nowhere is that more true than when it comes to creating kabobs. Here are some of my favorite combinations:

- Pieces of sausage add spicy appeal when threaded between other meats; they're especially good with chicken or lamb.
- Fresh sage leaves, prosciutto or bacon, and pork are delicious together.
- Try combining chunks of spicy Mexican or New Mexican sausage, chicken breast, and onion.
- Enjoy the contrast of a three-color fish kabob: salmon, tuna, and cod (or another white fish).
- Cubes of steak are wonderful when grilled beside shiitake mushrooms that have been marinated in olive oil.
- Shrimp in the shell marinated in olive oil, red pepper flakes, chopped garlic, and coarse salt is another favorite. Serve with wedges of lemon for squirting.
- Try polenta squares or triangles and portabello mushrooms. Brush them with a blend of garlic, olive oil, and fresh thyme as they grill.
- Lamb chunks (first steeped in your favorite red wine marinade),

onion, and sliced winter squash will soon become a family favorite, even among those who rebel at trying anything new. Serve it with chutney and a stack of warm flour tortillas or toasted French bread.

- Smoked chicken-apple sausage (See recipe in Chapter 18), red bell peppers, and asparagus go great together.

- Thread together zucchini, small or half ears of corn, clams, New Mexican sausages, and fresh tuna and then marinate them in olive oil, lemon juice, a pinch of chili powder and cumin, and lots of garlic. Wonderful!

- Try a selection of seafood, such as mussels, jumbo shrimp in the shell, squid, and crab. Brush them with a mixture of olive oil, garlic, and lemon juice as they grill. This combination is great when you serve it with a fruit salsa. (I provide salsa recipes later in this chapter.)

- For a new twist, try grilling vegetables and fruits together: eggplant, summer squash, bell peppers, sweet onions, cherry tomatoes, mushrooms, pineapple, or peaches. Cut vegetables into ½-inch slices or large chunks. Brush with warmed oil (seasoned with garlic or other herbs). Grill until tender. Turn only once. Fruit should be halved with pits removed. Grill as is (no oil needed), pulp side down. Or, thread a serving-sized combination onto each skewer.

If those suggestions haven't triggered some ideas of your own, not to worry. Go back and reread them and they soon will. The key to kabobs is having fun while you create them. If you really want to be *Lazy About* it, set out platters of the foods I've suggested in this section and let your family or guests build their own kabobs.

FLEX THOSE FINGERS FOR THESE

In many ways, appetizers outside at the picnic table and near the grill serve the same purpose as those you present to your guests at a cocktail party or before dinner. It keeps them busy chewing and mingling.

While the function is the same, the foods you serve outside for this purpose are usually a little different. Not vastly so. But you do need to take into consideration such factors as food spoilage possibilities; therefore, don't leave any shrimp or egg dishes out in the sun for hours. Some dishes, such as the mushroom paté I'm about to discuss, work well if you surround the serving bowl with chipped ice. You can grill stuffed mushrooms in shifts, so they come off of the heat at different times and don't sit around on the table for too long before the guests pop 'em in their mouths.

Stuffed Mushroom Caps and Meatballs

I like to use the same meat mixture to stuff mushroom caps that I use to create meatballs. That way, I don't have to worry about measuring precise amounts into each mushroom, so things come out even. I simply roll any leftover meat into meatballs and it looks like I planned the proportions I end up with. (It seems like there is always someone in a crowd who won't eat mushrooms. So, this variety serves two purposes.)

Servings vary

Button mushroom caps, cleaned with a brush. Remember, mushrooms contain plenty of water to begin with, so clean—never soak.

Most appetizers can be prepared the night before. Your job is much easier if the mushrooms are already stuffed and you shape the meatballs ahead of time so that they're ready to pop on the grill 45 minutes to an hour before you need to serve them. Salsa is a dish that tastes even better the next day.

1 Wash the mushrooms, pat dry, and remove the stems. (I reserve the stems to chop for mushroom pâté—recipe given later in this chapter).

2 Stuff the mushroom caps with about a teaspoonful of your favorite flavored ground meat. Here are a few options:

◔ Prepare the Haggis, Haggis, The Clan's All Here recipe on pg. 253. (I like to substitute ground pork and chopped beef heart for the lamb.) Use any leftover meat to shape into meatballs. Have dishes of barbecue or dipping sauce on the table to serve with this variety, such as the Peanut-buttery Pork Sauce recipe given later in this chapter.

◔ Flavor 1½ pounds of lean ground sirloin or ground round with the ingredients called for in the Calypso Caribbean Steak on pg. 101.

Add oatmeal, cracker crumbs, or breadcrumbs in ¼-cup increments until all liquid is absorbed. I love the flavor of this one as it is, but provide sauces or chutney for those who like adding that extra zing.

  Flavor 1½ to 2 pounds of lean ground sirloin or ground round with the marinade ingredients called for in the Pucker Up Grilled Steak from Chapter 8. Mix in ½ cup of diced onion and a tablespoon of Worcestershire sauce. Add oatmeal, cracker crumbs, or breadcrumbs in ¼-cup increments until all liquid is absorbed.

3 I sometimes adopt my brother's cooking method and wrap each and every mushroom individually in its own foil packet (for those times I put them on the back of the fire for the "chefs" to munch on during a long, slow-smoked meat grilling session). However, the most frequent way I grill these is by either placing the mushrooms cap-side down in buttered aluminum foil pie tins (to which I add a heavy-duty foil lid) or inside of foil packets. I put about a dozen meatballs in each foil packet; this works especially well if you need to stagger the grilling times. Place the packets on a medium grill for 45 minutes to an hour, depending on the size of the mushroom caps and the meatballs.

4 Remove the stuffed mushrooms and meatballs from the grill and set them out on serving platters surrounded by your choice of barbecue and dipping sauces. Provide holders containing toothpicks for those who wish to be dainty and not eat with their fingers. I usually place tongs beside the serving platters, too; this makes it easy for guests to transfer the meatballs and mushrooms to their plates.

Marvelous Mushroom Pâté

Get those crackers, toast points, and celery sticks ready. You're going to feel compelled to sample this one as soon as you make it. But go easy. You'll want to refrigerate the rest of it to serve your guests the next day; the flavors will be even better by then.

Makes 3 cups

4 tablespoons butter
1 cup fresh mushrooms
¼ cup shallots
½ cup chicken broth
One 8-ounce package of cream cheese
1 tablespoon scallions (white part)
Optional: fresh chives or scallion greens

1 In a grill-safe skillet, melt the butter and sauté the finely chopped mushrooms and shallots until tender. (I use the stems from the button mushrooms when I make stuffed mushrooms.) Add the chicken broth and simmer until all of the broth is absorbed by the mushrooms and the liquid evaporates. Remove from the heat and transfer to a serving bowl.

2 Stir in the cream cheese and the finely chopped (nonsautéed) scallions. NOTE: If you prefer a stronger spread, substitute 2 minced garlic cloves and ¼ cup of finely chopped scallion whites and greens for the shallots.

3 Chill until ready to serve. Garnish with finely chopped fresh chives or scallion greens, if desired.

Yep! It's time to make salsa. It's simple, as you'll discover.

Build Your Own Salsa

Everyone's tastes are different. But, as you'll soon discover, it's easy to accommodate those idiosyncrasies by adding and subtracting a few ingredients. I usually start out making a salsa base. Then I divide it into 1-cup increments and adjust the seasonings. Let me show you what I mean.

Servings vary

Basic Salsa

Tomatoes and tomato juice

1 Dice tomatoes. If you don't have time to plunge tomatoes into boiling water, remove the skins, and then chop your own—it's okay to use the kind that comes in a can. A 28-ounce can of diced tomatoes yields 3½ cups of tomatoes and juice. Enough for a lot of hungry appetites.

To each 1 cup of diced tomatoes and juice, add:

1 tablespoon chopped shallot or
1 small chopped onion or
½ cup of chopped scallions
2 tablespoons fresh, chopped cilantro (or 2 teaspoons of freeze-dried flakes)
2 tablespoons lemon juice or
2 tablespoons lime juice or

1 tablespoon vinegar (the choice of what kind is yours)
¼ cup extra-virgin olive oil

2 Choose your ingredients and mix together in a glass bowl.
Note: Lime juice is most often used in the spicier, traditional salsa.

3 Now it's time to add some variety. To each cup of salsa, add any or all of the following:

1 clove garlic, crushed
¼ cup chopped red or green pepper
¼ cup drained, canned corn (or better yet, grilled fresh sweet corn, cut from the cob)

4 Depending on how hot you like your salsa, I recommend you start with ¼-teaspoon increments of the following and adjust accordingly:

Chili powder
Cayenne pepper
Red hot sauce
Jalapeno pepper, chopped
Ancho chili powder
Chipotle purée

5 Choose your seasonings and mix them in with the basic salsa.

IF YOU'RE WATCHING YOUR FAT, YOU CAN ELIMINATE THE OLIVE OIL AND CREATE A FAT-FREE SALSA. JUST REMEMBER TO GREATLY REDUCE THE AMOUNT OF LEMON OR LIME JUICE OR VINEGAR, TOO. I RECOMMEND YOU START WITH ONLY 1 TEASPOON OF JUICE OR ½ TEASPOON OF VINEGAR AND ADJUST TO TASTE.

Minor's Base Salsa

Since my discovery of the Minor's bases (see Sources), not only do I dedicate shelf space in my refrigerator to these preservative-free timesavers, I've had a ball creating recipe variations as well. Here are a couple of my favorite salsa combinations. Remember that a little of Minor's Bases and Flavor Concentrates goes a long way. It's better to err on the side of caution and use a smaller amount than what's called for in a recipe and then add more later until you arrive at a salsa seasoned to your taste. (Don't panic if your resulting salsa is too strong; simply add more tomatoes and/or extra-virgin olive oil to "mellow" the flavor.)

Makes 1 cup

Basic

1 cup basic salsa mixture
½ teaspoon Minor's Roasted Garlic Flavor Concentrate
⅛ teaspoon Minor's Roasted Onion Flavor Concentrate
½ teaspoon Minor's Roasted Red Pepper Flavor Concentrate
Optional: chopped raw onions or scallions to taste

1 Add the bases to the cup of basic salsa and mix well.

Spicy Blend

¼ teaspoon Minor's Ranchero Flavor Concentrate
¼ teaspoon Ancho Pepper Flavor Concentrate
¼ teaspoon Chipotle Pepper Flavor Concentrate

1 Add one or all three ingredients to the base salsa, according to taste.

Peanut-Buttery Pork Sauce

As the recipe name suggests, this one is great with pork. (It makes a great basting sauce for grilled pork steak; just be careful because it will scorch easily.) It's also good as a dipping sauce for any of the meatball or stuffed mushroom recipes in this chapter. I often make it the night before, in either the microwave or on the stovetop. It's your call. I give you the grill-top directions below. However you decide to make it, I'm willing to bet you'll make it often!

Makes 1¼ cups

1 tablespoon butter
1 small onion
2 cloves garlic
½ cup ketchup
1 tablespoon Dijon mustard
1 tablespoon brown sugar
1 tablespoon honey
2 teaspoons paprika
1 tablespoon Worcestershire sauce
¼ cup creamy peanut butter
2 tablespoons soy sauce
1 tablespoon white wine vinegar

1 In a grill-safe skillet, melt the butter over medium heat and then sauté the diced onion and chopped garlic until the onion is transparent.

2 Stir in the ketchup, Dijon mustard, brown sugar, honey, paprika, and Worcestershire sauce, and continue to cook over a low heat for 10 to 20 minutes.

Gone Fishin'

3 Remove from the heat and stir in the peanut butter, soy sauce, and vinegar. Serve warm or chilled.

Note: For those who prefer a spicier dipping sauce, stir in ½ teaspoon of cayenne pepper and 2 teaspoons of ancho chili powder after you sauté the onion and garlic. Then, after you remove the sauce from the heat and add in the other ingredients, include a tablespoon of pureed canned chipotle or ¼ teaspoon of Chipotle Pepper Flavor Concentrate.

FRUIT SALSAS

These chunky fruit sauces are a great complement to most grilled meats, poultry, seafood, or grilled and toasty cheesy tortillas (see recipe on pg. 204). My recipes are on the mild side. If you like your salsa hot, add your choice of chilies, black pepper, and cayenne pepper to the mix.

Peach Salsa

3 ripe peaches
1 tablespoon red onion

1 tablespoon lime juice
⅛ teaspoon salt

1 In a glass bowl, mix the peeled, pitted, and coarsely chopped peaches (or nectarines), chopped red onion, lime juice, and salt, stirring gently to combine.

2 Cover and refrigerate at least 1 hour to blend flavors. You can store this mixture in the refrigerator for up to 2 days. (You can substitute mangoes for the peaches, if you prefer.)

Plum Salsa

3 ripe plums
1 scallion
1 teaspoon freeze-dried basil leaves
1 tablespoon balsamic vinegar
Pinch sea salt

1 In a glass bowl, mix the pitted and coarsely chopped plums, chopped scallion (white part only), basil, balsamic vinegar, and salt, stirring gently to combine. Cover and refrigerate for at least 1 hour to blend flavors; this one may be kept in the refrigerator for up to 2 days.

Mix leftover fruit salsas together in a microwave-safe bowl. Cook on high 5 to 10 minutes, stirring after each minute, until juices evaporate and mixture thickens. You've just created what those of us with Pennsylvania Dutch heritage call a mincemeat-tasting sauce. Others call it chutney. It's great served alongside grilled meats, and it will keep up to a week in the refrigerator.

Watermelon Salsa

1 cup watermelon
⅛ cup red onion
1 teaspoon freeze-dried cilantro
½ teaspoon honey
¼ teaspoon cinnamon
1 teaspoon candied gingerroot

1 In a glass bowl, combine the seeded and finely diced watermelon, minced red onion, cilantro, honey, and finely chopped candied gingerroot, and toss lightly to mix.

2 Chill for an hour in the refrigerator to blend the flavors.

Note: If you don't have candied ginger and must use fresh, don't fret—just increase the amount of honey to taste.

Grilled Flour, Corn, or Cheesy Tortillas

Now that you have all of those great dipping sauces and salsas for your guests, you need something for them to do the dipping with. Sure, you could set out a couple of bags of packaged chips, but why? Especially when it's so easy to make these great variations. Again, get ready to build your own.

Servings vary

Garlic Oil

¼ cup olive oil
2 cloves garlic

1 (a) In a grill-safe pan, sauté the minced garlic in the olive oil, strain, and set aside to use to brush onto the tortillas as you grill them. (See instructions below.)

Chili Butter

1 tablespoon olive oil
½ cup onion
¼ teaspoon chili powder
1 tablespoon ancho chili powder
2 tablespoons lime juice
Sea salt
Freshly ground black pepper
½ pound butter

1 (b) In a grill-safe pan, heat the olive oil and then add the chopped onion and sauté it until transparent. Add the chili

powders and continue to cook over low heat for 2 minutes. Remove from the heat and allow to cool slightly. Then add the lime juice and salt and pepper to taste and mix well. Add the butter and mix until well-blended. (You can substitute clarified butter, also known as "ghee," for the butter; ghee can withstand higher temperatures so it is less likely to burn.)

2 Brush flour or corn tortilla shells with either the Garlic Oil or Chili Butter. Place oiled side down on the grill and brush the tortilla tops with the same mixture.

3 Grill until lightly browned and crisp, about 1 to 2 minutes per side, if over low to medium heat. Move to a platter or napkin-lined basket. Break the tortillas into serving-sized portions.

Always use a grill-safe pan—one on which all parts can withstand the high temperatures of the grill (no plastic or wooden handles, for example). Grilling supply stores carry them or you can use one made completely of cast iron.

Cheesy Tortillas

1 Brush flour or corn tortillas with either the Garlic Oil or Chili Butter. Place oiled side down on the grill. Add grated cheese (such as cheddar, Swiss, mozzarella, or a combination of your favorites) to the center of each shell, being careful not to get the cheese too close to the edges of the tortillas; you don't want it to melt out of the shell and drip onto the coals and burn.

2 Place another tortilla atop of the grated cheese–topped tortilla. Brush the top of that shell with your choice of oil or butter. After about 1 to 2 minutes, or when the bottom shell is lightly browned, use tongs or a grill-safe spatula to turn the cheese-stuffed shells to grill the other side.

3 When the shells are lightly browned and the cheese is melted, transfer the shells to a serving platter and cut into wedges using a pizza cutter. Serve warm or slightly cooled with salsa or dipping sauce.

Optional: A "cheesy tortilla" by another name in another neck o' the woods would be a "quesadilla." (Check the "Quesa-Rah!-sa-Rah!-dillas" recipe on pg. 270 to see how to make 'em in a packet.) In other words, instead of putting the fixin's inside of a rolled or folded tortilla, you layer them between tortillas used as top and bottom crusts. You don't have to limit those fixin's to just cheese either. Go wild and add thinly sliced meat and some grilled onions, peppers, and other veggies tossed with salsa! Olé!

Chapter 15

The Grilled Finale

Desserts! Be they gooey and gloriously sticky or gummy and yummy or crunchy and punchy, for many of us, it's the conclusion of a meal that we crave. And best of all, there's no end to the sweet stuff you can fix on your grill.

Whether you want to relax over dessert, savor a cup of coffee or a drink with friends or your significant other, or whether you need something tempting to use to bribe the kids to eat their veggies, I'm here to help. Forget about taking time to stop and smell the roses; that can trigger allergies. I believe in slowing down the pace long enough to enjoy the truly sweet things in life: desserts!

Everybody needs balance in his or her life. Sometimes counterbalance is nice, too. And there's absolutely no need to feel guilty about scarfing down the sweet stuff. Instead, think of it as feeding your incentive to begin that exercise program, a much sweeter way to cool down the grill than dousing hot coals with water, which will warp your grill.

Here are some suggestions to get you started.

Savory Same Ol' S'Mores

Everybody loves this scout and campout staple. They're easy. They're quick. They're delicious.

Makes 4 servings

2 milk chocolate bars (1.55 ounces each)
8 large marshmallows
4 whole graham crackers (8 squares)

1 Break each graham cracker and chocolate bar in half. Place half of a chocolate bar and 2 marshmallows between each of the two graham crackers. Wrap them in lightly buttered foil pieces.

2 Place on grill over medium-low heat for about 3 to 5 minutes or until chocolate and marshmallows are melted. (Grilling time depends upon the grill temperature and whether it is open or covered.)

Join the back-to-basics movement. No dessert is simpler than toasted marshmallows. So grab those skewers with the wooden handles or your grilling mitts and a couple of sticks, stick a marshmallow on the end of each one, and spend some quality time creating some family memories.

(Simpler Than Rice Krispies Treats) Chocolate Mousse

Let your guests and family think you slaved for hours making this dessert. Don't tell them how simple it is to make. The taste certainly won't give away your secret.

Makes 6 to 8 servings

One 8-ounce package of cream cheese
1 teaspoon vanilla
One 12-ounce package of semisweet chocolate chips
One 8-ounce container of frozen whipped topping

1 In a large bowl, mix together the softened cream cheese and vanilla.

2 Melt the chocolate. There is less risk of burning the chocolate if done in a grill-safe double boiler; however, as long as you watch it closely and stir it often, you can use a grill-safe pan or skillet over medium to low heat. Adding a tablespoon or so of milk to the pan or skillet will make it easier to stir the melting chocolate chips to keep them from scorching. That small amount of liquid won't change the firmness of the mousse.

3 Pour the melted chocolate into the cream cheese and blend well.

4 Add the defrosted whipped topping and stir into the chocolate-cream cheese mixture until it's completely blended. Chill until ready to serve.

You don't necessarily need to heat up the grill to make the chocolate mousse recipe, especially if you plan to fix it the night before. You can either melt the chocolate chips in the microwave (on high, stirring it between 15- to 30-second nuking increments, being careful not to scorch the chocolate) or in a double boiler.

IF YOU'RE TIRED OF MELTED ICE CREAM MESSES, THE CHOCO-LATE MOUSSE IS FIRM ENOUGH TO SERVE LIKE ICE CREAM IN A BOWL, OR BETTER YET, ON A CONE.

Who Goosed the Mousse?

For an adult dessert, I recommend substituting 4 tablespoons of liqueur for the vanilla. The following is my favorite combination.

Makes 6 to 8 servings

One 8-ounce package of cream cheese
4 tablespoons (or more) coffee liqueur
One 12-ounce package of semisweet chocolate chips
One 8-ounce container of frozen whipped topping

1 In a large bowl, mix together the cream cheese and liqueur.

2 Follow steps 2 through 4 given for the (Simpler Than Rice Krispies Treats) Chocolate Mousse.

3 If you want to get fancy about it and make a big impression, don't just chill the mousse. Instead, spoon it into a pastry bag and pipe it into sugar cones or your dessert dishes.

This Pie's the Limit

This is dessert that, with a little foresight, you can bake on your grill so it's ready to serve when you finish the main course.

1 spice cake mix
1½ cups quick-cooking oatmeal
½ cup butter
1 egg
½ cup chopped nuts
½ cup brown sugar
One 21-ounce can of apple or peach pie filling
Optional: ½ cup grated cheddar cheese

1 In a large bowl, combine the cake mix, 1 cup of the oatmeal, and 6 tablespoons of the butter. Mix until crumbly, reserving 1 cup of the resulting crumbs.

2 To the remaining crumbs, blend in the egg; if you intend to use apple pie filling, also add the ½ cup of grated cheddar cheese. Press this mixture into a buttered 12-inch pizza pan or 13 x 9-inch sheet pan. Grill for 12 to 15 minutes.

3 Remove pan from the grill and spread the pie filling over the crust.

4 In a small bowl, mix the remaining oatmeal, nuts, 2 table-spoons butter, and the brown sugar. Sprinkle this mixture over the top of the pie filling.

5 Return to the grill for another 15 to 20 minutes. Serve warm or chilled, cut into wedges or squares.

Hot Fruit Salad

This will tempt you to heed that bumper sticker's advice: Life's short; eat dessert first. Instead, save the best for last. A fantastic finale for a fine feast.

Makes 6 servings

1 medium pineapple
2 large bananas
3 medium plums
2 medium nectarines or peaches
½ cup honey
1 tablespoon fresh lemon juice
¼ cup mint leaves or 2 drops peppermint oil

1 Cut the pineapple lengthwise into 6 wedges, leaving the leaves attached. Cut the bananas into thirds, the plums in half, and the nectarines or peaches into quarters.

2 In cup, stir together honey, lemon juice, and 1 tablespoon of the mint leaves or the 2 drops of peppermint oil.

3 With tongs, place all fruit pieces on grill over medium heat and grill for 10 to 15 minutes, turning the fruit occasionally until it's browned and tender. Brush fruit with some honey mixture during last 3 minutes of the grilling time.

4 To serve, arrange grilled fruit on large platter; drizzle with any remaining honey mixture. Garnish with fresh mint.

Stuck in a rut? Don't limit yourself to grilled fruit over ice cream. Grill angel food cake wedges over medium heat about 1 minute or until golden on both sides. For added flavor, brush with your favorite liqueur or some honey butter before you put the wedges on the grill.

Bananarama Razz Ma Jazz

Don't worry about the alcohol content in this dish. The alcohol burns off when you ignite the sauce, so that after showmanship grilling worthy of the most demanding audience, all you're left with is marvelously flavored bananas and sauce to foster your favorite feeding frenzy fantasies.

Makes 8 servings

4 ripe bananas
4 tablespoons butter
2 tablespoons light brown sugar
½ teaspoon ground cinnamon
¼ teaspoon ground nutmeg
¼ cup banana- or nut-flavored liqueur
¼ cup light rum

Grilling a ham and got some extra pineapple rings left over? Brush them with dark rum, grill a few minutes, turn the rings and brush with more dark rum. Sprinkle with brown sugar. Grill 6 to 8 minutes. Serve with a scoop of ice cream or sorbet nestled in the center or dollop of yogurt.

1 Peel and slice the bananas.

2 In a large grill-safe frying or sauté pan, melt the butter over medium high heat. Add the bananas and slowly stir them while they heat and soften slightly. Add the brown sugar, cinnamon, and nutmeg, and stir for another 30 seconds.

3 Remove the pan from the flame, and add the liquor and rum. Return the pan to the grill. Once the alcohol comes to temperature, it should ignite. If it doesn't, you can ignite it with a match. Leave the pan on the grill until the flame burns off.

4 Serve the bananas and sauce over vanilla or praline ice cream, pound cake, or hot waffles.

To guarantee dessert is ready when you're ready to serve it, plan its grilling time so that it's done by the time you're ready to serve your meal. Then turn off the grill or set at its lowest temperature. Move dessert to a low temperature area to keep it warm.

Polka Dot Apples

Served plain or over ice cream or cake, your family will love this.
Makes 4 servings

One 20-ounce can of apple pie filling
¼ cup raisins
1 teaspoon lemon juice
2 tablespoons butter
⅛ cup packed brown sugar
¼ cup oatmeal
Pinch salt
⅛ teaspoon ground cloves
¼ teaspoon ground cinnamon

1 In a large bowl, mix the apple pie filling, raisins, and lemon juice together.

2 Ready an 18-inch square of heavy-duty aluminum foil. Use 1 tablespoon of the butter to oil the "inside" portion of the foil that will be next to the food. Pour the apple pie filling mixture into the center of foil and spread it out a bit.

Note: If you prefer, you can butter an aluminum pie pan and use that instead. You can then just make your "lid" out of a single thickness of aluminum foil; use about a teaspoon of the butter to oil the inside of the foil lid.

3 In a small bowl combine the brown sugar, oatmeal, salt, ground cloves, and ground cinnamon. Mix well and sprinkle over the top of the apple pie filling mixture.

4 Melt remaining tablespoon of butter and drizzle it over the oatmeal mixture.

5 Bring the edges of the foil up and over the mixture, folding over the top to make a tent and crimping the ends by folding them over to seal the packet. (Or, if using an aluminum pie plate, cover the pie plate with a loose-fitting piece of foil, butter side down, pinching the perimeter so it clings to the foil pan, but leaving some space against the top.)

6 Place packet over medium coals and grill for about 30 minutes. Serve warm.

Go ahead. Be adventurous. Experiment. Substitute ⅔ cup of your favorite granola for the oatmeal, brown sugar, and spices.

Gone Fishin'

Crust Isn't Just For Pizza Anymore Rolls

The next time you make up a batch of "Pam's Breaking All of the Rules But It Works Pizza Crust" from Chapter 12, keep back some of the dough to use for breakfast or dessert rolls. I'll give you some suggestions, but these are only a guide. Use your imagination and create desserts of your own.

Why make only one batch of rolls? Mix up a double batch of the crust recipe and turn half of it into rolls. Roll it up with your choice of ingredients inside and freeze the roll before slicing. Bring to room temperature and allow dough to rise a bit and grill or bake later.

1 Roll out the section of dough as usual but rather than pregrill the result, use it to create one of these:

- Generously butter the top of the crust and then sprinkle it with cinnamon, sugar, and some grated lemon rind. Drizzle on some vanilla. Add some chopped walnuts, if you like. Roll up and then slice, placing the rolls close together on a buttered pan. Drizzle maple syrup over the top of the rolls and grill for 15 to 20 minutes.
- Spread the dough with peanut butter and grape jelly or peanut butter and honey, roll, slice, place on a buttered pan, and grill for 15 to 20 minutes.
- Follow the steps in the first option, except substitute grated orange rind for the lemon and pecans for the walnuts.

Go wild! Come up with your own combinations.

THE VERSATILE DO-IT-YOURSELF DESSERT

Whether you need a dessert treat for the kids or the kid in you, one of these suggestions is sure to be just what the sweet tooth ordered. You see, s'mores isn't the only campout trick I know. Another favorite is what some people call:

Hobo Popcorn

Peanut or vegetable oil
Unpopped popcorn kernels

1 In the center of an 18-inch square of heavy-duty or a double thickness aluminum foil, place one teaspoon of oil and one tablespoon of popcorn. Bring foil corners together to make a pouch. Seal the edges by folding, but be sure to allow room for the popcorn to pop. Tie each pouch to a long stick with a string. Give everyone a pouch and have them hold it over the hot coals, shaking constantly until all the corn has popped.

2 Season the popcorn with:

- Salt and butter
- Soy sauce and toasted sesame oil
- Melted chocolate
- Melted peanut butter
- Melted caramels

Or season with your favorite flavored salt, be it a cheese, chili, or herb blend.

Chapter 16

The Whole Shebang: Preparing Entire Meals on the Grill

There are very few indoor cooking methods that allow you to start a meal and then safely walk away from it. Sure, you can do that with a crockpot and, in some cases, with meals that you roast in the oven. But nothing lends itself to a haphazard, afterthought style of cooking like grilling does. With grilling, family activities can be your priority; the stuff cooking on the grill is secondary. In many cases, you can start your meal on the grill and only return to check on its progress when it's convenient for you.

Case in point: I have a friend who combines grilling, exercising, and entertaining her kids. Not an easy feat! But she has it down to a science. She starts her meal on the grill and then plans walks around the block, the number of which depend on the steps required to complete the meal. Families as large as hers are rare these days. But, as you'll soon see, she's figured out how to handle it.

Once she has the food on the grill, this mom then begins a trip around the block. She leads her procession pushing the baby in a stroller followed by the next child on a tricycle, and the next one on a bike with training wheels. The eldest is on foot, keeping the kids in line and bringing up the rear in what looks like an unchoreographed

Don't discard those outer leaves from kale and other greens. Use them to create a serving dish. Arrange them on a coated paper or plastic plate and ladle your salad on top. It makes an attractive presentation and nobody will notice that you're not using your best china.

version of the elephant's parade from Disney's *The Jungle Book* or *Dumbo*.

It doesn't matter if you're able to get your spouse or your teenagers to cooperate with that sort of plan (which, in part, depends on whether or not one of them will still fit in a stroller), you can still adapt your outdoor cooking steps to accommodate your lifestyle—not the other way around.

WE'LL SALAD IN THE SUNSHINE

The recipes in this section can serve as an entire meal. I'll show you others that can accompany and complement an entrée in the "Side Dishes NOT To Be Pushed Aside" section.

It's Grilled Vegetable Salad Lime!

This salad's succulent fresh sweet corn, zucchini, yellow squash, and tomatoes acquire robust flavors from the citrus- and chili-infused dressing and smoky perfection from the grill. Serve this salad with the suggested lightly grilled cheese-and-onion-filled flour tortillas and you have a complete meal.

Makes 4 servings

Chili-Lime Dressing

½ cup extra-virgin olive oil
3 tablespoons lime juice
¾ teaspoon chili powder
½ teaspoon ground cumin
½ teaspoon salt

¼ teaspoon garlic powder
Optional: 1 teaspoon sugar

Salad Fixings

4 small ears yellow corn
2 medium zucchini
2 medium yellow squash
4 small ripe plum tomatoes
4 green onions
Four 6-inch-diameter flour tortillas
½ cup shredded sharp cheddar cheese
Lettuce leaves

You want food to stick to your ribs, not your grill rack. Therefore, don't just season the meal, season the rack, too. Herbs and spices go on the former; for the rack, either coat it with a generous amount of cooking oil or use nonstick vegetable cooking spray. I prefer the latter. It goes on fast sans mess.

1 Coat grill rack with nonstick vegetable cooking spray.

2 In a glass jar with tight-fitting lid, prepare the Chili-Lime Dressing by combining the oil, lime juice, chili powder, cumin, salt, and garlic powder until well mixed. Add the sugar, if desired. Set aside.

3 Carefully pull back husks from corn, leaving them attached at base, and remove all the silk. Lightly brush corn with some Chili-Lime Dressing. Place corn on tray while preparing the other vegetables.

4 Use your discretion as to whether or not you first peel the zucchini and yellow squash. Cut them crosswise in half, then cut the halves lengthwise into ¼-inch-thick slices. Remove and discard the seeds. Place both varieties of squash on the tray with the corn. Brush slices on both sides with some dressing. Cut tomatoes lengthwise into halves and brush with some dressing.

So it'll be easier to handle when it comes time to cut the kernels off of the cob, refrigerate sweet corn first or cool it under cold running water. Be sure your knife is sharp. And, of course, cut away from your body in case the knife slips. Otherwise, it couldn't be easier!

5 Grill the corn over medium-hot coals until kernels are lightly browned, 8 to 10 minutes. Once it's done, transfer the corn to a tray.

6 Grill zucchini and yellow squash, turning occasionally until lightly browned, 2 to 3 minutes. Also transfer these to the tray once they are done.

7 Grill tomatoes, turning once, until just softened, which should take 1½ to 2 minutes. Transfer tomatoes to the tray with the other vegetables and set aside.

FEEL FREE TO SUBSTITUTE FROZEN CORN, CARROTS, AND GREEN BEANS FOR THE FRESH VEGETABLES. TOSS THE THAWED VEGETABLES WITH THE DRESSING AND DIVIDE EVENLY BETWEEN FOUR FOIL PACKETS. MAKE PINHOLES IN THE PACKETS SO THE VEGGIES PICK UP SMOKE FLAVOR. PLACE THE PACKETS ON THE RACK OVER MEDIUM-HOT COALS; GRILL AT LEAST A HALF HOUR BEFORE YOU PREPARE YOUR TORTILLAS.

8 Finely chop the white portion of the green onion. Heat flour tortillas over low coals, turning often just until softened, 15 to 20 seconds. Sprinkle half of each tortilla with 2 tablespoons shredded cheese and one fourth of the chopped green onion. Fold tortillas in half and grill just until cheese softens. Fold tortillas in half again and transfer to tray with corn.

9 To serve, line 4 plates with some lettuce leaves. Cut corn kernels off cobs and set aside. Arrange one fourth of zucchini and yellow squash alternately with each other on one side of each plate. Mound corn in center and garnish with tomato halves and folded tortillas.

10 Serve with the remaining Chili-Lime Dressing.

Skewered Caesar-Style Chicken Salad

Many people assume that Caesar salad, a food fit for the gods, originated in Rome. Not so. It was actually created by a Tijuana chef, using what he had left on hand, to serve a large crowd of late diners. At the last minute, he threw in some bread crumbs…and the rest is history. I think you'll like my version, too.

Makes 4 servings

½ cup olive oil
4 cloves garlic
2 teaspoons dried rosemary
4 large boneless, skinless
    chicken breasts
32 1-inch cubes Italian bread
2 tablespoons lemon juice
1 teaspoon Worcestershire sauce
¼ teaspoon dry mustard
¼ teaspoon ground black pepper
Torn romaine lettuce leaves
½ cup green olives
½ cup black olives
4 tomatoes
4 tablespoons grated Parmesan cheese

1 Soak 8 bamboo skewers (to be used for the bread cubes) in water for a half hour.

2 In a small grill-safe saucepan, heat oil over medium heat and add minced garlic and cook 1 minute or until golden. Remove from heat and add the rosemary.

You can substitute purchased Caesar salad dressing for the garlic- and rosemary-flavored oil. Just be sure to get the regular dressing; while you can use the fat-free kind over your salad, it won't work as a coating for the chicken and bread.

3 Rub the chicken breasts with one fourth of the seasoned oil and set aside for the 5 minutes it takes you to prepare the bread cubes.

4 Brush bread on all sides with about 1 tablespoon garlic-flavored oil and thread onto the bamboo skewers.

5 Place chicken breasts on the grill over medium-hot coals, grilling until done (15 to 18 minutes), turning once.

6 During the last few minutes of the chicken grilling time, place the skewered bread cubes on grill rack, turning frequently, until golden brown. Transfer bread to tray or plate.

7 Just before serving, stir the lemon juice, Worcestershire sauce, mustard, and pepper into remaining garlic-flavored oil; pour into small pitcher and set dressing aside. Ready 4 individual platters with 2½ cups of romaine on each. Divide the olives and chopped tomatoes between the salads. Top with 2 bread skewers.

8 Either place a chicken breast to the side of each salad or cut each breast into cubes and toss with the romaine.

9 Sprinkle each salad with 1 tablespoon of freshly-grated Parmesan cheese.

10 Pass dressing to serve over salad.

Not Just Another Chicken Salad

The spinach makes this salad colorful. The sautéed walnuts add an extra dimension you must taste to believe! This salad will impress your friends and, best of all, it's easy to make!

Makes 4 servings

2 boneless, skinless chicken thighs
1 cup walnut pieces
1 tablespoon olive oil
¼ teaspoon ground ginger
½ teaspoon candied ginger
4 tablespoons orange juice
2 tablespoons white wine vinegar
4 cups fresh spinach leaves
2 oranges or drained mandarin orange slices
1 cup sliced, fresh mushrooms
4 slices red onion

1 Place your grill wok or a grill-safe, heavy skillet over hot coals to preheat.

2 Cut the chicken into cubes and coarsely chop the walnuts.

3 Once the wok or skillet is warm, add the olive oil. When it starts to sizzle, add the chicken cubes and walnuts, stirring to coat them with the oil.

4 Sprinkle the ground ginger over the chicken and walnuts. Add the chopped candied ginger. Stir-fry until chicken is done, 5 to 10 minutes, depending on the temperature of your skillet.

5 Add 2 tablespoons of the orange juice to the skillet and continue to stir-fry until some of it is absorbed by the chicken. Remove the skillet from the heat and add remaining orange juice and white wine vinegar.

6 Tear the spinach into bite-sized pieces, then toss with orange sections, sliced fresh mushrooms, and red onion slices and divide among 4 plates.

7 Spoon the chicken mixture over the tops of the spinach salads and serve immediately.

Salad Smarts

1. A salad should always be simpler than, say, brain surgery, so expand your horizons. Don't limit yourself to complex salad preparations. Combine a mixture of chopped raw vegetables and chilled pasta and toss with your favorite dressing.

2. Improvise. If you have an herb garden, substitute the woody stems from your thyme or rosemary plants for skewers for the Caesar-Style Chicken Salad. Read more about this in Chapter 14.

3. Keep bags of frozen vegetables at the ready in your freezer. Most will work great in salads if you grill them until they're crisp and tender, either inside a foil packet or stir-fried in your grill wok. (See Chapter 2, "Equipment Education.")

THE WORKS: CASSEROLE-STYLE AND MARVELOUS MAIN DISHES

During the summer, there's no reason to introduce even more heat into the kitchen by using your oven. Not when you have a grill. The recipes in this section show you what I mean.

Personal Pumpkin Casseroles

This recipe calls for canned vegetables. If you prefer to use fresh or frozen, you'll need to precook them a bit in order for them to get to the soup-tender consistency required of this dish. So that they experience the full hearty flavor of this dish, be sure to instruct your family or guests to use their spoons to scrape a portion of pumpkin into each bite.

Serves 4

4 pumpkins (small enough to sit on the grill rack with the lid closed, about 1 pound each)
1 pound lean ground beef
1 small onion
¼ teaspoon basil
¼ teaspoon thyme
¼ teaspoon rosemary
¼ teaspoon marjoram
¼ teaspoon cinnamon
1 can creamed corn
1 can whole kernel corn
1 can French-cut green beans
2 tablespoons brown sugar

1 Cut out a lid on each pumpkin and remove the seeds and clean the inside.

2 Either in a grill-safe heavy skillet atop the grill rack or on your stovetop (if assembling the pumpkins in advance), brown the ground beef with the chopped onion, basil, thyme, rosemary, marjoram, and cinnamon until it is completely cooked. Drain the fat from the ground beef.

3 In a large bowl, mix the ground beef with the creamed corn and the drained whole kernel corn, drained green beans, and brown sugar.

4 Divide the mixture between the 4 pumpkins and put the pumpkin "lids" back in place.

5 "Bake" in a medium grill with the lid closed for 1½ hours or until a toothpick can easily prick the flesh of the pumpkin.

6 Use pie plates as your individual serving dishes, so that if a spoon pierces the outside skin of the pumpkin, the juices will be contained. Garnish by placing the lid to the side in a dollop of sour cream.

PUMPKINS AREN'T THE ONLY VEGETABLES IN THE SQUASH FAMILY THAT CAN SERVE EXTRA DUTY. A STUFFED ACORN SQUASH CAN ACT AS ITS OWN CONTAINER, TOO. AND DON'T FORGET DUAL-DUTY FRUIT; NOTHING IS MORE ATTRACTIVE THAN MIXED FRESH FRUIT SERVED IN A WATERMELON "BOWL."

Lemony Herb Roasted Chicken

Among my circle of friends, this recipe is known by an acronym created from the list of ingredients: MR. T Lemon Butt Chicken. Marjoram, Rosemary, Thyme, Lemon, Butt(er). Whatever you call it, I call it delicious.

Makes 2 to 4 servings

¼ cup butter
¼ teaspoon marjoram
¼ teaspoon rosemary
¼ teaspoon thyme

1 lemon
2½- to 3-pound whole chicken

1 In a grill-safe saucepan, melt butter and add the marjoram, rosemary, and thyme.

2 Make a small incision in the lemon and squeeze about a tablespoon of juice into the butter mixture. Then, pierce the lemon in several other places and place inside the chicken cavity.

3 Brush half of the herb-butter mixture over the chicken and then place it breast side up on grill rack.

4 Grill for 1¼ to 1¾ hours, uncovered, until done, brushing the chicken with the butter mixture several more times. (If chicken browns too quickly, cover loosely with a "tent" made of aluminum foil.)

Salmonella is a major concern with chicken. Take every precaution to avoid cross-contamination. The best way to ensure that chicken is done is to use a meat thermometer to verify when the white meat has reached 175°F (or 185°F if you check the dark meat).

When You Don't Have Time to Be Impressive but Still Wanna Steak-and-Potatoes Meal

Yikes! Your spouse forgot to tell you that the boss and his or her spouse is coming for dinner: TONIGHT! You need something in a hurry, or preferably, faster. As long as you keep an emergency package of strip steaks in the freezer, you'll always be prepared. Seat everybody around the picnic table with a frosty-cold beverage in front of them (you'll find suggestions at the end of this chapter), light the grill, and within 10 minutes, you'll be ready to join them.

Makes 4 servings

Four 8-ounce strip or loin steaks
Lea & Perrins Worcestershire sauce
Balsamic vinegar
Garlic powder
4 baking potatoes, or 12 to 16 red potatoes
Salad fixings of your choice

1 Remove the steaks from the freezer, put them on a microwave-safe plate, and partially thaw them in the microwave.

Note: Do not rush this step. If you use the high setting on your microwave, you'll partially cook the steaks and they'll be tough. Follow the manufacturer's directions for your specific machine. When in doubt, use the 50 percent setting for 3 minutes. You don't want them completely thawed because they'll set outside for about 10 minutes before you place them on the grill.

2 While the steaks thaw, select and wash the potatoes. Here are three suggestions on how to prepare them to impress your guests:

☾ Pierce each of the 4 large baking potatoes, put on a microwave-safe plate, and once you remove the steaks from the microwave, cook the potatoes on high for 5 to 8 minutes. Have 4 pieces of foil ready to use to wrap the potatoes once they're done in the microwave. I like to butter the portion of the foil that will wrap against the potato. Place a potato on each foil piece, then make an incision on the top of each potato into which you place a pat of butter. Wrap the foil around each potato.

☾ Once you've determined the number that will be sufficient for each serving, wash and pierce the small red potatoes. Follow the instructions in the bullet point above, only place 3 to 4 potatoes on each foil section.

☾ Clean and dice your choice of potatoes. Put them in a microwave-safe covered bowl and cook for 5 to 8 minutes, until just tender. (Be careful when you remove the lid so that you don't get burned by the steam.) Divide the potatoes equally and spoon them onto 4 buttered foil pieces that are large enough to wrap around the pota-toes. Top with some butter and sprinkle with dill, or for an even better taste sensation, some chopped shallots. Shallots impart a flavor that I find is hands-down better than that which you get from onions or garlic!

3 While the potatoes are in the microwave, arrange your salad greens in individual bowls or, if you prefer to let your guests make their own, into paper towel-lined baskets. Most people don't mind assembling their own salads, so simply grab a few

bottles of salad dressing from the refrigerator to take with you to the picnic table.

4 Place the steaks on a platter to take them to the grill. Collect your dinnerware and napkins, the foil potato packets, the salad fixings, and the bottles of Worcestershire sauce, balsamic vinegar, garlic powder, and salad dressings, and you're ready to move outside.

At this point, unless you prefer to be a martyr, now is the time to yell for everyone outside to get up and help you do the carrying. (Be sure to make that request with a smile on your face so it reflects in your voice.)

5 Smile again, this time so they can see you do so, thank everyone for their help, and pour them some more of their beverages of choice to keep them occupied awhile longer.

6 Place the potato packets on the grill. You now have about 10 minutes in which to enjoy a little something cold to drink your-self.

7 Place the steaks on the grill rack directly over the medium-hot coals. Sprinkle each steak with generous amounts of the Lea & Perrins Worcestershire sauce, the balsamic vinegar, and some garlic powder. (I believe at this point flare-ups are our friend, for they allow me to sear the meat and seal in the juices.) You're not running a restaurant here, so it's up to you whether or not you wish to take "requests" as to how everyone would like their steaks. Even if those requests range from medium (the

least done I prepare my steaks to ensure they've reached a temperature sufficient to destroy harmful bacteria) to well-well-done, by strategically moving the steaks to hotter and cooler portions of the grill, you can fix them so they all get done at the same time.

8 Once the steaks are ready to serve, instruct your guests and spouse (who should also be carrying your plate) to bring their plates to the grill. Slap a steak and a potato packet onto each plate, steer everyone back to the table, start fixing your own salad so they follow your lead, and now...after barely breaking a sweat...enjoy your meal!

GRILLING SEASON IS YEAR-ROUND FOR ME, DESPITE THE WEATHER. THE YEAR-ROUND PART IS EASIER FOR THOSE OF YOU WHO LIVE IN WARMER CLIMATES. HERE ON THE WEST COAST OF OHIO I HAVE FOUND THAT GUESTS DO COMPLAIN WHEN THEY HAVE TO TAKE TURNS WITH THE SNOW SHOVEL TO CLEAN THEM-SELVES A PLACE AT THE PICNIC TABLE, SO I SOME-TIMES EVEN LET THEM EAT INSIDE...IF THEY PROMISE TO BE NEAT ABOUT IT.

YooHoo Yogurt Chicken

Gone Fishin'

I follow the suggestions in Chapter 4 and keep a selection of condiments, salad dressings, and seasonings on a tray that I store inside the refrigerator in the garage. If you have the space for that luxury, it saves you the time of carting that stuff back and forth from inside the house.

Give this one a chance! You'll be glad that you did. The blend of sweet onion and tart yogurt creates a sauce that pleases the palate without pouring on the calories. I sometimes like to double the amount of sauce called for in the recipe and add small red potatoes to the skillet before I add the chicken. Other times I sprinkle on some paprika just so I can see the contrast of that pretty red color against the white background of the sauce.

Makes 4 servings

8 boneless, skinless chicken thighs
1 tablespoon olive oil
2 cloves garlic
2 large yellow onions
2 cups plain, fat-free yogurt
Optional: 1 tablespoon chopped fresh parsley
Optional: 2 teaspoons paprika
Optional: salt and pepper

1 Place the chicken over medium-hot coals and grill until juices run clear, 3 to 5 minutes on each side.

2 While the chicken is grilling, place a grill-safe heavy skillet (with a lid) over the hottest area of your coals to bring skillet up to temperature. Once it's hot, add the olive oil. When the olive oil sizzles, move the skillet to a cooler area of the grill and add the minced garlic cloves and onion slices. Sauté until onion is tender; do NOT brown.

3 Stir in the yogurt. Use tongs to move the chicken from the grill and place it in the skillet with the yogurt sauce. Spoon some sauce over the chicken. (I like to push the onions to the side, add the chicken, and then spoon the onions over the chicken. This helps prevent the onions from browning during the remainder of the cooking process.)

4 Cover the skillet and leave on the grill for 15 to 30 minutes. To serve, move the chicken to a platter and pour the onion-yogurt sauce over the top. (Now is when you'll sprinkle on parsley and the paprika if you wish to use them and season to taste with the salt and pepper.)

Note: Some brands of yogurt add gelatin as a thickener. This can cause the yogurt to separate during the cooking process. If this occurs, after you've removed the chicken to the platter you can thicken the sauce by stirring in some cornstarch slurry, arrowroot, Ener-G potato flour, or instant mashed potatoes, ¼ teaspoon at a time, until thickened. (If you use the cornstarch, you'll need to return the pan to the heat long enough to bring the mixture to a boil to complete the thickening process and remove the "starchy" taste.) This dish is delicious even if you omit the "thickening" step, but the presentation is much more attractive (i.e., it looks nicer) if you take the time to do so.

Add small red potatoes to YooHoo Yogurt Chicken before you cover the skillet. The amount of time you precook the potatoes in the microwave will depend on their size and how long you plan to leave the skillet covered on the grill before you serve the meal.

Coriander seed is the tan, peppercorn-sized seed of the cilantro plant. (That's the ingredient used as a flavor enhancer in the Luau-Luscious Pork Roast recipe.) Cilantro, which is also sometimes called Chinese Parsley or Mexican Parsley, is an herb popular in Latin cuisines. To add further confusion to the name possibilities, some spice distributors refer to dried cilantro as dried coriander. Ground coriander is ground coriander seed.

Luau-Luscious Pork Roast

This is another recipe that you can play with. Improvise to your heart's content. For example, when it comes to the sweetener, I prefer the robust, full-bodied taste imparted by molasses; I offer alternative suggestions for those who prefer a milder flavor. Likewise regarding the amount of pineapple juice; the amount suggested in the recipe acts as a tenderizer. If you want your roast to have more of the pineapple flavor, double the amount of pineapple juice called for in the recipe. Fixing the roast gives you time to grill your potato and veggies at the same time.

Makes 4 to 6 servings

One 2-pound boneless pork loin roast

Note: This marinade works great (and faster) if you wish to save money on the loin roast and serve cheaper, individual pork chops. With this marinade, your chops will taste anything but cheap.

Marinade

1 small clove garlic
⅛ cup olive oil
¼ cup unsweetened pineapple juice
¼ cup sweetener (dark corn syrup, honey, molasses, or maple syrup)
1 tablespoon lime juice
1 tablespoon brown sugar
1 tablespoon Dijon mustard
1½ teaspoons soy sauce
½ teaspoon coriander seed
¼ teaspoon ground ginger

1 In a microwave-safe bowl large enough to hold the roast, sauté the chopped garlic in the olive oil by cooking on high for 15 to 30 seconds in the microwave.

2 Add the pineapple juice, sweetener, lime juice, brown sugar, Dijon mustard, soy sauce, coriander or cilantro, and ground ginger to the olive oil and garlic mixture.

Reserve one fourth of this marinade to use to baste the meat during grilling; pour the reserved marinade into a covered jar and refrigerate until needed.

LUAU-LUSCIOUS PORK ROAST IS ANOTHER RECIPE THAT CAN BENEFIT FROM CREATIVE GRILLING. OMIT THE ¼ TEASPOON GROUND GINGER AND SUBSTITUTE ½ TEASPOON (OR MORE) OF CHOPPED CANDIED GINGER INSTEAD. YOU'LL LOVE THE SWEETER, SUBTLE DIFFERENCE.

Remember, each time you open the lid you can add up to 15 minutes to the grilling time. Only lift the lid when you have to, such as to turn the entrée. The food will be fine. You're a grill chef, not a babysitter.

3 Place meat in the dish, turning to coat it with marinade. Cover the bowl with plastic wrap and refrigerate 8 to 24 hours, turning the meat occasionally to distribute the marinade.

4 Grill over medium coals for 1 to 1½ hours, or until a meat thermometer placed in the center of the thickest part of the meat registers 170°F.

SIDE DISHES NOT TO BE PUSHED ASIDE

Nothing is easier to set in front of your family and friends than some dip and a selection of fresh veggies. My simple "base" is delicious by itself—how you doctor it is up to you. I offer some suggestions, but I'm sure you'll come up with lots of other flavor blends on your own.

Veggie Dip Base

1 cup fat-free sour cream
1 cup real mayonnaise
Optional: 1 tablespoon lemon juice

1 Stir the sour cream and mayonnaise together in a small bowl. If you decide to use it, add the lemon juice now. (See the Gone Fishin' sidebar with the Make-Ahead Magnificent Mint Lemonade Syrup recipe on pg. 246 for a suggestion regarding the lemon juice.)

2 Use a full batch of the dip base recipe above to create a Green Goddess Dip by adding the pulp of one ripe avocado, ¼ cup of chopped green onions, 1 teaspoon parsley, and sea salt to taste.

3 Doctor the dip by adding such ingredients as cream cheese, soy sauce or Bragg Liquid Aminos, chopped onion, fresh or dried herbs, crisp bacon pieces, chopped tomatoes, or minced garlic. Some additions will require some time for the flavors to merge; others are ready to serve immediately.

See Sources for information on Minor's bases. Many of those are fantastic for creating unique dips. By adding a scant ¼ teaspoon of each base per cup of dip, I've served such combinations as:

- sun-dried tomato and roasted red pepper dip
- herb-roasted onion (with a touch of the chicken or beef broth base as a flavor enhancer)
- bacon or ham and roasted onion
- roasted garlic
- fiery fiesta pepper dip from a combination of ranchero, chipotle, and ancho flavor concentrates

Cucumber Slaw

Because this recipe will keep three months in the refrigerator, you can mix up a batch today and it'll be there whenever you're ready to serve it. It's a tradition with my family's Thanksgiving meal.

Makes 8 cups

6 or 7 cucumbers
2 green peppers
2 large sweet onions
2 cups sugar

1 cup white vinegar
2 tablespoons sea salt
1 tablespoon celery seed

1 Have a large bowl nearby to hold all of the ingredients eventually.

2 Wash, peel, and remove the seeds from enough cucumbers to yield 7 cups when they are sliced very thin. Do the same with the green peppers, which when chopped or sliced should equal a cup.

3 Peel and chop the onions, which should also yield around a cup. Toss all ingredients together in the bowl and set aside.

4 Pour sugar and vinegar into a saucepan over a low heat, stirring until the mixture is warm enough to dissolve the sugar.

5 Add salt and celery seed to the vinegar mixture and stir.

6 Pour the warm vinegar mixture over the cucumbers, peppers, and onions and mix well. Transfer to glass jars and store in the refrigerator until served.

Sauerkraut Salad

Stop that! Don't wrinkle up your nose until you've tried this. You can substitute plain old cider vinegar for the sweet pickle vinegar (juice), but it won't be as good. Follow the recipe and you have a side dish that's good served alongside cottage cheese and even better if you use it in your Grilled Reuben sandwiches (lean corned beef, Swiss cheese, and sauerkraut on toasted rye bread).

1¼ cup sugar
¼ cup sweet pickle vinegar (or cider vinegar)
¼ cup extra-virgin olive oil or vegetable oil
¼ teaspoon salt
1 bag or large can of sauerkraut
1 cup celery
½ cup green pepper
½ cup sweet onion

1   In a large glass bowl, stir together the sugar, vinegar, oil, and salt until the sugar is dissolved.

2   Put sauerkraut in a colander and run cold water over it for a few minutes, until it is thoroughly rinsed. Use a spatula to press out the excess moisture, and then transfer the sauerkraut to the bowl with the vinegar mixture. Stir well.

3   Add the chopped celery, green pepper, and onion to the sauerkraut mixture and stir until well blended.

4   Store in the refrigerator in covered glass jars until ready to serve. Salad will keep several weeks in the refrigerator as long as the vinegar mixture covers all of the other ingredients. Add additional pickle juice if necessary.

Toss some of the Sauerkraut Salad together with chopped hard boiled eggs and grilled red potatoes for something different from the same ol', same ol' potato salad. Or, add the Sauerkraut Salad to a mix of sliced carrots, broccoli florets, and cauliflower.

It's Not Yucky Yogurt Cheese Pasta Sauce

Try this for an unusual pasta accompaniment to your meal, especially those times you're serving a grilled entrée that you've basted with Italian dressing. By the way, the recipe is correct. I don't use any salt in this one. It's tart and strangely appetizing all by itself!

Per single serving

1 tablespoon shallots
1 tablespoon olive oil
2 tablespoons yogurt cheese
1 teaspoon mayonnaise
Optional: Parmesan cheese

1   In a microwave-safe dish, sauté the chopped shallots in the olive oil. Stir in the yogurt cheese (that you made by draining fat-free, plain yogurt in a coffee filter–lined, covered funnel placed so it could drain into a jar overnight; you can substitute silken tofu for the yogurt cheese, if you desire). Mix in the mayonnaise.

2   Toss with cooked and cooled angel-hair pasta. Sprinkle with freshly grated Parmesan cheese if you wish. Serve immediately.

Bravo Bacon "Baked" Onions

This is definitely not a low-fat recipe, but sometimes it's just nice to splurge. It makes a great side dish for steak or hamburger sandwiches. Or use the bacon, add tomato, mayonnaise, and lettuce, and serve on thick slices of bread—toasted on the grill, of course!

Makes 4 servings

4 medium sweet onions
4 teaspoons butter
8 slices of bacon

1 Peel the onions. Crosscut the onions from the top two-thirds of the way down.

2 Divide a teaspoon of butter in between each of the 4 sections you've created in each onion.

3 Measure out 4 pieces of foil large enough to generously wrap the onions, overlapping the foil at the top to seal. Lay out two pieces of bacon in the shape of an "X" across each piece of the foil and place onion in the center. Bring bacon up and over the sides of the onion, overlapping at the top. Wrap the foil up over the sides of each onion, folding it over at the top to secure it.

4 Grill over medium coals for an hour, turning occasionally. (If you place the onion on a higher shelf in your grill and close the lid, it isn't necessary to turn the onion.) Keep in mind that if you're opening and closing the lid while you grill an entrée, the onions may take a bit longer to cook. Therefore, you may wish to start your onions and any other foil-wrapped vegetables 30 to 45 minutes before you're ready to grill your entrée, then move them to the higher rack for the remaining 15 to 30 minutes.

When you know you'll be having guests the next day, consider taking the time the night before to make one of the chilled soups suggested in Chapter 17. That advance preparation will free up more of your time to spend with your friends.

NOW FOR SOMETHING TO GO DOWN COOL AND EASY

Man does not live by canned soft drinks and fermented beverages alone. Sometimes it's nice to break out of a rut and try something different. For those times you're ready to do just that, may I suggest the beverage recipes that follow.

Energy Booster Punch

Years ago I heard a "home remedies" doctor on a radio talk show claim that this fruit juice mixture could boost your energy, especially if you add a teaspoon of cider vinegar to each glass. I skip the vinegar part; however, I do often use seltzer water in place of plain water to create a fizzy thirst quencher. This is one way to give your family a healthy soft-drink substitute.

1 can frozen apple juice concentrate
1 can frozen pineapple juice concentrate
1 can frozen grape juice concentrate
1 can frozen cranberry juice concentrate
Water per instructions on the cans

1 Mix all juice concentrates together. I prefer to store the concentrate mixture in a covered container (a 2-liter empty seltzer bottle, for example), add the appropriate amount to a pitcher or individual glasses, and mix in the water or carbonated water when I'm ready to serve it. (I also sometimes freeze the concentrate mixture in ice cube trays; once it's frozen, I transfer the cubes to a freezer-safe bag. I add a cube or two to a glass, top with water, and stir.) If you wish, you can add the water per the instructions on the cans immediately. Store in your refrigerator. Serve chilled.

Innocent Margaritas

As you'll see by the recipe that will follow this one, I don't like getting stuck in a standard lemonade rut, either. Variety is also the thirst quencher of life.

8 large limes
1 large Valencia orange
¾ cup sugar
6 cups water

1 Wash the limes and the orange, then slice them in half and squeeze their juices into a pitcher. Place lime and orange hulls into the pitcher, too.

2 Stir in sugar. Use a wooden or heavy plastic spoon to crush lime and orange hulls with juice and sugar to release the citrus oil.

INSTEAD OF ICE FOR THOSE COOL DRINKS, USE FROZEN MELON BALLS OR OTHER FROZEN FRUIT. MAKE AND FREEZE YOUR OWN MELON BALLS OR PICK UP A COUPLE OF BAGS OF 'EM FROM THE FREEZER CASE AT YOUR LOCAL SUPERMARKET. THE ADDED FLAVOR FROM STRAWBERRIES OR MELON BALLS WILL GIVE A BOOST TO SWEET ICED TEA OR ANY CITRUS SODA.

3 Add water to mixture and stir well.

When you're ready to serve, in a blender add 1 cup of ice to every ½ cup of lime/orange mixture. Blend well until you have a frosty, slushy drink. Pour into chilled margarita glasses and garnish with a lime slice, if you wish.

Gone Fishin'

Make-Ahead Magnificent Mint Lemonade Syrup stores well for several days in the refrigerator and, whether you make this recipe with the mint or leave it out, when you substitute seltzer water for plain water, you get a healthy alternative to sugar-laden soft drinks.

Make-Ahead Magnificent Mint Lemonade Syrup

According to my experience, you usually get around 1 cup lemon juice from 4 medium to large lemons. Keep that in mind when you're planning the amount of syrup you wish to prepare.

2½ cups water
2 cups sugar
1 cup fresh lemon juice
½ cup fresh orange juice
¾ cup mint leaves, loosely packed
Optional: mint sprigs for garnish
Optional: thin lemon slices for garnish

WHETHER YOU MAKE IT WITH THE MINT OR OMIT THAT STEP, I'VE FOUND THAT SUBSTITUTING A TABLESPOON OF MAKE-AHEAD MAGNIFICENT MINT LEMONADE SYRUP FOR THE LEMON JUICE ADDS A DELICIOUS DIMENSION TO ANY DIP.

1 Pour water and sugar into a grill-safe saucepan over medium heat. Stir until the sugar dissolves and then allow the mixture to simmer for 5 minutes. Remove from the heat and let the mixture cool while you ready the other ingredients.

2 Cut fruit in half and extract juice. Add the lemon and orange juices to the sugar syrup.

3 Rinse mint leaves and pat dry. Put the mint leaves in the bottom of a 4-cup glass measuring cup. Pour sugar syrup over the mint leaves and let stand for an hour. Strain resulting syrup into a jar. (This lemonade base can be stored, covered, for several days in the refrigerator. Freeze any that you won't use within that time.)

4 To serve: Mix ⅓ cup of lemonade syrup in a glass with ⅔ cup water or seltzer water. Fill the glass with ice cubes. Garnish with a mint sprig and a lemon slice, if desired.

Good Golly Good Ginger Ale Syrup

Here's one way to know the formula for your soft drink. It's up to you whether or not you divulge it to your friends.

Makes 4 servings

1 cup water
1 or 2 whole gingerroots
1 cup cane sugar
1 tablespoon vanilla
4 cups seltzer water

1 In a grill-safe pan over the hottest portion of the grill, bring water to a boil. Peel and slice enough gingerroot to fill 1 cup and move the pan to an upper rack or cooler area. Allow mixture to simmer for a half hour.

Double your efforts: If you want to take the time, the resulting Good Golly Good Ginger Ale Syrup will usually be twice as strong if—at the end of this step—you put the ginger-water mixture in a blender or food processor and purée the mixture. Strain the purée through cheesecloth, return it to the pan, and complete according to the remaining instructions, increasing the amount of sugar if necessary. Be sure to "test" the results to determine how much to use for each glass of beverage.

2 Remove the pan from the heat, and with a slotted spoon remove the ginger. (**Optional:** Strain the ginger water through cheesecloth to remove any ginger pulp.)

3 Add the sugar and stir until it dissolves. If necessary, return the pan to the heat long enough so no sugar crystals remain.

4 Add the vanilla.

5 For each serving, put ¼ cup of the resulting ginger ale syrup into a glass—over ice, if you wish. Pour in 1 cup of chilled seltzer water. This will mix with the syrup and cause a "head" to form on the drink. Store any leftover syrup in a covered glass jar in the refrigerator for up to a week.

There! This chapter should give you plenty of ideas about using your grill to help you prepare entire meals. But wait! That's not all! There's still Chapter 17, which includes soup, breakfast, tailgater party, sandwich, and packet meal recipes. And I haven't forgotten about your sweet tooth. Turn back to Chapter 15 for lots of dessert ideas, many of which you can leave unattended to "bake" on your grill while you enjoy your meal with the rest of your friends and family.

Chapter 17

Tailgating and All Kinds of Other Stuff

As you can probably tell, I'm a firm believer that slaving away in the kitchen is a poor excuse for missing a sunrise, noonday sun, dusk, or sunset.

This chapter contains around-the-clock suggestions for breakfast, a grilled sandwich, cold soups, packet meals, tailgating, and the occasional midnight eclipse snack, too.

Scrapple

Unlike the original Pennsylvania Dutch version of this recipe that uses pork parts I don't like to think about, this one is not only quick and easy, it uses sausage.

Makes 8 servings

1 pound sausage
One 12-ounce can of evaporated milk
¾ cup cornmeal
1 teaspoon sugar

1 Over medium heat, fry the sausage in a grill-safe skillet until meat is completely cooked. Use a spatula to turn the meat often so it doesn't get too brown. Break it into pieces as small as possible.

2 Add the evaporated milk and heat to the boiling point. Add the cornmeal and sugar and continue to cook, stirring often, for about 5 minutes or until the mixture thickens.

3 You can serve it directly from the pan in mush form. Or, if you wish to make it ahead, you can pack it in a loaf pan and chill it for later; then, cut it into 1-inch-thick slabs, coat it in some cornmeal, and fry it in butter.

Scrapple served with some eggs, hash browns, and fresh fruit makes a wonderful meal. If you're making an effort to cut the fat in your diet, see the suggestions in Chapter 18 on how to adapt the recipe.

Slumgolly

My dad invented and named this one. Contrary to what some politically correct people might have you believe, around our houses, slummin' it means dining on mighty fine but cheap food. Fix this for breakfast or brunch and you'll never look at scrambled eggs the same again.

Makes 8 servings

1 pound bacon
1 large yellow sweet onion
4 large potatoes
8 eggs
¼ cup milk
16 slices of bread
Salt and pepper to taste

IF YOU'D LIKE SOME COLOR AND AN ADDED FLAVOR BOOST, TOSS IN A HALF CUP OF DICED GREEN AND RED PEPPERS AND SAUTÉ THEM WITH THE ONION.

1 Cut the bacon into bite-sized pieces and fry over medium heat in a large grill-safe skillet.

2 While the bacon is frying, peel and dice the onion and potatoes. Drain most of the fat from the bacon and discard. Add the potatoes to the skillet and grill with the pan covered for 5 to 10 minutes, stirring and turning the potatoes several times during the process, until the potatoes are tender. Add the diced onions and sauté until they are clear.

3 Crack eggs into a large bowl and whip them together with the milk. Tear the bread into bite-sized pieces and toss in the egg mixture. Pour the egg and bread into the skillet and toss with the bacon, onions, and potatoes until it is well mixed.

4 Continue to fry uncovered on the grill until the eggs are set, 8 to 10 minutes. Use a flat-edged metal or heavy plastic spatula to turn the mixture often, scraping the bottom of the skillet as you do so to ensure the mixture is not sticking.

Note: Be sure to switch to a different utensil to stir the eggs during the last few minutes of frying time to avoid salmonella contamination.

PACKET MEALS, OR YOU DON'T ALWAYS HAVE TO FRY IT UP IN A PAN

There's no limit to the number of dishes you can create on the grill using the packet method. Keep in mind that the foil dimensions given throughout these recipes are intended as a guide only. As always, feel free to put your "fingerprints" on my suggestions and alter them to make them your own creations; simply adjust the size of the aluminum foil packet as needed. See Chapter 3 for additional information on how to create a packet.

Haggis, Haggis, The Clan's All Here

Feel free to don your kilt during the grillin'. You'll enjoy this other-wise Americanized recipe all the more if you do. Just don't get in a huff if anybody tries to call this one a "glorified meatloaf." Simply smile and say it's "authentic tasting" and everyone's life will be easier.

Makes 8 servings

1 pound boneless ground lamb
½ pound lamb liver
½ cup beef broth
1 small onion
1 large egg
¾ teaspoon salt
¾ teaspoon black pepper
½ teaspoon sugar
¼ teaspoon ground ginger
⅛ teaspoon ground cloves
⅛ teaspoon ground nutmeg
1 cup old-fashioned oatmeal
4 large potatoes
8 carrots

You can get some of that delicious smoke taste to leak into your food if, before turning a packet for the final time, you use a pin to prick several holes in the foil. Be careful, though. Make sure you keep the holes small—you want doorways for the smoke, but you don't want the juices to all escape.

1 In a large bowl, mix together the ground lamb, liver cut into cubes, beef broth, diced onion, and all of the other ingredients, except for the potatoes and carrots. Don't worry about getting it completely mixed at this point, because as you'll soon discover, you're about to get your hands dirty anyhow, so you might as well finish mixing it then.

2 Clean and slice the potatoes and carrots. Ready eight 12-inch or larger squares of heavy-duty aluminum foil by first spreading them across your counter. (You're gonna get your hands dirty here in a minute, remember? This will save you from having to wash your hands between steps, so stick with me on this!)

3 Grease a 6-inch circle in the center of each piece of foil. Layer the potato slices from half of one potato and one sliced carrot in the center of each circle.

4 Now return to that waiting bowl of haggis mix. Squeeze the meat between your fingers. Move it around in the bowl. You want to make sure it's completely mixed and that the oatmeal has absorbed the broth by this point.

Don't turn up your nose at the idea of mixing the haggis using your hands. Think of it as saving time! You will need to super-scrub your hands after handling the meat anyhow, so unless you like to do dishes, there's no reason to dirty mixing spoons, too.

5 Next, individually shape an eighth of the haggis mixture into a hamburger-sized patty portion and set it atop the potatoes and carrots. Once you've made all 8 haggis patties, you're excused for a minute to go wash your hands.

6 Seal each foil packet by folding over the edges. You'll turn these packets several times while they're on the grill, so you want to be certain they're well-sealed so that the potatoes and carrots benefit from the steam from the meat juices. I often place another piece of foil across the seam side (top) of the packet and then turn it over and fold the foil over on the other side; this ensures that it's well-sealed.

7 Place each packet over medium coals and grill for 45 minutes to an hour, or until carrots and potatoes are tender. Turn the packets every 10 to 15 minutes. Keep the grill lid closed between turns.

You can Americanize the haggis recipe some more and substitute ground beef and beef liver for the lamb.

Build a Better Bird's Nest

This one takes a little bit more preparation time (unless you sneak in thawed frozen hash browns in place of the freshly grated potato), but once it's on the grill, you can forget about it until it's done.

Per serving

2 slices of bacon
1 large potato
1 egg
Optional: grated onion
Optional: diced green and red pepper
Optional: salt and pepper

1 In the center of an 18-inch square of heavy-duty aluminum foil, crisscross the two pieces of bacon.

2 Clean (and peel, if you prefer) and grate the potato. Mix in the onions, peppers, and seasoning, if used, then shape it into a ball.

3 Place the potato ball in the center of the bacon cross. Press it down so it forms a base that rests on the bacon, then take your thumb and create a "nest" indentation in the center of the hash browns.

4 Crack an egg into that nest. Pull the resulting 4 ends of the bacon up and over the nest; then do the same with the foil, folding it into a packet that retains the shape of the nest.

5 Grill over medium heat for 30 to 45 minutes. Open the packet, being careful not to get burned by the steam that will escape. The nest is done if the bacon and potatoes are crisp on the outside and the egg is firm. If you wish to "crisp" it a bit more, return the packet to the grill with the top left open for another 5 to 15 minutes.

WHEN PLANNING A PACKET MEAL, REMEMBER

1 THOSE PIZZA CRUSTS YOU KEEP ON HAND IN THE FREEZER (SEE CHAPTER 12) AREN'T JUST FOR PIZZA ANYMORE. TOASTED OVER THE GRILL, THEY MAKE EXCELLENT FLATBREAD TO SERVE ALONGSIDE A PACKET MEAL.

2 THE PIZZA SAUCE YOU KEEP ON HAND TASTES JUST AS GREAT OFF A PIZZA. YOU CAN USE IT AS ONE OF THE LAYERS IN A PIZZABURGER-LASAGNA-STYLE PACKET MEAL MADE OF SLICED POTATOES, GROUND BEEF, PEPPERONI, MUSHROOMS, YOUR CHOICE OF CHEESES, AND, OF COURSE, PIZZA SAUCE. USE A LAYER OF THE MEAT MIXED WITH PIZZA SAUCE FOR THE TOP AND BOTTOM LAYERS; THIS HELPS PREVENT THE MEAL FROM STICKING TO THE FOIL.

3 THERE'S MORE THAN ONE WAY TO FIX A PIZZABURGER-LASAGNA-STYLE PACKET MEAL. YOU CAN FORGET THE POTATOES AND TRY IT WITH VEGETABLES, SUCH AS ZUCCHINI OR CABBAGE WEDGES. MOST OTHER VEGGIES HAVE A HIGHER MOISTURE CONTENT THAN POTATOES; VENT THE TOP OF THE PACKETS FOR THE LAST FEW MINUTES OF GRILLING TO ALLOW THE MOISTURE TO EVAPORATE.

Squash That Pork Chop, Honey

This is a meal you can prepare the night before and prebake it for 45 minutes in a 400°F oven, if you wish. Take the packets directly from the refrigerator and place on the grill rack over medium coals. They will be ready in about 30 minutes. Otherwise, follow the instructions given below.

Makes 2 servings

Two 1-inch-thick pork chops
1 acorn squash
2 tablespoons brown sugar
2 tablespoons honey
2 tablespoons butter

1 Place each pork chop on an 18 x 12-inch section of heavy-duty aluminum foil. Season to taste.

2 Cut the acorn squash in half and remove the seeds.

3 Place each squash half on a pork chop, cut side up. Fill the hollow of each squash with 1 tablespoon each of the brown sugar, honey, and butter.

4 Bring the foil up and over the pork chop and squash half to form a packet, folding it to secure it.

5 Grill for an hour over medium coals.

GRILLING A MEAL IN A FOIL PACKET COULDN'T BE EASIER. PLUS, YOU GET TO PUT YOUR FEET UP WHILE THE FOOD IS COOKING!

Toasted Ham Sandwiches

Dijon mustard goes through a subtle flavor change when slowly heated in this manner. You have to taste these to appreciate what that difference does for a ham sandwich.

Per serving

½ teaspoon Dijon mustard
1 deli-style hamburger bun
1 slice baby (mild) Swiss cheese
One ¼-inch slice of ham
½ teaspoon butter

1 Spread ¼ teaspoon of the Dijon mustard on the inside half of each bun. Place the cheese and ham on the bun to form the sandwich.

2 Spread ¼ teaspoon of the butter on the outside of both halves of the bun. Place the sandwich in the center of a 6 x 12-inch piece of heavy-duty aluminum foil. Bring the foil up and over the sandwich, folding it to close it and form a packet.

3 Grill over low heat for 15 to 30 minutes.

TAILGATING: TAKING YOUR SHOW ON THE ROAD

What better way to do the voodoo that you do so well than to take your show on the road and have a tailgate party? Here are some tips to get you started:

1 A day or two before the game:

- Decide on your menu.
- Do food prep work.
- Pack prepared food in disposable containers.
- Prepare a checklist of the items you want to take along; check off items once they're packed and loaded in the car. (This includes loading the grill, after you've checked to verify you have a full propane cylinder—or enough charcoal, if you're a true primitive.)

2 The day of the game:

- Appoint a designated driver, if one will be needed.
- Check off the checklist (again) before you leave for the game. Make sure your friends, spouse, and kids are in the car, if you have any and plan to let them ride along.
- Ice down the beverages and load the coolers in the car.
- Pack up the foodstuffs; be sure to include enough ice packs to keep everything at a safe temperature.
- Plan to leave early enough to have the food ready at least two hours before the start of the game.
- Show your colors: wear a team jacket or jersey.

3 Once you arrive at the stadium:

⤶ Park in a prime parking place—next to a grassy area or at the end of the parking row where there's more room, and preferably where there's a restroom nearby.

⤶ Show your colors some more: affix a flag or balloon to your antenna—or portable flagpole, if you travel with one—so your friends can find you.

4 Before the start of the game:

⤶ Delegate clean-up chores while you finally sit down to eat your meal.

⤶ If you don't travel with a big-screen, satellite TV and actually plan to enter the stadium to watch the game, be sure to allow time for the grill to be cool enough to pack away (around 10 minutes for the Grill2Go) when you secure everything else back inside the car. (If you have a friend who you know hates sports, invite him or her to join you at your "cookout." With any luck, that person will bring along a good book and be willing to stay behind to "guard the gear" while you enjoy the game!)

⤶ Offer to share your recipes and "secrets" while you watch every-body else around you cleaning up the mess. (Feel free to bring along a crate of *Lazy About Grilling* to hand out as door prizes to others in the parking lot!)

Prepare a replenishable portable paper and plastic products pack containing napkins, plates, towels, toilet paper (Joe Cahn of Tailgating.com calls this the "MVP of the parking lot"), trash bags, and utensils. Unless you know there are clean-up facilities nearby, include moist towelettes or extra water to use to wet paper towels. A supply of disposable latex gloves for when you're handling raw meat is also a good idea. Include a first-aid kit, complete with antacids (which are in no way meant to be a critique of the chef du jour), aspirin and anti-inflama-tories, feminine products, sunblock (or frostbite oint-ment, depending on your geographical location), etc.

5 Other considerations before and after the game:

⌣ Have a cooler of extra ice and beverages ready for after the game.

⌣ Have rain gear handy: come rain or shine, everybody will be counting on you to be out there grillin'.

⌣ Have a set of those extra-comfy insoles inside of your extra-comfortable shoes; you'll be spending a lot of time on your feet.

TAILGATIN' WITH THE GRILL2GO

Let the other folks mount a huge metal drum on a trailer and convert it into a portable BBQ pit, you are *Lazy About* this. This probably means that unless you hit the jackpot on the lottery anytime soon and "invest" all your winnings in the ultimate home-on-wheels—complete with a custom, fold-out kitchen equipped with Bobby Flay, Emeril, and Mario to do your grilling and BAM!ming and stand around looking cute in shorts for you, you'll want to keep things as simple as possible. (If you do win that lottery, I suggest you hire me to supervise; I'd bring along Gale Gand to do the pastries! If I'm not available, Sara Moulton could probably step in.)

Because of its convenient size and affordable price, I used the Thermos Grill2Go as the standard for all recipes in this section. It's available online and through major discount and department stores.

The Grill2Go is a portable gas grill that weighs in at only 25 pounds. It folds up for transporting to a bundle that's only 29 inches long, 13 inches tall, and 16 inches wide, so it takes up about the same amount of space as a cooler; you can even get an optional "suitcase on wheels"-style carrying case, if you like. Its dishwasher-safe, nonstick grill top consists of a 16 x 13-inch-ribbed grilling area, a

12 x 10-inch flat griddle, and an effective grease "trap." (Overall, the surface equals 310 square inches, which is big enough to hold 16 hamburgers!) To fuel the grill, you can either use one of those two-hour, one-pound propane cartridges—the kind used to run a camper-style lantern, or you can purchase an optional adapter hose to connect a standard 20-pound tank.

The Grill2Go has a built-in ignition (although I'd recommend bringing along matches to use on damp days), rust-resistant frame, retractable side shelves, and fold-down legs—with the means to level the grill, which is something you'll want to do if you plan to fix eggs on the griddle! The base the grill sits on reminds me of one of those collapsible workbenches. The Grill2Go also comes with a spatula, tongs, and a customized cleaning tool.

As I see it, there are only three disadvantages to the Grill2Go:

1. On cold days, it's sometimes difficult to get the grill to heat above medium; the recipes in this section take that into consideration, however.

2. The sealed burners that prevent flare-ups also mean that you don't get a smoky flavor. (You can compensate for this by preparing a couple of foil packets holding soaked wood chips. When you're ready to preheat the grill, prick a few holes in the top of the packets and place them on the grill. Close the lid. The packets should be providing some smoke by the time the grill is heated and ready to use.)

3. There isn't much clearance under the lid. It's only about 2¾ inches at its highest point and tapers down to 2 inches at one edge and 1 inch at the others.

GREEK WEEK MEAL

Don't be a Greek weakling! Tie back that toga to keep it away from the "fire," lace together some thyme sprigs for that requisite laurel atop your head, and get ready to party!

Great Greek Grilled Gyros

Feel free to substitute boneless, skinless chicken breast or pork loin for the lamb loin, if you prefer. I won't tell. Your goal is to encompass the spirit of the celebration, not to accept rigid ingredient lists. The *Lazy About* way is all about what works best for you—your budget and your taste.

Makes 8 servings

2 pounds lamb loin, sliced into 1-inch slices
¼ cup olive oil, plus 2 tablespoons to coat the bread
½ teaspoon dried basil
¼ teaspoon dried oregano
¼ teaspoon dried thyme
1 teaspoon garlic powder

Optional: sea salt and freshly ground black pepper to taste

8 large pita breads
2 cups plain yogurt
½ cup lemon juice, fresh
3 or 4 cucumbers
2 cups shredded lettuce
2 large sweet onions
4 large tomatoes

1. A night or two before the big game, cut meat into paper-thin slices. (It helps if you put the loin in the freezer for about 10 minutes first.)

2. In a large, heavy zip-closure plastic bag, mix the olive oil, basil, oregano, thyme, garlic powder, and salt and pepper, if using. Add the sliced loin to the bag and squeeze to coat all of the meat with the oil. Close the bag and store in the refrigerator.

3. Wash, peel, and remove the seeds from enough cucumbers to yield 4 cups when they are sliced very thin. Place the slices in a colander, and toss them with a pinch or two of sea salt. Allow time for excess moisture to drain. Pat the cucumbers with paper towels, if necessary.

4. In a sealable container, mix the yogurt, lemon juice, and cucumber slices together. Chill.

5. The night before, assemble the remaining sandwich fixin's. Put the shredded lettuce in a plastic bag. Peel and slice the onions into thin slices; store them in another bag. (If you prefer peeled tomatoes, first submerge the tomatoes one by one in boiling water. After about 10 to 15 seconds in the water, remove the tomato and immediately submerge it in ice water to stop the cooking process. Skins should now slip off easily.) Cut each tomato in half. Squeeze each half to remove excess juice and the seeds. Chop the tomatoes and store in a sealable container.

6. The day of the game, set up and preheat the grill.

7 Brush both sides of the pita bread with olive oil, evenly dividing the 2 tablespoons of oil between the bread. (If you prefer, keep olive oil in a plastic squirt bottle and spray the bread with oil instead of brushing it on.) Place the pita bread on the grill and cook for 2 minutes on each side. Use tongs to turn the bread, and then arrange each pita on its own plate.

8 Empty the container of lamb onto the grill and cook for 2 to 4 minutes, turning the meat frequently using tongs.

9 While the meat is cooking, have somebody begin to build the sandwiches. Divide the lemon-yogurt-cucumber mixture between the bread; spread it out over the bread. Divide the lettuce, onion, and tomato between the bread, spreading them across one half of each pita.

10 Remove the meat from the grill and layer it atop the lettuce, onion, and tomato. Fold the bread in half. Use a serrated knife to cut each sandwich into two slices, if desired. (If you have any dainty eaters in your crowd, you may want to provide pieces of parchment paper for them to use to wrap their sandwiches.)

Marinated Feta Cheese Plate

The amounts in this dish are up to you. You also have two other choices: you can either arrange the marinated cheese on a plate beside marinated artichoke hearts, marinated mushrooms, and an assortment of Greek olives, or you can leave all of the stuff in their individual jars and provide spoons or tongs so your guests can dish them out themselves. This cheese goes great with gyros. If you plan to serve simpler fare for your Greek Week feast, use some of the olive oil from the feta cheese jar to coat crusty pieces of bread and toast them on the grill. Set out the cheese and some fresh fruit and you have a meal!

    2 pounds feta cheese
    Dried oregano
    Dried parsley
    Dried thyme
    Dried basil
    Freshly ground black pepper
    Fennel seeds
    Dried red chili flakes
    Bay leaf
    Extra-virgin olive oil
    Optional: Marinated artichoke hearts
    Optional: Marinated mushrooms
    Optional: Greek olives

1 Spread the feta cheese out onto several layers of paper towels placed on a baking sheet. Use additional paper towels to pat the cheese as dry as possible.

2 Sprinkle the dried herbs over the top of the cheese. (Unless you know that everybody likes their food spicy, go easy on the chili flakes. Another option would be to use Mrs. Dash Tomato Basil Garlic seasoning in place of the herbs suggested in the recipe; have Mrs. Dash Extra Spicy on the table for those who want to perk up their sandwiches. See Chapter 18 for information on Mrs. Dash and other seasoning blends.) Pat the cheese with your fingers to press the herbs into it. Put the cheese in a jar and cover with olive oil. Allow time for the oil to settle, then add more, if necessary. (As long as the cheese is always covered with olive oil, it will keep in the refrigerator for up to two months.)

If you grow your own herbs—or even if you let the local produce stand grow them "fresh" for you, you'll want to check out the tips on drying herbs in Chapter 18.

One Humonga Frittata Sandwich

You'll do all the preparation for this sandwich in advance. Then you'll wrap it in a heavy-duty aluminum foil packet so you can toast it until it's heated through on the grill. Like the sandwich, the portion sizes are humongous, so you can stretch them if you're caught short. If you know in advance that you'll need extra servings, it's an easy recipe to double or quadruple or....

Makes 4 servings

An unsliced round loaf of deli or homemade bread
2 tablespoons olive oil
1 tablespoon butter
1 large sweet onion
1 green pepper
1 red pepper
1 tablespoon unsalted butter or ghee
1 tablespoon olive oil
Juice of one lemon
1 teaspoon sugar
6 eggs
½ cup mild cheese (Monterey Jack, Swiss, or goat cheese)
4 ounces cream cheese
Optional: sea salt and freshly ground black pepper

1 Cut the top third off of the bread to make the "lid." Scoop out most of the bread in the bottom two-thirds of the loaf; this hollows out an area in the sandwich "base" to hold the filling. (You can add the scooped-out bread to the egg mixture, if you desire. Otherwise, freeze it to use later for bread crumbs.) Place the bread on a generous piece of aluminum foil—one large enough to wrap the bread and make a packet. You'll want

the dimensions of filled bread to fit on the grill with the lid down; you may need to "squish" it a bit once it is filled and in the packet to get it to fit.

2 In a large, oven-safe skillet, heat the oil and butter until the butter is melted. Use this oil and butter mixture to coat the entire outside of the bread.

3 Peel and slice the onion. Wash, core, and seed the peppers; chop.

4 In the same skillet over medium-high heat, add the next amount of butter and oil; stir to coat the pan until butter is melted. Add the green and red peppers, reduce the heat to medium, and sauté until the peppers start to get soft. Add the sliced onion and sauté until transparent. (Be careful not to brown the vegetables.) Stir in lemon juice and sugar. Cover, reduce heat to low, and let simmer for about 30 minutes.

5 Preheat oven to 350°F.

6 In a bowl, beat the eggs. Season with salt and pepper to taste. (Stir in the reserved bread, if using it.) Pour this mixture into the cooked onion-peppers mixture and add the grated cheese. Stir to combine. Cut cream cheese into cubes and arrange over the top of the egg mixture.

7 Bake for about 45 minutes, or until the eggs are completely firm.

8 Flip the baked frittata out of the pan into the bread. Place the lid on the bread. Wrap tightly in the foil. Refrigerate.

9 At the tailgate party site, preheat the grill to low. Place the sandwich packet on the grill and heat covered for 30 to 45 minutes, or until bread is crisp, turning the packet every 10 minutes to prevent one side of the bread from burning. Unwrap the bread and use a large serrated knife to cut the loaf in half, and then in half again, to make 4 wedges. Serve immediately.

Plenty of (Other) Packet Possibilities

In addition to the Toasted Ham Sandwiches recipe earlier in this chapter, consider making:

Quesa-Rah!-sa-Rah!-dillas

For each serving: Brush one side of a flour or corn tortilla with olive oil. Place the tortilla oil side down atop a section of heavy-duty aluminum foil. Top with a mixture of grated cheddar and Monterey Jack cheese. Brush one side of another tortilla with oil and place it oil side up atop the grated cheese mixture. Press together and wrap foil up and around the tortillas, forming a packet.

To prepare: Place packet on a preheated, medium grill. After 3 to 5 minutes, turn the packet and grill for another 2 minutes, or until cheese is melted and tortillas are crispy. Unwrap and cut into 4 wedges. Serve with salsa. (These are also yummy when served as the "bread" alongside a chef's salad.)

Packet-Pleasin' Pulled Pork BBQ Sandwich

Three nights before the tailgate party: Put a boneless pork roast in a ceramic-lined crockpot and add enough water to cover the roast. (**Optional:** I also add ¼ teaspoon of Minor's Roasted Mirepoix Flavor Concentrate and 1 teaspoon of Minor's Pork Base.) Cook the roast on the low setting for 12–24 hours.

Two nights before the tailgate party: Remove the roast from the crockpot and "pull apart" using a fork, discarding any fat or gristle. (One option for the broth is to skim the fat, strain it, refrigerate it until the morning of the party, heat it up, put it in a thermos, and serve it as "cup of soup" along with the sandwiches. Otherwise, it's up to you whether or not you skim the fat and freeze the broth to use later. If you're not going the "cup of soup" route, I recommend saving it because it's delicious, especially in wonton soup; you just don't need it for this recipe—unless your roast is big enough to let you spoon some broth over open-faced pork sandwiches and mashed potatoes for your family's dinner. The pulled pork sandwiches will be different enough that nobody will feel like they're getting "leftovers.") Return the pulled pork to the crockpot and add enough of The Swiss Army Knife Equivalent of Barbecue Sauces from pg. 142 to cover the meat. Cook on the low setting for 12 to 24 hours. (If you prefer to use your own barbecue sauce, you may need to thin it with some broth or water. The recommended sauce is "runnier" than most.)

The night before the tailgate party: Use a slotted spoon to remove meat from the sauce. (Put the extra sauce in a covered jar to take along to serve on the side.) For each sandwich, butter the outside of a hoagie roll. Spoon a generous portion of the drained meat inside each roll. Wrap in a foil packet.

At the tailgate party: Preheat the grill to low. Place packets on grill; cover and cook for 15–20 minutes, turning them halfway through the cooking time. (As an alternative to packets, preheat the grill to medium. Warm the pulled pork on the grill portion—a method that caramelizes the sugars in the barbecue sauce and adds another depth of flavor. Toast the rolls on the other portion of the grill. I recommend spreading the rolls with some garlic butter or roasted garlic-infused olive oil (see Chapter 13). Use tongs to put the meat on the toasted rolls. Keep in mind that because of the sweet sauce, the meat will scorch if the grill temperature is too high, so watch closely and adjust the grill temperature if necessary.) Be sure to have some Cucumber Slaw from pg. 240, fat dill pickles, and bread and butter pickles on hand to serve with the sandwiches.

Other possibilities

For the breakfast or brunch bunch: Layer cooked scrambled eggs and sausage or bacon between buttered pancakes or waffles. Wrap in packets. Warm for 15–20 minutes on a low grill, turning the packets halfway through the grilling time. Serve with syrup. Have a variety of fresh fruits, fruit juice, and coffee on hand.

Double-Crust Pizza Pleaser: Everybody loves pizza! Assemble packets by using the Grill2Go cooking grid as a pattern to roll and measure (or cut) prebaked pizza crusts. Spread olive oil on the outside of each crust. Spread the inside of each crust with pizza sauce. Place the bottom crust on a piece of heavy-duty aluminum foil a little more than twice the length of the crust. Top the sauce with your choice of fixin's and cheese. Lay the other crust "pizza sauce"-

side down on top. Seal the packet. Grill for 25–35 minutes on a medium grill, turning the packet every 10 minutes. Use a pizza cutter to slice into wedges and serve. Take along a salad and antipasta plate.

Appealing apple desserts: The night before, prepare packets that each hold an egg roll wrapper that you've lightly buttered on one side. Put the egg roll wrapper butter side down on a piece of foil. Fill half of the wrapper with thinly sliced apples tossed in lemon juice. Sprinkle some cinnamon and sugar over the apple slices. Fold the egg roll wrapper over to form a "pie," lightly wetting the edges with water and using a fork to crimp them to make a "seal." Wrap foil around the pie. Grill for 15–20 minutes on low, turning every 5 minutes.

Literal Grilling2Go: Don't have a Grill2Go grill? Don't fret. Some tailgaters swear by the "grill packets on the engine" method. Here's how it works: First you drive for twenty minutes. Next you pull over and raise the hood; find the warmest, flattest surface under the hood; and place your well-wrapped packet meal there. Use extra bunched-up foil, if necessary, to make sure the packet it wedged into place. Drive for another 60 minutes, or until the meal is done. This obviously won't work for home games. (I'll admit, I've never tried this method. My philosophy is that life's too short for me to spend time doing anything under the hood of my car!)

Gone Fishin'

Use a soup base (see Sources) to make broth. In most cases, you simply dissolve 1 teaspoon of base into each cup of water. If a recipe calls for a bouillon cube, use ¾ teaspoon of a base in place of each cube. Soup bases are much lower in sodium than bouillon cubes.

Slurps On

Soup and a sandwich can make a meal. Here are three suggestions for cold soups you can prepare ahead of time. See the instructions with each recipe for information on how long you can store these soups in the refrigerator.

Ruby Doobie-Do

This recipe calls for tomato juice, but I think it's just as good if you use a tomato-vegetable juice such as V-8 instead. This one is good hot or cold. It can be kept in the refrigerator for 4 days.

Per serving

⅓ cup beef broth
⅓ cup tomato juice
⅓ cup water

1 Stir the ingredients together in a coffee mug. Place the mug in the microwave on high for 30 to 60 seconds if you prefer a warm soup. Otherwise, serve immediately.

2 If you wish to store the soup in the refrigerator, do so in a covered jar.

A Cucumber Number

This soup is meant to be savored cold. Its subtle green color looks great when you serve it up in a crystal mug. It'll keep for 48 hours in the refrigerator. Just remove the covered jar of soup and shake it up to blend any ingredients that may have separated or settled, pour it into a mug, and serve.

Makes 4 servings

2 medium cucumbers
1½ cups buttermilk
1 teaspoon sea salt
⅛ teaspoon pepper
1 teaspoon dried minced onion

1   Clean (and peel if the skin is tough) the cucumbers. Cut into quarters and remove seeds, then purée in a blender or food processor along with ¼ cup of the buttermilk and the dried minced onion.

2   Add the salt, pepper, and remaining buttermilk and process until well-blended.

3   Chill in a covered container until ready to serve. (It's best to chill this soup for at least 2 hours before serving so the flavors can meld.) Serving cold soup adds pizzazz to your grilled dinner and making it is so quick and easy. The best of both worlds!

Not Your Grandma's Chicken Soup

Okay, I'm gonna cheat a bit with this one and use instant mashed potatoes. This is another soup with some versatility. It's delicious hot or cold if you serve it as stated in the recipe. It'll keep for 3 days in the refrigerator, so I'm giving you instructions on how to make a big batch.

1 small onion
2½ cups chicken broth
1¼ cups instant mashed potato mix

1 In a grill-safe saucepan over medium coals, grate the onion and add it to 1 cup of the broth.

2 Heat the mixture until it boils, reduce the heat (or move to a cooler spot on the grill), and simmer, covered, for 10 minutes.

3 Remove from the heat and add the instant mashed potatoes; beat with a fork until the potatoes are fluffy.

4 Stir in the remaining broth and heat until the mixture once again comes to a boil.

5 Remove from the heat and serve, or cover and chill for later.

THIS IS ALSO GREAT IF YOU SUBSTITUTE MILK FOR HALF OF THE BROTH AND VICHYSSOISE IT UP A BIT. THAT VERSION IS MADE EVEN BETTER IF YOU FLOAT SOME HALF-AND-HALF ON THE TOP OF EACH SERVING AND SPRINKLE ON SOME SNIPPED FRESH CHIVES.

Midnight At the Oh Taste Us

Now for those promised late-night snacks. This is another build-your-own-flavor recipe. I'll give you some suggestions. Once you get the hang of it, you'll then want to create your own. This recipe provides a great way to keep the kids busy outside (yet close enough so you can keep an eye on them) when the inevitable munchies strike during your child's sleepover or slumber(less) party.

Servings will vary

Basic ingredients
Graham crackers
Butter
Sweetened condensed milk

Suggested ingredients:
Coconut
Caramels
Pecans
Chocolate chips or kisses
Bananas
Marshmallows
Peanut Butter
Jelly

1 If you're letting the kids assemble their own, you'll need a piece of foil for each dessert. I recommend creating a packet, but that's optional. You can place all of the snacks on a grill-safe tray if you prefer; if you do, I recommend you line it with foil, as these are messy.

2 Butter each side of a graham cracker. (This creates the crust.) Drizzle some sweetened condensed milk over the top of the

graham cracker and then top it with your choice of ingredients. Some suggested combinations are:

- pecans, caramels, chocolate chips
- peanut butter, banana slices, another layer of sweetened condensed milk, chocolate chips
- peanut butter, jelly, marshmallows
- pecans, caramels, chocolate chips, coconut, marshmallows

3 Grill for 5 to 10 minutes, using an indirect and low heat method, until the chocolate is melted and the sweetened condensed milk bubbles. Watch these carefully or the graham cracker will burn.

4 The individual foil packets can serve as serving plates. Otherwise, if you prepared these on a grill-safe tray, use a spatula to lift each snack and serve it on a paper plate. (Now take a break while the crowd enjoys their treats, but be ready to hose off a bunch of sticky kids when they're done eating.)

Chapter 18

Healthier Food Fundamentals: Heart-Healthy Considerations

Every time you read the latest health news, you're probably thinking the same thing that I do: "If it tastes good, it's bad for us."

While that may be (okay, is) an exaggeration, it's still sometimes difficult to figure out what things you should cut where and in what ways so that you still retain that great flavor you've come to know and love.

The biggest out-to-hurt-your-heart culprits are:

- Fat
- Salt (Sodium)
- Sugar

Because people's metabolisms are different, consuming (the scientific word for feeding your face with) foods high in fat, sodium, or sugar won't affect everybody in the same way. Complicating things further is that no two experts agree on the best advice for you to follow. Some say "absolutely no sugar," while others tell you to "avoid artificial sweeteners without prejudice!"

Regardless of the advice, moderation seems to be the key. One dietician I know recommends that to learn moderation, you begin by filling up your plate as usual, then scraping one third of what's on your plate into the trash. (Some hosts frown on this practice at their cookouts. This also doesn't work if there's the possibility of going back for "seconds.")

Whether your life requires that you make a lifestyle change because of a personal goal ("I want to lose these pesky extra pounds") or a forced change because of illness, allergies, diabetes, or heart disease, moderation is again the key as you adapt your palate. It may seem overwhelming at first, but with time and patience, you will eventually develop new taste preferences. Just don't try to do so all at once.

In this chapter, I'll give you tips and recipes to get you started. I will also provide nutritional analysis, complete with protein-carbohydrate-fat ratios (PCF), so you can keep track of exactly how healthy you're being.

FIRING FORBIDDEN FATS

Okay, let's see if we can keep this straight: There are good fats, there are bad fats. Therefore, the total elimination of fat isn't always the best answer, while the reduction of fat is. Now all we have to do is to figure out the difference.

Saturated fats are the bad guys. They're the fats found in dairy products like butter and fatty cuts of meat. A diet high in saturated fat restricts the blood vessels and lowers the amount of healthy cholesterol (HDL) in the bloodstream.

I know what you're thinking: If butter is one of the bad guys, why is it used so often in this book? One reason is that I like the flavor. (Like my friend David Hebert says, "Butter by itself isn't bad. Buttering your bacon is bad.") But it does go beyond that. Recent studies have shown that the trans-fatty acids in no-cholesterol foods like margarine actually increase the amount of cholesterol in the body! Used within reason, and unless your doctor or dietician has advised otherwise, butter is usually the heart-healthier choice—if used in moderation.

Unsaturated or healthier fats—such as fish oil, oil from nuts like walnuts, unsaturated vegetable oils like olive or canola—have been shown to have the opposite effect of saturated fats. That's why it's important to not only limit the amount of fat in your diet, but also when you do add fat, to use healthier unsaturated fat as often as possible.

Whether it's a good fat or a bad fat, it's still a fat. And fat has calories. Lots of them! That's why it's wise to keep track of the fat in your diet.

The problem is, most of us like fat. Fat adds flavor. That's why gourmet restaurants use prime, marbled (read: fatty) cuts of meat and add lots of butter, cream, and sour cream to the potatoes! They also use lots of salt, but I'm getting ahead of myself.

The secret is to figure out the best way to get that added flavor while removing as much of the fat in your diet as possible.

Here are some suggestions on how to cut the bad fat from your diet:

- Prepare meat using a method that allows the fat to drain away from the meat rather than using a method like frying in which the meat sits in the fat. (It's a good thing you have this book about grilling, isn't it?)
- Eat smaller portions of meat and eat more greens and vegetables. One way to do this is to fool the eye with creative plate presentations. For example, when you slice meat on the diagonal and fan it out on the plate, it looks like there's more there.

- When grill-roasting meat in a pan for which you don't have the right-sized roasting rack, elevate the meat on pieces of celery. The celery raises the meat so the fat drains away; discard the celery when done.

- Slower grilling temperatures and the resulting increased grilling time allows more fat to drain out of the meat.

- Include more lower-fat meat choices in your meal plans, limiting higher-fat meats to three times a week.

- Stretch lean ground meat by adding bread crumbs, finely chopped vegetables, or tofu to the meat. (Note: Do not use bread crumbs with regular hamburger; it'll simply absorb the fat.)

- Trim off visible fat before and after cooking.

- Do not eat the skin of poultry. If you grill poultry with the skin on, remove it before you put the meat on your plate. (For example, rub Chicken à la Rub from pg. 67 on the outside of and under the skin of the chicken. Follow the directions in the recipe. Before serving, discard the skin. The chicken remains moist and flavorful, yet you throw away most of the fat calories with the skin.)

- Use arrowroot, cornstarch, or potato flour to thicken defatted pan drippings to make low-fat gravy or sauce to use in soups or stews. If you must have a bit of fat flavor in the gravy or sauce, use the method the French call "monter"—adding a small amount of butter to "finish off" a sauce at the end of the cooking time; this gives you the benefit of fat flavor without the disadvantage of lots of saturated fat calories.

- The ratio of oil (fat) to vinegar in salad dressing is usually three parts oil to one part vinegar. Try substituting broth or tofu for some of the oil. In fact, with low-fat tofu (about 70 calories and 7 grams of fat in a half cup) you get the benefit of additional protein. Plus, because it absorbs the flavor of what it's combined with, you'll seldom notice a difference in taste if you mix equal parts of tofu and mayonnaise (over 900 calories and 78 or more grams of fat in a half cup) together. Now I realize that you probably seldom eat a half cup of mayo as a single portion, but if you make a half-batch of dressing for your potato salad and substitute tofu for the other half, you'll see what I mean. You may need to adjust the herbs and seasonings to the full recipe amount, but herbs and seasonings don't add calories, so you benefit overall.

- Use an egg substitute or egg whites instead of whole eggs.

- Learn how to make so-called comfort foods so that they're low in fat and calories. For instance, use fat-free broth or some Lazy About "Cream" (recipe follows) in mashed potatoes and season them with roasted garlic and herbs. If you must use butter, add a small amount at the end. Even better would be to use a little infused or flavored olive oil instead. White truffle oil is excellent for this. If you have nonfat sour cream on hand, you can almost go hog-wild with that!

- Cut the fat in dips and spreads by using fat-free cream cheese, fat-free sour cream, or nonfat yogurt. If you're using a commercial dip, mix it with an equal amount of tofu or one of the other fat-free choices.

- Mix two parts olive oil with one part butter to use as a healthier-fat spread on bread. Even better is to use infused olive oil, such as that in which you've stored roasted garlic or roasted red peppers (see Chapter 13). **Better yet:** Toast the bread on the grill and spread it with roasted garlic!

Lazy About "Cream"

You can use this recipe as a substitute for heavy cream in gravy, mashed potatoes, or sauces. It's much richer tasting than skim milk. The yield will differ according to whether you use instant nonfat dry milk or the non-instant variety usually sold in health food stores.

Makes 1¼ cups, depending on type of nonfat milk used

1 cup skim milk
¼ cup nonfat dry milk

1 Put the milk and nonfat dry milk in a blender and process until mixed. Store in the refrigerator until the expiration date on the milk carton.

Nutritional analysis

Lazy About "Cream"	Heavy Cream
Calories per serving: 146.61	Calories per serving: 515.02
PCF ratio: 39-57-3	PCF Ratio: 2-3-95
Protein per serving: 14.32 g	Protein per serving: 3.06 g
Carbohydrate per serving: 20.75 g	Carbohydrate per serving: 4.17 g
Fat per serving: 0.56 g	Fat per serving: 55.27 g
Saturated fat: 0.37 g	Saturated fat: 34.40 g
Cholesterol: 7.96 mg	Cholesterol: 204.79 mg
Sodium: 220.73 mg	Sodium: 56.16 mg
Exchange approximations:	Exchange approximations:
2 Skim Milk	20 (Saturated) Fat

"South" of Van Wert County, "West" Coast of Ohio Guacamole

This recipe isn't low in fat, but the fat in the recipe is the healthier avocado oil kind. For my taste, the Bragg Liquid Aminos and Worcestershire sauce provide enough salty flavor for this dip—even if I use the homemade Worcestershire sauce in this chapter instead of a commercial version. (I prefer the milder French's brand rather than Lea & Perrin's Worcestershire when I use a commercial variety.) This guacamole makes a great dip for grill-toasted corn tortillas. Spread it on toasted whole-grain bread, add a thick slice of fresh tomato and a grilled, lean hamburger or sausage patty, and you've got yourself one great sandwich!

Makes 8 servings

¼ cup cider or unsweetened apple juice
1½ teaspoons cider vinegar
1 clove garlic
1 teaspoon Bragg Liquid Aminos
½ teaspoon Worcestershire sauce
2 teaspoons extra-virgin olive oil
1 avocado

1 In a blender or food processor, combine the cider or apple juice, vinegar, minced garlic, Bragg Liquid Aminos, Worcestershire sauce, olive oil, and avocado pulp.

2 Process until smooth. Unlike regular guacamole that is left somewhat "chunky," you want to purée this one.

Note: If you won't be serving the guacamole immediately, omit the oil when you purée the mixture. After you transfer the guacamole to a covered container, add the olive oil, covering the top. This helps prevent the guacamole from turning dark. When ready to serve, whisk the mixture until smooth to blend in the oil.

Nutritional analysis:

Calories per serving: 55.54

PCF ratio: 4-20-75

Protein per serving: 0.63 g

Carbohydrate per serving: 3.03 g

Fat per serving: 4.98 g

Saturated fat: 0.77 g

Cholesterol: 0.00 mg

Sodium: 34.38 mg

Fiber: 1.27 g

Exchange approximations: 1 Fat, 1 Free Condiment

Saving Sausage in Your Diet

Cutting the fat and sodium in your diet doesn't mean that you have to go without the spicy taste of pepperoni on your pizza or sausage for breakfast. If you make your own sausage, you can control the ingredients and avoid preservatives and artificial coloring and flavorings in the process.

Seasoning Suggestions: Sausage making isn't an exact science. In fact, you probably already have favorite brands or butcher shop blends based on how the meat is seasoned. The recipes given in this section are intended to be guidelines. Feel free to experiment. If you know you'll want more zip than the recommended amount of red pepper flakes will provide, add more. I suggest until you arrive at proportions that suit your tastes, that you err on the side of caution at first. Go easy on the seasonings, make a small test patty, pan-fry it, check the results, and then adjust accordingly. (Keep in mind that the flavors usually intensify if, before you grill it, you allow the meat to rest in the refrigerator overnight.)

For example, because pepperoni is a meat that is usually associated with a saltier flavor, my recipe includes 1 tablespoon of salt. However, while I omit the salt entirely, my friend uses 3 tablespoons, which increases the nutritional analysis for the sodium in her version from 92 mg to about 250 mg.

One of my quirks is that I don't like the taste of dried sage, which is a staple in many sausage recipes. If you like sage in your stuffing or dressing, you'll probably like it in sausage, so feel free to add some.

Grinding Instructions: If you have a meat grinder, follow the manufacturer's instructions. To grind meat in a food processor, it helps if you first cut the meat into 1-inch cubes and freeze those chunks for about 20 minutes. Then put them in the bowl of your food processor and pulse until the meat is ground, scraping down the side of the bowl as necessary.

Mixing Instructions: In a large bowl, measure all ingredients. Then get ready to get your hands dirty, using the "gonna have to wash 'em anyhow, so why have dirty utensils too" method! Squish everything between your fingers repeatedly, until you're absolutely certain that all ingredients are well mixed.

Cooking and Smoking Instructions: For sausage patties, shape and grill the meat as you would hamburgers. For sausage with a smoky flavor, I recommend stuffing the mixture into casings. Refrigerate overnight. Follow the instructions for your smoker. In most instances, you'll slow-smoke the sausages for about 6 hours, or until the meat reaches an internal temperature of 152°F.

Use the sausage mixture within 3 days; otherwise, either cut the recipe according to what you'll need or freeze the additional amount to use later.

Confused about which knife to use to trim the fat from the meat—or which knife to use for any purpose, for that matter? Check out the "world-wide" link on the J. A. Henckels Premium Cutlery Web site (www.zwilling.com). The site also includes tips on knife care.

Bravo for Bratwurst!

The settlers in my neck o' the woods were primarily Pennsylvania Dutch or German. The festivals around here start in August, and occur pretty much every weekend until well into October. While it's a staple of these festivals, I think bratwurst is good any time of the year. This sausage recipe works great for the "Bratwurst and Beer" recipe on pg. 143. If you don't want to bother with putting the meat in casings, shape it into patties, grill until well done, then add it to the beer and sauerkraut mixture as recommended in that recipe. For a change of pace, substitute cider or apple juice for the beer. Equally delicious!

Makes 5 pounds

3 pounds lean pork butt roast or loin
2 pounds boneless, skinless chicken thighs
2 teaspoons ground caraway seeds
1½ teaspoons ground mace
¾ teaspoon ground ginger
2 teaspoons kosher or sea salt
¾ cup nonfat dry milk
¼ cup water
2 teaspoons sugar
2 teaspoons ground black pepper

Optional:

1 cup dried bread crumbs

Nutritional analysis (per ounce, without bread crumbs):

Calories per serving: 64.21

PCF ratio: 49-3-48

Protein per serving: 7.59 g

Carbohydrate per serving: 0.44 g

Fat per serving: 3.33 g

Saturated fat: 1.11 g

Cholesterol: 24.78 mg

Sodium: 82.73 mg

Exchange approximations:

½ Lean, ½ Medium Fat Meat

Note: If you add the bread crumbs, you may need to increase the amount of water by up to another ¼ cup. Adding bread crumbs will also result in a milder-tasting sausage. In fact, you can go wild with this (or any other) recipe. Use beer or apple juice instead of the water. If you're making an effort to increase the amount of fiber in your diet, use oat bran instead of bread crumbs. (Just remember that when you add more fiber to your diet, you'll probably need to increase the amount of water that you drink, too. Chances are you should be drinking more water anyhow. I recommend strapping a canteen with a long straw to your belt.)

Pepperoni Pizzazz-a-ma-tazz

If you'll be using this pepperoni on pizza, I recommend cooking it first. It's fine grilled as patties and then crumbled on the pizza. If you're a purist and demand "slices" of pepperoni, use the sausage casings method described earlier. The chicken thighs replace the pork fat usually called for in pepperoni recipes. The nutritional analysis assumes beef is used, but it will remain similar if you use lean pork instead.

Makes 6 pounds

5 pounds round or flank steak, trimmed of all visible fat
1 pound boneless, skinless chicken thighs
1 tablespoon kosher or sea salt
¾ cup instant nonfat dry milk
¼ cup water
2 tablespoons sugar
1 tablespoon cracked black pepper
1 tablespoon (fine ground) black pepper
3 tablespoons chili powder
1 teaspoon dried thyme
1 teaspoon dried oregano
1 teaspoon whole anise
   seeds
1 teaspoon ground cumin

Nutritional analysis (per ounce):

Calories per serving: 60.05

PCF ratio: 62-3-35

Protein per serving: 8.94 g

Carbohydrate per serving: 0.41 g

Fat per serving: 2.26 g

Saturated fat: 0.74 g

Cholesterol: 27.17 mg

Sodium: 92.03 mg

Exchange approximations:

1 Lean Meat

Kicked-Up Kielbasa

To prepare the spiced whiskey called for in this recipe, put 2 teaspoons of bourbon in a microwave-safe bowl and add a pinch of dried pepper flakes. Microwave on high for 15 seconds, or until mixture is hot. If you want a really spicy sausage, double the amount of whiskey and go for an entire teaspoon of the pepper flakes! Shoot, add some ground cayenne pepper while you're at it! Allow the mixture to cool before adding it to the other ingredients.

Makes 3 pounds

2 pounds pork shoulder
1 pound beef chuck
2 teaspoons freshly ground black pepper
1 teaspoon ground allspice
2 teaspoons garlic powder
2 teaspoons spiced whiskey

Optional: kosher or sea salt to taste

Nutritional analysis (per ounce, without salt):

Calories per serving: 70.18

PCF ratio: 47-0-53

Protein per serving: 7.99 g

Carbohydrate per serving: 0.00 g

Fat per serving: 3.95 g

Saturated fat: 1.50 g

Cholesterol: 24.56 mg

Sodium: 15.02 mg

Exchange approximations:

1 Medium-Fat Meat

Ideal for the Indoor Grill Kielbasa

The brown sugar in this recipe helps add that caramelized flavor you get when meat's grilled outside over high temperatures. Whether you fix this one indoors or out, you'll like this variation.

Makes 3 pounds

2 pounds pork shoulder, trimmed of all visible fat
1 pound beef chuck, trimmed of all visible fat
4 teaspoons minced garlic
2 teaspoons freshly ground black pepper
2 tablespoons brown sugar
1 teaspoon ground allspice
1 teaspoon dried marjoram

Optional: sea or kosher salt

Nutritional analysis (per ounce, without salt):

Calories per serving: 72.21

PCF ratio: 46-4-51

Protein per serving: 8.00 g

Carbohydrate per serving: 0.64 g

Fat per serving: 3.95 g

Saturated fat: 1.50 g

Cholesterol: 24.56 mg

Sodium: 15.28 mg

Exchange approximations: 1 Medium-Fat Meat

Dedicated to Johnny Appleseed Chicken Sausage

If you like you can substitute lean ground chicken or turkey for any of the pork or beef called for in the recipes in this section. This one calls for all chicken. Feel free to mix in some lean pork if you prefer. The apples make this a dish that validates all that hard work Johnny did on his journey across America!

Makes about 5½ pounds

2½ pounds boneless, skinless chicken breasts
2½ pounds boneless, skinless chicken thighs
2 teaspoons kosher or sea salt
1 tablespoon freshly ground black pepper
1 teaspoon dried basil
1 teaspoon ground cloves
1 teaspoon dried rosemary
Tart baking apples
½ cup dry white wine, sherry, or unsweetened apple juice

1 Wash, peel, core, and finely shred enough apples to equal 1 cup. Add to the other ingredients and mix well.

Nutritional analysis (per ounce, using white wine):

Calories per serving: 47.75

PCF ratio: 63-2-36

Protein per serving: 7.03 g

Carbohydrate per serving: 0.20 g

Fat per serving: 1.78 g

Saturated fat: 0.48g

Cholesterol: 21.65 mg

Sodium: 71.47 mg

Fiber: 0.03

Exchange approximations:

1 Lean Meat

Substitute the seasonings called for in any of the sausage recipes in this chapter and create your own sausage varieties by trying these combinations:

- **Italian:** Add a Taste of Italy (herb) Blend
- **Hot Italian:** Add a Taste of Italy (herb) Blend and Mrs. Dash Extra Spicy.
- **Roasted Stuff:** Mix in some roasted red pepper and garlic in addition to or in place of some of the other seasonings; another option is to use roasted sun-dried tomatoes and Mrs. Dash Tomato Basil Garlic.
- **Marvelous Maple:** During the last two minutes of grilling time, brush both sides of the sausage with maple syrup.
- **Fruit-Filled:** Soak dried fruit like cherries, cranberries, or raisins in some water to reconstitute (puff up and make juicy) and use it in place of some of the meat.
- **Sage Advice:** While he can't convince me to try it (yet), I have a friend who swears by a sausage he makes combining ground turkey, fresh sage, and toasted pine nuts.
- **Greek Revival:** Substitute a fruity wine for the water or other wine in the recipe and add some freshly grated orange zest or dried orange peel.

SHUNNING THE SALT SHAKER

I've never been a big fan of salt, so this one was easy for me to adapt—which is a good thing because after years of low blood pressure, my body's decided it's time for a change of pace and leans toward the other extreme now if I'm not careful. I don't eat a salt-free diet. As I've mentioned elsewhere in this book, I just don't use table salt. I've found that, for me, kosher or sea salt doesn't seem to have that dreaded adverse effect on my blood pressure, and it takes less kosher or sea salt to achieve the salty flavor that pleases my palate.

Except for the amounts called for in baked recipes (for which I also substitute kosher or sea salt, depending upon whether or not I want a coarser or a finer-grain, easier-to-dissolve salt), you can reduce the amount of salt called for in most recipes. This is especially true if you season the dish with herbs and spices. If you use Worcestershire or soy sauce, omit the salt entirely. Just remember to have some at the table for those whose palates aren't quite as refined as yours. (You may have noticed by the ingredient proportions given in this book that I also don't suggest a lot of pepper. Remember, not everyone's tastes are the same. I've found that providing a pepper grinder at the table for those who want to add more is easier than putting tweezers beside the plates of those who want less.)

Sauce or stew too salty? Drop in a peeled, raw potato and let it simmer with the other stuff for a bit. The potato will absorb some of the salt. (Whether you then discard the potato or feed it to one of your salt-lovin' friends is up to you.)

Homemade Worcestershire Sauce

The main difference between traditional Worcestershire sauce and this version is that the commercial variety is made from anchovies and lots of salt. This delicious version can be used in any recipe that calls for Worcestershire. It's so good, you won't mourn the missing anchovies. Even though it's much lower in sodium than its commercial cousin, your taste buds won't complain. (Your heart will thank you and you'll feel better because by consuming less salt you'll be helping to keep your blood pressure levels under control.) As an added bonus, it's a celiac-safe (gluten-free) sauce, too.

Makes 1 cup (16 1-tablespoon servings)

1½ cups cider vinegar
¼ cup Smucker's Red Plum Jam or Plum Preserves
1 tablespoon blackstrap molasses
1 clove crushed garlic
⅛ teaspoon chili powder
⅛ teaspoon ground cloves
Pinch cayenne pepper
¼ cup chopped onion
½ teaspoon ground allspice
⅛ teaspoon dry mustard
1 teaspoon Bragg Liquid Aminos

Nutritional analysis (per tablespoon):

Calories per serving: 14.31

PCF ratio: 3-97-0

Protein per serving: 0.11 g

Carbohydrate per serving: 4.12 g

Fat per serving: 0.01 g

Sodium: 14.79 mg (Compared to 65 mg in Lea & Perrin's Worcestershire Sauce)

Fiber: 0.05

Exchange approximations:

1 Free Condiment

1 Add all ingredients to a large, grill-safe saucepan over direct heat and mix well. Stir until mixture boils.

2 Move the pan to an indirect heat area of the grill and simmer uncovered for 1 hour, stirring occasionally. Store any leftovers in a covered jar in the refrigerator.

Soy Sauce Substitute

Bragg Liquid Aminos, like its counterpart soy sauce, is made from soybeans. However, for this product, the company uses only purified water and doesn't add any preservatives, coloring agents, alcohol, additives, or chemicals. Bragg Liquid Aminos is certified kosher. Unlike soy sauce, it is not fermented—an important consideration for anyone with mold allergies.

While Bragg Liquid Aminos is not sodium-free, a half teaspoon only has 110 mg of sodium, compared to regular soy sauce, which has 171 mg. (In fairness, low-sodium soy sauce only has around 86 mg of sodium; I just find that Bragg Liquid Aminos tastes better than the reduced-sodium option, so it makes a great compromise.)

Bragg Liquid Aminos comes in a pourable version or a squirt bottle; the latter makes it easy to use to season foods on the plate. The company also has organic apple cider vinegar and extra-virgin olive oil products, too (see Sources).

Simply Sensational Salt Substitutes and Seasonings

Herb blends are a great way to add flavor. Even if you still have a hankering to salt your food, you'll be able to get by using less if it's already seasoned with one of these mixtures.

The directions are easy: Unless the recipe states otherwise, for these blends you put all the ingredients in a covered container, shake it up, and store it in a cool, dry place until needed.

WHEN IT COMES TO HERBS AND SPICES, LEAFY PLANTS ARE USUALLY HERBS; NUTS, SEEDS, AND ROOTS ARE SPICES.

Bodacious BBQ Blend

Try this one on beef, lamb, or pork, or sprinkle it over veggies before grilling.

3 tablespoons dried basil
3 tablespoons dried oregano
2 ground bay leaves

2 tablespoons dried rosemary
1 tablespoon dried savory

PDQ BBQ Blend

This one goes with fish and poultry, or it can be sprinkled onto tomatoes before grilling, or added to salad dressings made with extra-virgin olive oil and balsamic or red wine vinegar.

2 tablespoons dried basil
2 tablespoons dried sage
2 tablespoons dried thyme
2 teaspoons cracked black
    pepper

2 teaspoons dried savory
½ teaspoon dried lemon peel

Calypso Islands Blend

Use this on any food to which you want to add a Caribbean flair.

2 tablespoons curry powder
2 tablespoons ground cumin
2 tablespoons ground allspice

2 tablespoons ground ginger
2 teaspoons ground cayenne
  pepper

Kitchen Garden Blend

This blend can be used as a substitute for table salt in salads, soups, or on grilled vegetables.

4 teaspoons dried basil
4 teaspoons dried chervil

4 teaspoons dried tarragon
5 teaspoons dried thyme

British Blend

Jolly Old England may not be the first thing that comes to mind when you think of grilling, but this blend goes great on almost anything.

1 tablespoon crushed juniper
  berries
1 tablespoon dried thyme
1 teaspoon ground cloves

1 tablespoon onion powder
1 teaspoon cracked black
  pepper

Fishy, Fishy in a Brook Flavoring

Sprinkle this one onto fish or seafood before grilling.

5 teaspoons dried basil
5 teaspoons crushed fennel seed

4 teaspoons dried parsley
1 teaspoon dried lemon peel

French Herbes

Use this to season omelettes or scrambled eggs, fish or poultry before grilling, or hot vegetables.

3 tablespoons dried parsley
2 teaspoons dried chervil

2 teaspoons dried chives
1½ teaspoons dried tarragon

Herbes de Provence

This traditional French blend is good in egg dishes. It's also used to season rice and grains, or meat, fish, or poultry before grilling. Whisk some into wine vinegar and extra-virgin olive oil to which you've added a little Dijon mustard and it makes a delicious vinaigrette.

4 teaspoons dried oregano
2 teaspoons dried basil
2 teaspoons dried sweet
   marjoram
2 teaspoons dried thyme
1 teaspoon dried mint

1 teaspoon dried rosemary
1 teaspoon dried sage leaves
1 teaspoon fennel seed
1 teaspoon dried lavender
   (optional)

A Taste of Italy Blend

Use this on anything to which you want to add an Italian flavor.

1 tablespoon crushed dried basil
1 tablespoon crushed dried
   thyme

1 tablespoon crushed dried
   oregano
2 tablespoons garlic powder

Tex-Mex Temptation

Try this one on about anything to which you want to add a Texas sensation: grilled game or other meats, poultry, seafood, or vegetables, or to season a dip made with plain, nonfat yogurt.

3 tablespoons dried cilantro
2 tablespoons dried Mexican oregano
2 tablespoons chili powder
2 tablespoons cracked black pepper
2 tablespoons ground cumin
2 small crushed dried chili peppers
4 teaspoons dried thyme
1 teaspoon garlic powder

1 Combine all ingredients in a blender or food processor. Grind to desired consistency.

For those times you don't feel like coming up with your own spice and herb seasoning concoctions, try the ones available from Mrs. Dash.

- Classic Italiano
- Extra Spicy
- Garlic & Herb
- Lemon Pepper
- Minced Onion Medley
- Onion & Herb
- Original Blend
- Table Blend
- Tomato Basil Garlic

Even though some of the Mrs. Dash varieties include a "dash" of sweetener (fructose), they still qualify as a Free Exchange for diabetics. (See Sources)

SLASHING SUGAR

Sugar, like salt, is a flavor enhancer. In fact, a pinch of sugar in a recipe helps boost the salty flavor. While it's sometimes given a worse rap than it deserves, sugar is still an empty calorie. In other words, the only benefit you get by adding it to a recipe is that oh-so-sweet boost in flavor; sugar adds a big zip, but nada, nothing in the way of nutritional value. (Despite studies that show that for the diabetic, sugar has about the same adverse affect—increased blood sugar levels—as do other refined starches like white bread and rice, the choice as to how a diabetic should use sugar is between the diabetic and his or her dietician. The rest of us are on the honor system.)

Some painless, ways to be *Lazy About* decreasing the amount of sugar in your diet include:

- If you can tolerate them, use artificial sweeteners. Just keep in mind that you won't be adding any nutritional value to your diet when you do so. Diabetics should consult with a dietician because some artificial sweeteners can still adversely affect blood glucose levels.
- Eat more fruit! This satisfies your sweet tooth, has that needed extra nutritional value of vitamins and minerals, and increases the amount of fiber in your diet. Fresh or unsweetened frozen fruit is best. When you must use canned fruit, select the unsweetened kind packed in water or its own juices.
- Eat whole-grain snacks. For most people, baked goods made with whole grains need less sugar to taste sweet enough to enjoy, plus there's the added benefit that whole grains seem to reduce that sugar rush followed by another craving for sugar that is caused by

eating pastries and candy. (The reduced metabolism time for sweets combined with whole grains is based on studies done determining the glycemic index for foods, which is a still somewhat controversial method of analyzing how a food converts to sugar in the bloodstream. You can read more about the glycemic index at *www.mendosa.com/gi.htm*.)

⌔ Replace the soda that you drink with one of the healthier drink suggestions in Chapter 16.

Don't throw out leftover fresh herbs that you can't use immediately. Once the grill has cooled to about 200 to 225°F, place the herbs on foil or a baking sheet on the grill and cover. It'll take around an hour for the herbs to dry. Once they're dry, crush them between your fingers, put in a sealed jar, and store in a cool, dry place until needed.

I've been testing recipes using a new, all natural, low-glycemic, reduced calorie one-to-one sugar replacement product that I'm crazy about! Depending on the "formula"—regular Whey Low Granular or Whey Low Powder (confectioner's sugar variety), or Whey Low Granular, Type D (diabetic version)—and on whether or not you're diabetic, the glycemic index for this sweetener ranges from 12 to 20; granulated cane sugar is 100. While none of the Whey Low products is free of calories, they do only have 25 percent of the calories in cane sugar, or four calories a teaspoon versus the 16 in sugar. A very important consideration if you want to substitute sugar in a grilling marinade is that unlike artificial sweeteners, Whey Low can withstand high temperatures. Unfortunately, this product isn't expected to be available in stores nationwide until sometime in 2003. For now, however, you can order it from the company's Website at www.wheylow.com.

If you're ready to see recipes for some easy ways to make healthy desserts while letting a gadget do the work for you as you grill, check out Chapter 20.

Otherwise, continue on to Chapter 19 to learn all about some indoor grilling tools and tricks.

Chapter 19

Bringin' It Indoors: Indoor Grills and Gadgets

This chapter has information about and recipes for your indoor grill or grill pan. There are also details about other gadgets that let you maintain your *Lazy About Grilling* attitude and fix flawless fantastic feasts in a flash.

I specify names for the gadgets I use mainly because then I know how to label the attachments or processes. Different brands call things by different names. It isn't because I'm on some sort of "my way is the best way" power trip. You can just as easily use your (insert brand name here) gadget to do the task explained; just be sure to grab the correct, equivalent (insert name here) attachment when you do so. (In fact, I can do that "name the parts properly" stuff because I keep my manuals beside me here at the computer. If you were working alongside me in the kitchen, I'd probably ask you to hand me the "hoochie" so I can hook it up to the "thing-a-ma-jig.")

Speaking of my kitchen, please indulge me while I digress for a bit. My current kitchen is small and "putting equipment away" would mean truly "digging stuff out" to get at 'em once they're stored. Because I don't like getting things out and then putting them away again, being *Lazy About* gadgets in my house means lining up as many as possible across my countertops. I keep the attachments behind each one in little baskets slid under these half-counter-width shelves I use under the cupboards, so I can set out even more gadgets behind the gadgets at the front of the counters! Delegating is great, but that isn't always possible. Therefore, my philosophy is if you can't get *someone* to do a task, then have *something* close by that'll do as much of it as possible for you.

So, while you already know that I'm not opposed to grilling outdoors in snowy weather, there are times—like during thunderstorms—when it's better to give in and fix things inside. Get ready to fire up that indoor grill and prepare a good meal—and have a good time in the process.

WHY I SELDOM USE MY CAST-IRON SKILLET ON THE STOVE ANYMORE

Why? Because I'm in love with the results I get using my Cuisinart Hard Anodized Nonstick Grill Pan. Talk about being *Lazy About* breaking in a pan; this one is so well-seasoned that oil just beads up if you pour it in the pan!

It can take temperatures up to 450ºF, so it'll go from the stovetop to the oven.

The instructions for the recipes in this section are based on using that pan.

Laura's Lean Beef

It's now a fallacy that beef has to be heavily marbled to be flavorful. Gone, too, is that myth that you need to wrap a strip of bacon around a beef tenderloin for it to be tasty. Laura's Lean Beef is from cattle raised without antibiotics or growth hormones. A four-ounce beef tenderloin has only 140 calories and 4.5 grams of fat! (For a one-ounce serving, that scooch over 1 gram of fat means that it qualifies as a Very-Lean Meat if you're on a Food Exchange diet.) It's even earned the right to use the American Heart Association's heart-healthy logo on its label. Laura's Lean Beef is available at supermarkets nationwide (see Sources).

As you consider the recipes in this section, remember that Laura's Lean Beef requires less cooking time. Therefore, plan to add a minute or two to compensate if you're using other beef when you prepare these dishes.

You can achieve the succulent flavor of "seared" meats (that you once thought you could only achieve at the high temperatures on an outdoor grill) if you add a little brown sugar to your rub or marinade.

Extra-Oomph Stovetop-Grilled Beef Fillets

Sweet, savory, succulent, seared beef with a punch of peppery pizzazz! Is your mouth watering yet? It will be once you read this recipe. I served this to my brother's family; Dennis has now forgiven me for every mean thing I did to him as a kid.

Makes 4 servings

2 teaspoons paprika
2 tablespoons garlic powder
1 teaspoon freshly ground or cracked black pepper
1 teaspoon onion powder
¼ teaspoon cayenne pepper

If you don't have a stovetop grill pan, in a pinch you can use a well-seasoned cast-iron skillet. You just won't get any of those nifty, seared grill-type ridges across the meat.

¼ teaspoon dried oregano
¼ teaspoon dried thyme
1 teaspoon brown sugar
Four 4-ounce Laura's Lean Beef tenderloins
Olive oil

1 Mix all dry ingredients well.

2 Rub about ¼ teaspoon of olive oil onto each side of the beef, then coat each half of each fillet with ½ tablespoon of the dry mixture. Rub the dry seasoning into the beef. (It's called a "rub" for a reason, you know!) Set fillets aside for about a half hour and allow them to come to room temperature.

3 When ready to stovetop "grill" the meat, heat the Cuisinart Hard Anodized Nonstick Grill Pan over high heat until a drop of water dropped in the pan sizzles and evaporates in a flash.

4 Add the beef fillets to the skillet. Lower the temperature to medium-high. (You may want to top the skillet with a splatter screen if you got carried away with the oil.) Allow the meat to cook for three minutes on one side, then use tongs to turn the tenderloin fillets and cook for another two minutes for medium, or three minutes for medium-well. (Be sure to use tongs so you don't puncture the meat.)

5 Remove the pan from the burner and allow the meat to rest for 1 to 2 minutes in the pan, then for another 3 minutes on the plate before serving. The resting time allows the juices to redistribute throughout the meat so the fillets are nice and juicy when you cut into them.

Fruity Fantasy Strip Steaks

Who says cranberries are just for Christmas? This sweet-without-the-sour steak sauce proves otherwise! Dried cherries and cranberries are available online or by mail order (see Sources). See the Sit-Back-and-Watch-It-Steam Wild Rice and Broccoli recipe on pg. 329 for my suggestion on how to stretch the 2 steaks called for in this recipe into 4 servings.

Makes 2–4 servings

Two 8-ounce Laura's Lean Beef boneless strip steaks

Olive oil

¼ cup sugar

1 tablespoon dried cherries

1 tablespoon dried cranberries

2 tablespoons (⅛ cup) water

1 orange

Crystallized (candied) ginger

1 teaspoon Worcestershire sauce

Optional: sea salt and freshly ground black pepper to taste

1 Preheat oven to 375°F.

2 Dry boneless strip steaks (at room temperature) with paper towels, then rub lightly with olive oil. Spread the sugar onto a plate and roll the steaks in the sugar, pressing to ensure all surfaces are coated. (You can use a mixture of white and brown sugar, if you prefer.)

3 Bring the Cuisinart Hard Anodized Nonstick Grill Pan to the correct temperature over high heat. Add the steaks and pan-sear them for a minute on each side.

4 Place the pan in the oven and bake for 5 minutes, or until the internal temperature of the meat reaches 160°F for medium.

5 While the steaks bake, in a covered microwave-safe bowl, add the dried cherries, cranberries, and water. Microwave on high for 40 seconds. Allow mixture to steep, covered, to reconstitute the fruit.

6 Remove meat from pan and place on a platter to rest before you carve the meat. Place the pan over medium heat and add ½ cup of fresh orange juice, grated orange peel to equal 1 teaspoon, finely chopped candied ginger to equal 1 teaspoon, the Worcestershire sauce, and the dried fruit and water mixture. Bring to a boil, then reduce heat and simmer for 5 minutes. (If you prefer a sweeter sauce, as the mixture simmers, taste the sauce and add sugar a teaspoon at a time until it's sweet enough for your taste. If you want some extra kick to the sauce, feel free to stir in some steak sauce at this point.)

7 Slice the steaks into ½-inch-wide slices and fan out across the serving platter. Pour the orange juice and fruit sauce over the meat. Season with additional sea salt and freshly ground black pepper, if desired.

Lemon Pepper-Dashed Orange Roughy

This is one of my favorite indoor grilled foods! Grill chefs who live near a coast—or near a reliable fresh fish market with a ready supply of choice seafood flown in fresh daily—may like fish grilled to medium rare. Because I start with frozen fillets, I like mine a bit on the dry side. This recipe reflects that. Adjust the cooking time if you're stovetop-grilling fresh fish.

Makes 2 servings

Two 8-ounce orange roughy fillets
2 teaspoons olive oil
2 teaspoons Mrs. Dash Lemon Pepper
1 teaspoon extra-virgin olive oil

1 Pat the fillets dry with paper towels. Rub ½ teaspoon of olive oil over the curved portion of each fillet. Sprinkle 1 teaspoon Mrs. Dash Lemon Pepper evenly over the top of each fillet. Pat the seasoning onto the flesh of the fish.

2 Bring the Cuisinart Hard Anodized Nonstick Grill Pan to temperature over high heat. Add the fillets to the pan, curved side down. Drizzle the remaining 1 teaspoon of olive oil over the flat, exposed side of the fillets, rubbing into the fish with the back of a spoon. (Alternatively, you can either spray or brush the olive oil onto the fish.)

3 Grill for 4 to 5 minutes, or until the flat side of the fish begins to lose its transparent color. You'll want the fish to just begin to

For those times you want to get every last scrumptious bite of sauce out of a hot pan, grab a heat-safe spatula and other handy kitchen utensils to get the job done. Not only can they stand the heat, they come in colors! (See Sources) I'm partial to all things blue, so guess which color I use in my kitchen?

blacken, but not burn. Reduce the heat, if necessary. Turn the fish and grill for an additional minute.

4 Transfer the fillets to plates or a serving platter. Drizzle the extra-virgin olive oil over the blackened top of the fillets.

Note: Lemon Pepper Dashed Soft-shell Crabs is another great dish. Allow at least 2 soft-shell crabs per serving. (see Sources) You'll generally need to reduce the pan temperature to medium or medium-high once you add the soft-shell crabs to the pan. Reduce the grilling time to 3 to 4 minutes on the "prettier" side of the crabs; turn and grill for another minute on the darker side.

SOFT-SHELL CRAB IS ALSO GOOD GRILLED IN ROASTED GARLIC BUTTER, GARLIC BUTTER, OR OLIVE OIL WITH OLD BAY SEASONING (SEE RECIPE IN CHAPTER 1). DIANE GOLDSMITH SAYS SHE PREFERS TO MARINATE THE SOFT-SHELL CRAB IN THE OLIVE OIL AND OLD BAY SEASONING MIXTURE FOR AN HOUR OR TWO. I PREFER A MILDER FLAVOR, SO I COAT MINE IMMEDIATELY BEFORE I GRILL THEM.

INDOOR GRILLS

The recipes in this section assume you're using an indoor grill with a "lid." George Foreman may have started the craze, but other manufacturers now make worthy contenders, too. Newer models have hinged lids that adjust to the depth of the food you're grilling. Others come with temperature controls. Some of the choices I've tried, also listed in the Sources after Chapter 20, are:

George Foreman's Grilling Machine
Meal Maker Express Contact Grill

Indoor Fare

It's my opinion that skinless, boneless poultry or boneless cuts of meat work best on an indoor grill. Other than that, the possibilities are almost as endless for grilling indoors as they are for firing up the grill outside.

Prime recipes in this book you should consider for your indoor grill include:

- Grilled Honey-Mustard Chicken, pg. 86
- To Live for Chicken Marinade, pg. 88
- Gulf Coast Hurricane Hamburgers, pg. 94
- Beefy Caesar Salad, pg. 108
- Garlic and Honey Pork Chops, pg. 117

There's a reason I'm starting out the recipes in this section with a salad and a marmalade. Stick with me and you'll see why!

Even the smallest George Foreman grill is large enough to use to fix yourself a complete breakfast in a flash. Plug in the grill, remove a sausage patty from the freezer, and put it on the grill near the bottom to allow any fat to drain away without getting the drippings on the rest of the grill. Close the lid and grill for 5 or 6 minutes, or until the juices run clear. Once you have the sausage on the grill, remove a frozen leftover waffle from the freezer. (I use yet another gadget to make mine: the Cuisinart 2-Slice Belgian Waffle Maker.) About 3 minutes before the sausage is done, add the waffle to the back of the grill. For a meal for "on the road," slice the waffle in half and use it to make a sausage sandwich; otherwise, serve the waffle with your favorite toppings alongside the sausage.

Ann's Very Veggie Salad

This salad is my winter equivalent for coleslaw. If the amount of sugar is a concern, use Whey Low instead; I've tried it with both Whey Low Granular and Whey Low Granular, Type D (see Chapter 18). It's versatile. As long as there's enough brine in the covered container to cover the veggies, it keeps (almost) forever in the refrigerator.

Makes 8 servings

1 teaspoon kosher or sea salt
1 cup sugar
¾ teaspoon cracked black pepper
¼ teaspoon celery seed
1 tablespoon water
¾ cup white wine vinegar
½ cup extra-virgin olive oil
Green pepper
Onion
Celery
1 can no-salt-added corn
1 can no-salt-added French-style green beans
1 can no-salt-added peas

I OFTEN SUBSTITUTE BLANCHED FROZEN VEGETABLE MIXES FOR THE CANNED VEGGIES, OR ADD BEETS TO IT AS WELL FOR A CHANGE OF PACE AND CHANGE OF COLOR.

1 To a microwave-safe container (I use a 4-cup glass measuring cup), add the salt, sugar, pepper, celery seed, water, and vinegar. Stir to mix. Microwave on high for 30-second intervals, stirring between each interval, until sugar is dissolved. Set aside to cool.

2 Wash, peel, seed, and chop enough green pepper to equal 1 cup. Peel and chop the onion to equal 1 cup. Clean and chop the celery to equal 1 cup.

3 To a large covered bowl, add the green pepper, onion, and celery.

4 Drain the canned vegetables and add to the bowl.

5 Pour the vinegar mixture over the vegetables. Add the olive oil. Mix well. Refrigerate until needed. Stir and serve. (The olive oil, which "gels" in the refrigerator, will liquefy once it comes to room temperature.)

Note: White wine vinegar has a milder flavor than most vinegars; however, it's still a good idea to have extra-virgin olive oil at the table to drizzle over the salad for those who feel the salad is too tart.

TJ Robertson's Triumphant Zucchini Marmalade

Here's a way for you to deal with that seemingly never-ending abundance of zucchini from your garden. TJ says, "This is my blue-ribbon-winning, tri-state fair entry and a wonderful spread on toasted homemade bread; the zucchini adds crunch."

Makes 5 half-pints

2 pounds young zucchini squash
2 lemons
Grated lemon peel (lemon zest)
One 13½-ounce can of crushed pineapple, drained
1 package powdered fruit pectin
5 cups sugar
Crystallized (candied) ginger

NOTES ABOUT TJ'S RECIPE:

IF YOU USE OLDER SQUASH, PEELING WILL GIVE YOU A BETTER PRODUCT; YOU MAY ALSO WANT TO "CORE" THE ZUCCHINI TO REMOVE THE SEEDS. I PREFER TO USE YOUNGER, SMALLER ZUCCHINI BECAUSE I THINK THE INTERESTING COLOR OF THE PEEL ADDS GREAT CONTRAST TO THE MARMALADE, PLUS IT GIVES IT SOME CRUNCH.

THE IDEAL CONSISTENCY AFTER COOLING IS FOR THE MARMALADE TO BE THICK BUT STILL "STIR-ABLE" IN ROOM TEMPERATURE STATE. IT WILL THICKEN CONSIDERABLY IN REFRIGERATOR.

1 Clean and cut squash into paper-thin slices to measure 6 cups. (Now would be a good time to put a gadget into action. Use the 4 mm Slicing Disc or Medium Shredding Disc on your Cuisinart PowerPrep Plus Food Processor to prepare the zucchini.) Put sliced zucchini into a large kettle.

2 Add juice from the lemons to equal ½ cup, 1 teaspoon lemon peel, and crushed pineapple to the pan. Bring to a boil over medium heat. Lower heat and simmer, uncovered, until squash is tender but holds its shape, about 15 minutes.

3 Add fruit pectin. Place over high heat and bring to a boil. Stir in sugar and finely chopped candied ginger to equal 2 tablespoons. Bring to a full rolling boil and boil hard for 1 minute. (Be sure to watch this closely; it is better to boil too little than to boil over 1 minute, because boiling for even a few seconds too long will give you a stiff product. It may even be unspreadable if used straight from the refrigerator.)

4 Remove from heat (slide pot off the burner); skim off any foam. Stir and skim 5 minutes to cool slightly and prevent fruit from floating.

5 Ladle into hot, sterilized jars; seal with hot paraffin or cover with 2-piece canning rings that have been sterilized and kept sitting in slowly simmering water.

Recipe may be doubled (not tripled) but you will have to boil a few seconds longer than 1 minute, and stir and cool about 7 minutes before ladling into jars.

From-the-Freezer-to-the-Plate (With a Quick Stop in Between) Grilled Chicken Breast

When you buy frozen chicken breasts, the fillets are usually a split chicken breast. An entire chicken breast would serve two. I'm still using a George Foreman indoor grill—the kind you plug in and the temperature it gives you is the temperature you get. If your grill allows for temperature adjustment, I'd recommend you use a medium-high setting.

For one serving

1 frozen boneless, skinless half chicken breast

1 Remove the chicken breast from the freezer and put it on the grill. Plug in the grill. Allow 5 to 7 minutes for the meat to defrost and cook completely.

Serving suggestions:

- Put grilled chicken breast in a salad bowl and top with a generous helping of Ann's Very Veggie Salad. (Ann's Very Veggie Salad is good over cold, leftover grilled chicken, too.)
- Put grilled chicken on a serving plate. Season with sea salt and freshly ground black pepper to taste. Serve with a generous helping of TJ Robertson's Triumphant Zucchini Marmalade, either atop the chicken or on the side.
- Serve with orange marmalade thinned with a little lemon juice, soy sauce, Bragg Liquid Aminos, or Worcestershire sauce.
- Serve with 2 teaspoons of mayonnaise mixed with 1 teaspoon of seedless raspberry or red currant jelly.
- Serve with a tablespoon of apple butter or Queen's River Cinnamon Pear Jam (see Sources).

Getting the Other Gadgets Involved

Put those other kitchen gadgets to work helping you prepare fine foods. Here's how I use some of mine:

Bread Machine Recipe: Seven-Grain and Oat Bran Bread

The seven-grain cereal I use already contains oats, but I still add oat bran to this recipe because it not only increases the healthy fiber, but I think it makes the bread taste sweeter, too. Get ready to fire up the bread maker and enjoy this heart-healthy, fiber-rich bread.

Makes a 2-pound loaf

1 tablespoon honey
1¼ cups skim milk
1 tablespoon olive oil
1 medium egg
1 teaspoon sea salt
2 tablespoons nonfat dry milk
½ cup oat bran
½ cup King Arthur whole-wheat flour

¾ cup seven-grain cereal (see description below)
2¼ cups King Arthur unbleached bread flour
2½ teaspoons dry yeast
Optional: 1 tablespoon Ener-G Dough Enhancer

1   Add the ingredients to your bread machine in the order given (unless instructions for your machine specify otherwise).

2   Set machine to bake on the whole-grain bread setting. Check bread at the "beep" and adjust liquid or flour amounts if necessary. (I've found that this bread bakes better if it is not in a firm ball that pulls away from the side of the pan. In other words, the dough should be a bit more "wet" than it would be if you were kneading it by hand.)

Notes about this bread:

★ You can reduce the fat and cholesterol in this bread, plus increase the fiber if you use this egg substitute: Put ¼ cup water and a tablespoon of ground flaxseed in a microwave-safe container. Microwave on high for 30 seconds. Stir. (Mixture should have the consistency of egg whites. If not, continue to microwave in 10-second segments until mixture thickens.)

★ Again, make sure that salt doesn't come in contact with the yeast. If that happens before the yeast has had a chance to work, salt can kill the action, leaving you flat.

★ Instead of trying for 24 thin slices, the serving size for this bread is easier to achieve if you slice it into 12 thick slices and cut each slice in half.

★ Seven-grain cereal is a mixture of cracked wheat, rye grits, barley grits, millet, cornmeal, flaxseed, and oats. The kind I use is organic Country Life Seven-Grain Cereal (see Sources). Join me in avoiding artificial flavorings! This company also offers a wide selection of all natural ones—like almond, butter, and fruit and mint flavors.

★ The dough enhancer I use in this recipe is by Ener-G, which also makes cultured buttermilk powder, salt-free baking powder, potato flour, and a wide assortment of other products (see Sources).

Nutrient Analysis for 24 Servings:

Calories Per Serving: 82.47

PCF Ratio: 14-73-12

Protein Per Serving: 3.02 g

Carbohydrate Per Serving: 15.30 g

Fat Per Serving: 1.14 g

Saturated Fat: 0.21 g

Cholesterol: 8.09 mg

Sodium: 108.42 mg

Fiber: 1.22 g

World's Greatest Grilled Cheeseburger Sandwich

Use your indoor grill to make this delicious sandwich, made with ground round served on toasted seven-grain bread with a savory cheddar cheese. I list some "optimal" optional ingredients with this one; they're the things I think you should use to top the sandwich to add to the perfection. This recipe illustrates one way to "stretch" a meat portion, as suggested in Chapter 18.

Makes 4 servings

1 tablespoon olive oil
1 teaspoon butter
2 thick slices of Seven-Grain and Oat Bran Bread
1 ounce cheddar cheese
8 ounces Laura's Lean Beef ground round

Optimal optionals:

⌣ Worcestershire sauce, garlic, and balsamic vinegar to taste

⌣ Lots of fixin's, like stone-ground honey mustard, mayonnaise, etc.

⌣ A side salad of fresh greens and tomato, red onion, and avocado tossed with lemon juice, some fresh herbs, and extra-virgin olive oil.

1 Preheat your indoor grill.

2 To prepare the toasted cheddar cheese sandwich, combine the olive oil and melted butter. Use half of the mixture for "buttering" the outside portion of each slice of the bread. Place

the cheddar cheese atop the inside portion of one slice of bread and top with the other slice, "buttered" side up. Set aside.

3 Combine the ground round with the Worcestershire sauce, garlic, and balsamic vinegar, if you're using them. Shape the ground round into a large, rectangular patty, a little larger than a slice of the bread.

4 Put the ground round patty on the grill. (If you're using a larger grill, position the "hamburger" so that it's at the bottom of the grill, near the area where the fat drains away from the meat. That way you can grill the cheese sandwich at the top area of the grill.) Grill according to manufacturer's directions, which will probably be about 4 to 5 minutes.

5 Two minutes before the hamburger is done, place the cheese sandwich on the free portion of the grill.

6 Once the cheese sandwich is done, separate the two slices of bread, being careful not to burn yourself on the cheese. Top one slice with the "hamburger" and add your condiments and fixings to taste. Put the "lid" back on the sandwich and cut into 4 wedges.

Notes about this sandwich:

◟ You can cut more fat out of the World's Greatest Grilled Cheeseburger Sandwich by using Cabot's 50% Light Cheddar Cheese or Cabot's 50% Light Jalapeño Cheddar Cheese if you're craving more zip. Unlike some reduced-fat cheeses, Cabot's 50%

Light Cheddar melts great. It's also kosher-certified, gluten-free, made with vegetable-based rennet, and low in sodium, too.

ᴗ Once you've used the olive oil and butter mixture to "butter" the bread for a toasted or grilled sandwich, you'll never want to use just plain butter again! The olive oil helps make the bread crunchier and imparts a subtle taste difference to the sandwich.

Nutritional Analysis for 4 Servings, Sandwich Only:

NOTE: Be sure to allow for your choice of condiments and side dishes when you calculate additional exchange approximations, fats, and calories.

Calories per serving: 261.97

PCF Ratio: 26-24-50

Protein Per Serving: 16.94 g

Carbohydrate Per Serving: 15.39 g

Fat Per Serving: 14.54 g

Saturated Fat: 5.40 g

Cholesterol: 60.19 mg

Sodium: 186.96 mg

Fiber: 1.22 g

Exchange Approximations: 2 Meat, 1 Fat, 1 Starch/Bread

There may be days when you don't have time to fire up the grill, but you still want the convenience of...admit it!...no cleanup! No problem. Packet meal convenience is as close as your countertop and electrical outlet if you have an indoor grill—the kind where you close the lid so food is grilled on both sides simultaneously.

Definitely Not Roughin' It
Orange Roughy Fillets Packet

You can substitute any mild fish in this recipe. Farm-raised catfish, snapper, or halibut are all good choices.

Makes 2 servings

2 orange roughy fillets, about ¾ inch thick
Sea or kosher salt
Freshly ground white or black pepper
1 cup sliced fresh mushrooms
¼ cup chopped basil leaves
2 tablespoons dry white wine
2 teaspoons extra-virgin olive oil

1 Plug in your indoor grill and allow it to preheat.

2 Rinse fillets in water and dry thoroughly between pieces of paper towels.

3 Tear off a piece of heavy-duty aluminum foil about twice the width of the fish fillets laid side by side. Spray the middle of the foil with nonstick cooking spray, leaving about a two-inch perimeter around the foil uncoated.

4 Arrange the fillets side by side and flat-side down on the foil. Season with salt and pepper.

5 Top the fillets with the mushrooms and basil. Drizzle the wine and olive oil over the fillets. (If not using fresh basil, you can substitute 1 teaspoon of dried basil per fillet or substitute ½ teaspoon of Mrs. Dash Lemon Pepper per fillet instead.)

6 Fold the foil over and crimp the edges to form a packet. Tear off another equal-sized piece of heavy-duty foil. Place the fish packet in the center of this piece of foil. Fold the ends up over the packet so the resulting seam is at the top and crimp the other edges. (This should prevent any of the juices from escaping the packet and running onto the grill. Why should you have to clean it when you're done? This helps ensure that you don't.)

7 Place the packet on the grill, close the lid, and grill for 20 minutes. Allow to rest for a minute or two before you open the packet. Serve hot, garnished with lemon wedges.

It takes less kosher or sea salt to season a dish than it does with ordinary table salt. This is an important consideration for anyone watching his or her sodium intake. If you must avoid salt altogether, you can substitute lemon pepper or Mrs. Dash Lemon Pepper herb blend in most seafood recipes. (Be careful. Check the label: Some brands of lemon pepper and other seasonings contain salt!)

Pretty Red Packet Potatoes

The instructions assume you are starting out with raw potatoes. If you don't have any leftover steamed or baked potatoes to use, this will dirty one dish. Once you experience the savory goodness of these potatoes, you'll agree that it's well worth that tiny bit of inconvenience.

Makes 2 servings

2 medium-to-large red potatoes
½ red onion
1 teaspoon butter
1 teaspoon olive oil
1 teaspoon fresh dill
1 teaspoon extra-virgin olive oil

1 Clean the potatoes and either thinly slice them or cut them into cubes. Put into a microwave-safe covered dish.

2 Thinly slice the red onion. Add it to the dish along with the potatoes.

3 Microwave on high for five minutes, or until potatoes are fork-tender and onion is steamed and transparent. Allow to sit, covered, while you prepare the packet.

4 Plug in your indoor grill and allow it to preheat.

5 Tear off a strip of heavy-duty aluminum foil, about one and a half times as wide as your indoor grill. Spray the middle of the

foil with nonstick cooking spray, leaving about a two-inch perimeter around the foil uncoated.

6 Remove the cover from the microwave-safe dish, being careful not to burn yourself on the steam. Stir the potatoes and onion slices to mix. Transfer them to one half of the nonstick spray-treated portion of the foil. (The other half of the treated portion will be the packet "lid.") Divide the butter and drizzle the olive oil over the potato-onion mixture. Sprinkle with dill.

7 Fold the foil over and crimp the edges to form a packet. Tear off another equal-sized piece of heavy-duty foil. Place the potato packet in the center of this piece of foil. Fold the ends up over the potato packet so the resulting seam is at the top, and crimp the other edges.

8 Place the packet on the grill, close the lid, and grill for 10 minutes. Allow to rest for a minute or two before you open the packet. Serve hot. Season with sea salt and freshly ground pepper, if desired.

GADGETS AND OTHER HANDY STUFF

Here's some handy stuff that I believe no one can be *Lazy About Grilling* without, indoors or out:

- Zester: There is a wide assortment of graters and zesters; however, many grill chefs are finding that a razor-sharp, stainless steel rasp meant for the woodshop works even better when used for food! A "coarse grater" rasp is best for grating cheese and chocolate. You can use a "long grater" for tasks that require a finer texture, like zesting citrus fruit or fine-grating garlic, ginger, or hard cheeses.

- Oil spritzer or spray bottle: The manufacturers (and prices) for these gadgets range from those who make inexpensive plastic spray bottles (look for ones that let you select a "mist" setting) to gourmet versions with self-priming, pump sprayers. Used instead of a brush for adding a thin coating of oil or liquid-only marinade.

- Cuisinart Turbo Convection Steamer: Fill the water reservoir, add your ingredients, and you can use this steamer to steam up to 5 cups of rice at a time. The "60" model comes with an extra-large, 6-quart steaming tray and a removable water reservoir with cooking and time indicators. It has easy-to-use dial controls, an additional steaming tray, and an automatic turn-off, so I like it because it's a no-brainer way to fix side dishes.

- Cuisinart Automatic Frozen Yogurt–Ice Cream and Sorbet Maker: Fill this no-ice-required machine with your fixin's, plug it in, and it'll freeze up to 1½ quarts (6 cups) of dessert for you while you eat your meal.

Sit-Back-and-Watch-It-Steam Wild Rice and Broccoli

This recipe is almost as easy as finding someone to cook it for you. It's a low-fat way to add fiber to your meal. Using the Cuisinart Turbo Convection Steamer makes it easier to fix than doing it on the stovetop, because you don't have to keep checking the pot. For more flavor, you can substitute nonfat chicken or vegetable broth for the water. The hearty portion sizes for this dish make it a good choice to stretch the servings for Fruity Fantasy Strip Steaks from 2 to 4.

Makes 4 servings

½ cup wild rice
½ cup brown rice
1 large onion
2 carrots, diced

2 stalks celery, diced
2 cloves crushed garlic
2 cups water
4 cups broccoli florets

1 Mix the brown and wild rice together and spread them evenly in the rice bowl.

2 Fill the water reservoir of the steamer and place it in the reservoir holder. Insert the large steaming tray into the base, then place the rice bowl on top of the tray.

3 Add the chopped onion, diced carrots to equal ¼ cup, diced celery to equal ¼ cup, and garlic to the bowl of the food processor. Process until finely chopped. Being careful to hold the blade from the bottom of the food processor, pour the mixture over the rice. Lightly stir to distribute the mixture over the rice. Pour the water into the rice pan.

4 Insert the turbo convection fan onto the top of the lid, making sure the prongs are properly fitted into the slots. Push down with light pressure to engage. Place the lid on the steamer and plug it into the wall outlet.

5 Use the dial on the control panel to set the steaming time to 50 minutes. Near the end of the steaming time, prepare the broccoli and put it in the upper tray. (If you're using frozen broccoli, make sure it's completely thawed.)

6 At the end of the 50 minutes, unplug the unit. Wait one minute before removing the lid, taking care not to get burned by the steam.

7 Remove the lid and fluff the rice with a fork, adding an additional ½ cup of water if more moisture appears to be needed. (Odds are it won't be. In fact, don't be alarmed if not all of the moisture is absorbed by the rice. Wild rice sometimes needs to be drained when it's done cooking.)

8 Add the upper tray holding the broccoli. Check the water reservoir and add more water to it if necessary. Cover the steamer and plug it back in. Set the timer for 10 minutes. At the end of the steaming time, unplug the unit. Wait 10 minutes before uncovering the steamer. Serve immediately. Have sea salt, a pepper grinder, Bragg Liquid Aminos or light soy sauce, and your choice of Mrs. Dash or one of the herb blends from Chapter 18 at the table to use to season the rice and broccoli. (The broccoli is good served as a warm salad topped with a little extra-virgin olive oil, Bragg Liquid Aminos or light soy sauce, and toasted sesame seeds or toasted ground or slivered almonds.)

Reverse Smoothie

Most smoothie recipes have you add frozen fruit or ice to the blender or bowl of your food processor and you process until it's, well...smooth. This method lets you take advantage of fresh or unsweetened canned fruit. Simply start the Cuisinart Automatic Frozen Yogurt–Ice Cream and Sorbet Maker as you're about ready to start eating your meal and a half hour later, dessert will be ready and waiting for you.

Makes 8 (½ cup) servings

1 recipe Lazy About "Cream" (see Chapter 18)
1 cup nonfat plain or vanilla yogurt
Fresh or drained canned fruit

Optional: ¼ cup sugar or Whey Low Granular (see Chapter 18)

1 In a blender or the bowl of a food processor, add the "cream," yogurt, and enough fruit to equal 2 cups. Also add the sugar, if you're using it. If you're using plain yogurt, throw in a teaspoon of pure vanilla extract or natural almond flavoring if you wish. Process until smooth.

2 Turn the ice cream maker to ON and pour the smoothie mixture into the freezer bowl through the ingredient spout. (If you're pouring it from the bowl of a food processor, be sure to follow the manufacturer's directions about keeping the blade in place while you pour.)

3 Let freezer run for 25–30 minutes, or until the smoothie has thickened to the consistency of soft-serve ice cream.

Go wild with the fruit! Strawberries and bananas are always a good choice, but about any type of berries thrown into the mix tastes great, too. Peaches are another excellent choice. Remember that being Lazy About things often means you take advantage of what you have on hand. If you're uncertain about which flavors to combine, use unsweetened fruit cocktail.

Gone Fishin'

If you don't want to dirty up one more "dish," skip using the blender or food processor, roughly chop the fruit, and make a chunky, less-smooth smoothie. The Reverse Smoothie dessert is meant to be served with a spoon anyhow. Just remember that if you're adding the sugar, stir the mixture until it's dissolved before you move on to Step 2.

A Quick Sherbetish Sensation

Go beyond lazing around and save yourself the hassle of cleaning and chopping fresh fruit. I list the ingredients below. Follow the mixing and freezing instructions for the "Reverse Smoothie" recipe to make this dessert.

Makes 8 (½ cup) servings

1 recipe Lazy About "Cream" (see Chapter 18)
1 cup nonfat plain or vanilla yogurt
One 12-ounce can frozen 100% juice concentrate
Optional: ¼ cup sugar or Whey Low Granular (see Chapter 18)

Note: The choice of which 100% juice concentrate you use is up to you. Orange-strawberry-banana is a great choice, as is pineapple with some natural coconut extract or flavoring. You can even use lemonade concentrate and water (instead of the Lazy About "Cream" and yogurt) to make a sorbet!

A Round of Sodas for Everyone!

Here in the Midwest, we call carbonated beverages "pop." You make a "soda" when you pour pop over ice cream. This recipe works if you don't have an ice cream maker to make the "Reverse Smoothie" or "A Quick Sherbetish Sensation" fresh, or as a way to use the leftovers if you've used a machine. Frozen desserts that use a base of skim milk (like the ones here with Lazy About "Cream") get hard as a rock in the freezer. This method works better than trying to scoop them out for those times you can't do the fresh, soft-serve style.

If one of your guests is too refined to indulge in a soda, serve a nouveau cuisine-style teeny-tiny, itty-bitty petite pastry-shaped frozen dessert placed dead center on the plate, of course, with white and dark chocolate sauce drizzled from Timbuktu and back across the top of it. Don't forget the sprig of mint!

Leftover or unfrozen Reverse Smoothie or A Quick Sherbetish Sensation mix

1 (a) Spoon the mixture into nonstick-coated mini-muffin pans, (see Sources). Cover with plastic wrap and freeze until solid. To unmold the "cubes," either dip the pan in hot water or lightly heat the bottom of the pan using a hair dryer. Cover the pan with a baking sheet and invert to release the "cubes."

1 (b) Spoon the mixture into a flexible mold that can be used in the freezer or the oven. Cover with plastic wrap and freeze until solid. To unmold, push up on the flexible mold from the bottom.

2 Add 3 or 4 cubes to a 12-ounce glass. Pour chilled sparkling water over the cubes. Serve with an iced tea spoon and a straw.

Bonus Project: Getting the Kids Involved Churning Butter

In a pinch, you can use a chilled glass jar with the lid on tight and have the child shake it until butter is formed. However, not only is this method not as much fun, there's the risk that the jar will slip out of the child's hands and break.

A Donvier ice cream maker is handy for making single or double servings of frozen desserts. (Any more than that, I don't want to "crank" that long!) I found what I believe to be an even more fun use for mine! On a recent visit with the grandkids, I let them do the cranking and we used it to make butter.

Makes several ounces of butter (amount depends on the percentage of butterfat in the cream; 18% butterfat should yield at least 2½ ounces of butter).

1 pint chilled whipping or heavy cream

1 Chill the freezer bowl for the ice cream maker in the refrigerator for at least 8 hours. (Do not put it in the freezer!)

2 Sit down at the table with the ice cream maker in front of you and at least one child close by. Place freezer bowl in the plastic holder and pour in the cream. Insert the blade into the bowl, put the plastic cover in place, and insert the crank.

3 Slide the ice cream maker across the table to give it to the child. Let him or her begin to crank away!

4 The child will probably figure this part out by him- or herself, but just in case, be sure to point out that the lid is a "window." Use it to watch for when the cream begins to look "fluffy." When that happens, remove the lid, hand the child a spoon,

and let him or her taste the whipped cream. (Okay, this step isn't mandatory, but it's fun, which in my book, makes it a requirement!)

5 Put the lid and crank back in place and have the child keep cranking until the butter separates from the cream. Pour off the resulting buttermilk. (It doesn't taste anything like that cultured stuff you buy in the store. If you can get the child to taste this, great! If not, use it in a loaf of bread or batch of pancakes.)

6 Show the child how to use an icing spreader or small spatula to press the butter into Flexipan or candy molds. Chill until ready to use, then punch the butter pats out of the molds and enjoy!

Now that you've spent this much time indoors, you're probably ready to go outside again. The next chapter will give you some electrifying suggestions on doing just that.

Chapter 20

Outdoor Electric Cooking: The New Millennium Way to Zap Your Meals

There once was a time you had to sacrifice flavor for the convenience of an electric grill. That's no longer the case. In my experience, the electric grills that I use from Char-Broil (see Sources) reach temperatures high enough to sear meat just the way I like it. That's good news for apartment dwellers who can't use a gas or charcoal grill on the patio. It's great news for anyone whose chemical sensitivities require them to avoid propane fumes.

Electric grilling isn't the only outdoor convenience. Now there are smokers and fryers designed for that purpose, too.

To round out your meal, you can even bring some of the indoors outside if you have a space where you can plug in the appliances I discussed in Chapter 19, such as a steamer or ice cream maker.

Gone Fishin'

OUTDOOR ELECTRIC GRILLS

I like the convenience of an electric grill. There's no tank to fill or charcoal to buy (and the mess that comes with getting it started).

The electric grills I mention in this chapter run off of standard electrical current, using a grounded plug—one that plugs into a standard 110 grounded outlet, ideally with a ground fault interrupter. You'll need an outlet near where you want to use the grill. Using even a heavy-duty extension cord can be a fire and safety hazard.

One of the biggest downsides to using an electric grill is that unless you're inside a well-ventilated, protected patio area or garage, you can't grill during stormy weather.

Another grilling concern is cold weather, but you can compensate for the chill by placing unglazed quarry tiles or a pizza stone in the grill. The principle with either of these is the same as when you use them in your oven: They absorb a lot of heat, so the grill retains more heat and therefore reheats faster once you close the lid after a peek inside. Just make sure you allow plenty of circulation around the tiles or stone. In other words, use ones small enough so that they don't take up all of your grilling space.

A brick or two inside the grill works just as well; just be sure to check with the building supplier from whom you obtain the bricks (to make sure you're getting untreated bricks safe for this purpose.)

Another trick is to place some sort of barrier between the legs of the grill and the floor. This is especially important if the grill sits on concrete. Even something as simple as several layers of cardboard will help prevent the concrete from sapping heat from the legs of the grill.

For more information, see Chapter 3 for "indirect grilling" methods on an electric grill.

Patio Bistro

At first glance, you might question the design of this Char-Broil grill, but it's curved for a reason. That feature means you can work at the grill from a seated or another *Lazy About* position. An insulated liner wraps around the grilling surface, which helps prevent burns if you do accidentally lean too close to the grill. The lid is even designed so that you don't have to reach across the grill to close it once it's open. It's hinged so that it opens to the side. The handle on the lid stays cool to the touch, too.

The inside of the lid contains a patented liner that helps reflect the heat of the grill when the lid is closed. There's a temperature gauge on top of the lid so you can keep track of the heat levels.

The grid for grilling is porcelain-coated steel, so it's durable and easy to clean. Rather than using standard lava rocks, the grill comes with Char-Broil's exclusive (hickory) wood-embedded briquettes.

To the right of the grilling area is a work surface, complete with a dishwasher-safe, slide-out cutting board. There's a cooler under the cutting board and a place to hang your grilling utensils off to the side, too. The grill is even on 3-inch casters, which makes it extremely easy to move from one spot to another, another important consideration for those of us with mobility concerns.

Patio Caddie

This grill is Char-Broil's scaled-down version of the Patio Bistro, which makes it perfect for an apartment patio. (Basically it has a bit smaller grilling surface sans the work space area to the right of the grill.) It has a rust-resistant porcelain body that's a rugged base, while at the same time being lightweight and tip resistant.

Canny, Clever Chicken Creations

The basic principle of this recipe is that you want to grill the chicken slowly (2 hours on a 350ºF grill; 4 hours or longer if you want to slow-roast or smoke it at 250ºF). The canny secret: a half a can of beer or other flavored liquid in its belly. In fact, because most chefs drink the unneeded half can of beer before they put the chicken on the grill—or even more, if they're preparing more than one chicken—I'm going to do things backward and give you the major ingredient first, then list the instructions, then tell you about some possible variations.

Makes 2–4 servings

One 4-pound whole chicken

1 Preheat grill or smoker to 250ºF or 350ºF, depending on your preferred cooking method.

2 Remove any unwanted parts from inside the chicken. (Reserve the giblets for gravy or broth-making, if you desire.) Wash the chicken thoroughly, inside and out. Pat dry with paper towels.

3 Coat outside of chicken with olive oil and rub with your choice of seasoning or salt and pepper to taste.

Note: If you're grilling or smoking more than one chicken using this (or any other) method, try to get chickens that weigh the same so they're done cooking at the same time.

4 Fill an empty 12- or 16-ounce aluminum can with your choice of steaming liquid. (See recipes that follow the instructions.)

5 Stand the chicken up over the open can. Holding the chicken upright, fit the chicken's cavity snugly over the upright can. In other words, the can will set on the grill and the chicken will "rest" atop the can. Place chicken with its legs crossed over its new roost and put foil on the ends of the legs to prevent them from burning. Place assembled chicken and "roost" on preheated grill. (Some grill chefs like to put a whole head of garlic at the neck opening and fold the neck flap of skin over the top of it. This results in a bit of extra flavor for the chicken and lots of cloves of roasted garlic which can be squeezed out to spread on bread.)

6 Cook with the grill lid down or the smoker covered for 4 hours, if using a 250°F setting; 2 hours if at 350°F. You want the chicken to reach an internal temperature of 165°F or to cook until the juices run clear.

7 Remove chicken from grill or smoker. Place on platter and let rest. Cut chicken in half for 2 servings; in quarters for 4. Carve the chicken if you need to stretch the meat to serve more.

Be sure to discard the can and its contents after use. Be careful because the liquid will be hot!

Here are the variations. Unless other instructions are given, everything goes in the open can. The rest is according to the preceding instructions.

Basic Beer Belly Chicken

6 ounces of beer for each chicken
1 clove of garlic, cut in half

Basic Your-Choice-of-Liquid-in-the-Belly Chicken

One empty, 12- or 16-ounce aluminum can
6 ounces apple juice, root beer, or other soft drink, or white wine
1 clove garlic, cut in half

Zap-Spice That Beer Chicken

1 teaspoon hot sauce
3 tablespoons cider vinegar
One 12-ounce can of beer
1 tablespoon stone-ground or Dijon mustard
1 tablespoon Worcestershire sauce
¼ cup soy sauce
2 cloves minced garlic

1 In a measuring cup, combine all ingredients. Pour half of the mixture into the open aluminum can. Use the remaining mixture to baste the oiled chicken.

The possibilities for fixing tender, moist chicken using this method are endless. You can fill the can with one of the brining recipes later in this chapter, if you wish. You can mix half citrus juice with half water and add your choice of seasoning blends mentioned in Chapter 18. Be creative and have fun!

While I haven't experienced any problems or ill effects for from this cooking method, some general concerns have been raised about the safety of using aluminum. I'm no expert on whether or not aluminum—or in this case, dyes used on the can—can leach into the food, but I continue to experience no problems with this method. If you have qualms about the dyes, you could cover the can's exterior with baking foil. I have been trying to find a stainless steel container to use as a substitute for the can. Once I figure out whether a 12-ounce martini shaker (sans lid) is the right size for achieving the same effect, I'll post the results on the Lazy About Grilling web site at www.ricehahn.com/grill/. Look for "Build a Better Beer Can."

SMOKING ON A SMALL SCALE

There are times when you want to smoke foods and don't want a smoky flavor for the rest of the foods on your grill, or maybe you only need to smoke a small portion of food and don't want to have to use the quantity of wood chips required for the usual grill-top method. Smoking on a small scale (read: being *Lazy About* smoking) usually means you don't want to set up your smoker. I know I save mine for when I'm cooking for a crowd. In this section, I give you two easy suggestions for smoking small quantities of food.

Build-It-Yourself Cast-Iron Smoker

This works for smoking small amounts of food, whether you want to do so outside on your electric (or other) grill, or inside in a 250°–350°F oven. It's the ideal way to smoke one or two servings of seafood.

To assemble the makeshift smoker:

1. Get out your trusty cast-iron skillet.

2. Tear off two pieces of heavy-duty aluminum foil that are a little wider than your skillet. (The long edges will be the width of the foil as it comes off the roll; heavy-duty aluminum foil is usually 18 inches wide. The width of your skillet means you'll end up with two pieces, each about 18- x 15-inches wide.)

3. Center both pieces of foil in the skillet, one on top of the other, so that an equal length extends over two "sides" of the skillet.

4. Put at least 1 tablespoon of dry wood chips in the center of the top piece of foil. (I also add a bay leaf to the chips. Feel free to add other herbs as well.) Fold the two edges of foil loosely across the wood chips so that they're covered. Use a fork to prick small holes through the resulting two layers of foil over the chips. Be careful that you don't pierce through the foil under the chips. (If you do, there's no more being *Lazy About* it; you'll have to clean the skillet, and who wants to do that?)

5. Spray the pierced section of foil with nonstick spray. Place the food to be smoked on top of the treated foil.

6. Fold the remaining foil up and over the food, tenting it to allow smoke to circulate, and crimping the edges to form a tight seal so that the smoke doesn't escape.

7. Place on a medium grill or in the oven and cook for the length of time suggested in the recipe.

It's a Cinch Cider-Smoked Salmon

A craving for some smoked salmon is what brought about the "invention" of my Build-It-Yourself Cast-Iron Smoker and the creation of this recipe.

Makes 1 serving

¼ cup cider or apple juice
1 tablespoon brown sugar
¾ teaspoon kosher or sea salt
1 bay leaf
Pinch each of fennel seeds, ground allspice, cracked pepper, red pepper flakes, and dried thyme
One 8-ounce salmon fillet

1 In a microwave-safe bowl large enough to hold the salmon fillet, add the cider, brown sugar, salt, and bay leaf. Microwave on high for 30 seconds. Stir. If sugar and salt have not dissolved, microwave at 10-second intervals until they do.

2 Remove the bay leaf and either discard or set aside to add to the wood chips when you assemble your Build-It-Yourself Cast-Iron Smoker. Add the spices and stir well, enough to cool the brine to room temperature.

3 Wash the salmon fillet and pat dry with paper towels. Add it to the marinade. Be sure to coat all sides of the salmon. (The salmon should remain in the marinade at room temperature for about 20 minutes. After 10 minutes, turn the fillet so that the other side rests in the marinade.)

Unlike other methods of smoking, you use dry wood chips in the Build-It-Yourself Cast-Iron or Camerons Stovetop Smoker.

4 Preheat the grill or oven. Assemble the Build-It-Yourself Cast-Iron Smoker. I usually use the finely ground alder chips that come with the Camerons Stovetop Smoker described later in this chapter for this recipe. (See Sources). At the end of the marinating time, place the salmon fillet on the foil and tent the remaining foil above the fish as described earlier.

5 Smoke the salmon for 20 minutes, or until it flakes with a fork.

Camerons Stovetop Smoker

Whether you use this on the grill, on the stovetop (as recommended by the manufacturer), or in the oven (the *Lazy About* favorite—probably because of my commitment to spending as little time as possible slaving over a hot stove), this smoker will come in handy for smoking medium amounts of food—four servings, for example. It's a great way to test a brine. Simply prepare enough brine for 4 chicken breasts and use this smoker to smoke them. Once the food is ready, you can perform your own taste test to see whether or not you like the flavor enough to fill up your smoker with chickens or turkeys brined using that method!

Smokers of this type consist of a stainless-steel roasting pan (usually with a 10½ x 14-inch cooking area), drip tray, smoking rack, and sliding, removable lid. Mine came with a small cookbook that includes suggested smoking times. Whether I'm using the smoker in the oven or on the stovetop, being *Lazy About* cleanup means coating all interior surfaces with nonstick spray. Then, to make cleanup even easier, I distribute the dry wood chips under the drip tray on several small pieces of foil. I fold the foil over, but don't seal them. This allows the smoke to escape. (I didn't do this the first time I used the smoker and as a result, the roasting pan has a few darkened areas in it. It took a bit more scrubbing to clean up that first time, too. So here's your opportunity to learn from my mistake and save yourself that avoidable hassle.)

Rub-a-Dub Oven-Smoked Chicken Breast

Here's one that I make inside the oven. The honey or syrup on the skin helps the chicken absorb the smoke flavor.

Makes 4 servings

4 whole bone-in, skin-on chicken breasts
1 teaspoon garlic powder
1 teaspoon dried parsley
¼ teaspoon paprika
¼ teaspoon freshly ground black pepper
¼ teaspoon kosher or sea salt

¼ teaspoon lemon pepper
4 teaspoons honey or dark corn syrup
2 teaspoons Worcestershire sauce
2 teaspoons Bragg Liquid Aminos or soy sauce
½ teaspoon Dijon mustard

1 Preheat the oven to 275°F. Assemble the smoker as described earlier, adding your choice of wood chips.

2 Wash the chicken breasts and pat dry with paper towels.

3 In a small bowl, mix the garlic powder, parsley, paprika, pepper, salt, and lemon pepper. Divide the mixture and rub it over and under the skin of the breasts. Place the breasts on the smoker rack.

4 In a small bowl, mix the honey or syrup, Worcestershire sauce, Bragg Liquid Aminos or soy sauce, and mustard. (The syrup will give the chicken a stronger flavor.) Evenly divide the mixture and spread it over the top of the breasts. Put the lid on the smoker. Bake for 1½ hours, or until juices run clear.

Easy, Tender, and Juicy Slow-Smoked Pork Ribs

Here's another recipe I smoke in the oven. There's just no being any more *Lazy About* than this!

Makes 4 servings

2 pounds bone-in pork ribs
¼ cup white wine
2 teaspoons Mrs. Dash Garlic and Herb, or to taste
Optional: 1 teaspoon brown sugar
¼ cup maple syrup
1 tablespoon white wine

1 Preheat the oven to 275°F.

2 Wash the pork ribs and pat dry with paper towels.

3 Assemble the smoker according to the instructions earlier in this chapter. Arrange the ribs on the rack, fat side up.

4 Pour the wine evenly over the meat. Sprinkle the Mrs. Dash seasoning over the ribs. Sprinkle the brown sugar over the ribs at this time, too, if you're using it. Put the lid on the smoker and place in the oven for 2 hours.

5 In a small mixing cup, stir the wine into the maple syrup to thin it a bit. Remove the ribs from the oven, (turn the exhaust fan

on over your stove if you're bothered by light smoke fumes), carefully slide back the lid, and evenly pour the maple syrup and wine mixture over the ribs. Return to the oven for another half hour.

6 Remove the ribs to a serving platter and allow them to rest for about 10 minutes before you serve them.

ELECTRIC WATER SMOKER

Water smokers are designed to slow-cook food using the steam created from water into which you introduce wood chips and your choice of herbs, spices, and vegetables.

I use a Char-Broil Electric Water Smoker. (It's available in a gas model, too.)

Let's get what some may consider the bad news out of the way first. The drawback of an electric smoker is that it may not be able to achieve its maximum cooking temperature when used outside during cold weather. But being *Lazy About* smoking means we're prepared to navigate such shortcomings! I let others use the methods of checking and adding to their coals every half hour or fiddling with changing a tank that always runs out halfway through cooking. (That propane tank stuff is the seldom discussed, unwritten rule of cooking in weather too cold to let you make a fist, let alone think of holding a wrench! Until I can attach the tank with Velcro, I'm sticking to electric!)

As long as the method you use doesn't restrict the air from circulating, you can use some of the same suggestions mentioned earlier in this chapter for electric grills to help maintain the cooking temperature inside the smoker.

My water smoker holds 8 quarts of water, which is usually sufficient for an 8-hour smoking session, although it's a good idea to
check it halfway through the smoking time. It has two chrome grates
on which you can smoke up to 50 pounds of food at one time.
There's a temperature gauge in the lid, so it's easy to keep track of
that. It has an adjustable heat-setting dial on the side of the unit. Last
but not least, when you consider it does need electricity, it comes
with a 5-foot cord.

The manufacturer recommends that (because you will be using water
with the smoker) the outlet into which you plug it not only needs to be
grounded but must have a ground-fault interrupter, too—something
usually required in new home construction, but not always in place in
older garages or outdoor outlets.

Pam's 22-Pound Smoked Turkey Tale

On a cold, crisp December day here on the west coast of Ohio, I
set up my electric water smoker in my daughter's garage (well, son-
in-law's, too, but I wouldn't be a proper mother-in-law if I didn't semi-
ignore him) and, without inhaling, I smoked a turkey. Because it was
frozen and because it was already injected with that keep-it-moist,
salt-added stuff the frozen turkey people inject in birds, we simply
thawed the turkey and filled the water reservoir with the requisite
quarts of water, mesquite chips, and some onion peels and celery
leaves for good measure. Then we heated up the smoker, put a drip
tray on the bottom rack, and set the turkey on the top rack.

Well, actually we did some other stuff before we put the turkey on
the rack. We stuffed the cavity with several small peeled onions and
whole potatoes that had been pricked with a fork. This added to the

cooking time, but because the moisture from the potatoes is drawn up into the turkey, those taters gave their lives to keep the bird moist. (We threw the rock-hard potatoes into the compost heap when we were done. Ditto the onions.)

Other than that, the only prep work was to rub the turkey with some vegetable oil and wrap the legs in foil, which is the height of avoidance and how to be truly *Lazy About* trussing the bird.

We smoked the turkey for 6 hours, which brought the internal temperature to about 150°F. If I were morning person, "we" might have gotten things organized early enough to allow for the recommended eight hours of smoking. As it was, we finished off the turkey (sans foil around the legs and with some butter rubbed on the skin for the heck of it) in a 350°F oven for about an hour while we set the table and finished up the other fixings for our meal.

After our meal, we carved the rest of the meat from the turkey and my daughter Lara saved it in a roasting pan along with the resulting juices. She then simply warmed up those leftovers to serve alongside the ham and other stuff for a Christmas Eve buffet she (and that guy she married) had for the in-laws.

Brining Recipes

For those times you smoke a "proper" fresh turkey, you may want to introduce some flavor by first soaking it in a flavored, brining solution.

Years ago, further back than even I can remember, brining was developed as a way to mix salt and sugar and use them to preserve foods when the temperature was too high to dry-cure. As a general rule, salt was added to water that's almost boiling to the point where the water wouldn't dissolve any more; it was then considered to have 100 percent saline content. Sugar was added to impart the desired sweet taste, such as a ratio of 2 parts sugar to 5 parts salt for ham.

Chances are, even if you decide to "brine" food before you grill or smoke it, you also plan to use storage methods other than sticking the stuff in a root cellar once it's cooked. Because you can take advantage of your refrigerator or freezer to store meat, the salt ratio becomes a matter of taste. That's one way of saying that, in the recipes to follow, feel free to adjust the salt up or down, according to your taste and dietary restrictions.

Venison "Corned Beef" Pastrami

You can just as easily use a beef roast for this recipe. Go with a brisket if you want to call it corned beef. Go with whatever boneless cut is on sale if you want to test it first. When I first created this recipe, I used about ⅓ cup juniper berries—crushing some and leaving others whole. Then I tried using straight gin instead, and now I prefer it that way. However you make it, be sure to try some on a grilled Reuben sandwich!

Makes about 2 pounds cooked meat (if using a bone-in cut of venison)

¼ cup gin
3 cups water
½ cup packed light brown sugar
2 tablespoons kosher salt
2 tablespoons black peppercorns

1 tablespoon dried thyme
3 bay leaves, crumbled
2 teaspoons whole cloves
¼ cup dried minced garlic
One 3-pound venison roast

1 In a saucepan, over medium heat, combine the gin, water, brown sugar, and salt. Bring to a boil and stir to dissolve the sugar and salt. Remove from the heat and add the peppercorns, thyme, bay leaves, cloves, and minced garlic. Let steep and cool for an hour.

2 Place the venison roast in a glass or plastic container, or heavy-duty zip-closure bag. Pour in the seasoned brine. It needs to cover the brisket completely; if not, add more water. Cover and refrigerate for 3 weeks, turning the brisket every couple of days.

3 Preheat the smoker. Remove the roast from the brine and place it on the rack inside the smoker. Smoke for 2 to 4 hours, depending on the amount of smoky flavor you prefer.

4 Remove from the smoker and cool for 30 minutes.

5 Place the roast in a large Dutch oven, cover with water, and place over high heat. Bring the liquid to a boil. Lower the heat and simmer for two hours. Remove from the pan and cool completely. Slice thinly and serve.

Brining Poultry

It's impossible to give you exact amounts for brining an entire chicken or turkey because the size of those birds can vary considerably. That's why the recipes in this section are in "test-batch" sizes, or enough to brine two boneless, skinless chicken breasts, one bone-in chicken breast, or an equivalent amount of turkey. For these recipes, you'll marinate the poultry in the brine for up to two hours. Grilling or smoking time will depend on the size of the poultry pieces you're using, and whether or not they are boneless or bone-in. As you would with a whole bird, you'll aim for an internal temperature above 160°F. (In fact, the resting time will be less before you carve the meat, which means there's less time that the poultry continues to cook once you remove it from the heat source. Therefore, if you prefer, you can usually let the pieces reach an internal temperature of 170°F before you remove them from the oven without the risk of drying them out.)

The ratio of salt and sugar to water for brining an entire bird is usually 1 cup each of salt and sugar for each 2 gallons of water. You then increase the spices or other ingredients accordingly. As I already mentioned earlier, because you're not using the brine to preserve the bird, the amount of salt that you use is up to you. These "test recipes" should help you determine what ratio of salt to water you

In case you ever find yourself—heaven forbid—without this book's list of suppliers close at hand, remember all links for the products and ingredients suggested are listed online at the CookingWithPam.com website, as well as at www.ricehahn.com/grill/ for your surfing pleasure.

like best. As I've also mentioned elsewhere in this book, although I do use some, I go easy on the salt. Keep that in mind if you're a salt junkie.

When you brine an entire chicken or turkey, you'll want to cover the entire bird in brine for 4 to 24 hours. Because you won't be using a full-strength saline solution, it'll need to be refrigerated, or kept at a safe temperature in a cooler, during the entire brining process.

Another Kind of Apple Cider Brine

Johnny Appleseed must have known I'd be his future friend when he traveled through this area. I probably use cider as often as I do beer or wine when I grill. In this case, though, because it is a brine, the recipe calls for apple cider vinegar instead of salt.

¾ cup water
¼ cup cider vinegar
1 tablespoon Worcestershire sauce
1 teaspoon dried minced onion
½ teaspoon dried minced garlic
½ teaspoon dried rosemary
¼ teaspoon dried thyme
¼ teaspoon dry mustard
¼ teaspoon cracked pepper
Optional: ¼ teaspoon dried sage
Optional: ⅛ teaspoon red pepper flakes

Pride of the Hive Brine

1 cup hot water
1 tablespoon kosher salt
1 tablespoon honey
1 tablespoon lemon juice
1 tablespoon whole cloves
1 tablespoon whole black peppercorns
¼ teaspoon dried thyme

Lemon Entertain You: Orange You Glad It's Brine(?)

You'll want to use hot water for this brine, so that the salt will dissolve. Once that happens, you can add the other ingredients.

½ cup hot water
1 teaspoon kosher salt
2 teaspoons brown sugar
½ small orange, thinly sliced with seeds removed
½ small lemon, thinly sliced with seeds removed
½ teaspoon dried rosemary
¼ teaspoon dried thyme

Turducken

Warning: Assembling a whole turducken is the least *Lazy About* procedure in this book. (For that reason, and until you know how you prefer to season your custom-built "bird," I recommend starting with boneless, skinless chicken and duck breasts, and a turkey breast with enough skin left on it to wrap around all three.) Roll up the duck breast so that you can wrap the chicken breast around it. Wrap the turkey breast around the chicken breast. Secure the skin. Regardless of your grilling or smoking method, you'll want the turducken breast to reach an internal temperature of 165°F. If you're the type who never wants to do anything halfway, follow along and learn how you can assemble a new and better bird!

Yield will vary according to the size of the birds and how good you are at wielding a knife!

1 fresh turkey
1 fresh chicken
1 fresh duck

1 First, you need to remove the bones from the turkey. (I warned you that this wouldn't be easy!) To do so, place the turkey breast-side down on a large, easy-to-clean, cutting-board-style surface. Remember, a sharp knife is a safer knife. Starting at the neck, use the tip of a sharp, deboning-type knife to make a cut along the entire length of the spine through the skin and flesh. Follow as close to the bone as possible, carefully pulling the skin and meat away from the skeleton. Near the neck end, feel to locate the shoulder blade and cut through the meat to expose it, then cut the meat away from around the bone. You should now be able to sever the bone at the joint and remove the blade.

2 Wiggle the wing between the second and third joint to disjoint it, then remove the heavy "drumstick" of the wing, being careful to leave the skin intact. Continue working the meat away from the backbone, moving toward the thighbone, making sure you leave the "oyster" (pocket of meat on the back) attached to the skin; you do NOT want to remove that succulent meat with the bone.

3 Next wiggle the ball-and-socket joint to release the thighbone so you can cut it from the carcass. The turkey should now be at the point where you can open it up to see what bones remain. Continue to work the meat away from the carcass until you reach the center front of the breastbone. At this point, carefully

LAZY ABOUT GRILLING

separate the skin from the breastbone at the midline without piercing the thin skin.

4 With the turkey still breast down, repeat this deboning procedure on the remaining side of the turkey. When both sides are finished, carefully remove the carcass. (Put it, along with the other bones, in that bowl you've got beside you, ready for your helper to take to the kettle to make the broth.)

5 Now you're ready to remove the thighbones and leg bones. Using caution so you don't break through the skin, use a small hammer to break the leg bone completely across, about two inches from the tip end. Next wiggle both ends of the bone to verify the break is indeed complete. Leaving the tip of the bone in, remove the leg bone and thighbone as one unit by using the tip of your knife to cut the meat away from around the thighbone. After you've done this, hold the thighbone up with one hand and use the other hand to carefully cut the meat away from the joint joining the leg and thigh. Scrape the meat away from the leg bone using the blade of the knife, then remove the leg-thigh bone. (Do not cut through the joint. A lot of meat will probably remain on these bones, but it'll go into the broth, so don't worry about that.) Use the knife and some needle-nose pliers to remove as many pin bones from the leg meat as possible. Repeat with the other leg and thigh.

6 If necessary, turn the meat to the inside so the skin is on the outside and it looks like a turkey again. Refrigerate.

7 Get out the chicken and place it breast-side down, following the same procedure you used to debone the turkey, only remove all of the bones, instead of leaving in part of the wing and leg bones.

8 To remove the bones from each wing, cut off the first two joints of the wing. Save them for the broth. Leave the wing's drumstick, but cut the meat from around the drumstick and remove that bone.

9 At the thigh, with the knife blade, follow the thigh and leg bone to separate the bone as one unit, being careful not to cut through the skin.

10 Trim off any excess skin and fat around the neck area and discard. Refrigerate.

11 Repeat Steps 7–10 to debone the duck.

12 Now it's time to be Dr. Frankenstein: To build your turducken, open the turkey skin-side down on the flat surface so that as much meat as possible is exposed. Season the meat with kosher salt and freshly ground black pepper, or your choice of herbs or seasoning blend.

13 On top of the turkey, place the chicken skin-side down. Season the exposed meat, if desired.

14 On top of the chicken, arrange the duck skin-side down. Season the exposed meat, if desired.

15 Moving your new bird to the roasting pan (or, even better, to a "turkey lifter"—a steel rack with folding handles that wrap around the bird so that you don't have to truss it) can be a bit tricky. If you're using the turkey lifter, you can carefully position the turducken breast-side up on the rack, so that the open bottom of the bird is folded over onto itself and tucked under the bird. (This is why some people prefer to use stuffing in the turducken; the stuffing "fluffs" it up to compensate for those missing bones. I prefer the safer sans-stuffing method.) If you're putting the turducken directly into a roasting pan, you may want to sew it closed. To do that, fold the sides of the turkey together to close the bird. While your helper holds the turkey closed, sew up the openings with stitches about an inch apart. Tie the legs together just above the tip bones, and, remembering that it needs to end up breast-side up in the pan, tuck the wings under the bird. Season the outside of the bird and rub with oil, if desired. Refrigerate until ready to bake.

16 Grill or smoke at 200°–250°F until done, or for about 12 to 13 hours, or until a meat thermometer inserted through to the center reads 165°F. You will need a roasting pan under it to collect the accumulated drippings. You may also need to dump those juices from the pan periodically. If the turducken is directly in a roasting pan, every few hours you'll need to drain the juices from the pan so that the turducken doesn't continually rest in that hot oil.

17 Once you remove the turducken from the grill or smoker, you need to move it to a serving platter or carving board. If you aren't using a turkey lifter, you'll need a helper similarly equipped with a large, strong spatula in each hand to use to lift and hold the turducken. Because there aren't many bones left in the bird, this part can be tricky! Allow the turducken to rest for up to an hour before you carve it. Make your cuts so that each slice contains some of each kind of meat.

18 Use some of the pan drippings to make gravy, if desired.

Lazy About Bird Surgery and Stuffing

Turn deboning the birds for your "turducken" into an assembly line process. (This method won't work if you insist on stuffing your turducken and need the dressing ready in advance. Some outdoor chefs insist this helps plump up the bird and keeps it "purdier." I go for the safer method of grilling, smoking, or frying an unstuffed bird and make my dressing as it cooks.) Spread a heavy plastic tablecloth across your picnic table and lay out the tools you'll need to perform the chores. While you're tackling the turkey, so to speak, have a helper get a huge kettle of boiling water ready to make the broth you'll need for the dressing. Even if you plan to fry your turducken, it's okay to use the turkey fry pot (see information later in this chapter) as your stewpot for boiling the bones. Remember to make sure your helper adds the appropriate amount of onions, carrots, and celery or Minor's Roasted Mirepoix Flavor Concentrate to the water. As you transfer the bones to a bowl, your helper can be carrying them to the pot to drop them in the boiling water. Your helper can also be in charge of taking the deboned bird to the refrigerator and bringing you the next one. (That way you won't have to be the one constantly washing your hands!) By the time you have the turducken assembled, your helper can have the broth made, and the turkey fryer cleaned out and ready to prep to use to fry the turducken.

BEYOND FRYIN' IT UP IN A PAN!

Another popular piece of electric outdoor cooking equipment is what's generally referred to as a "turkey fryer." These huge units are made for French-frying turkeys, but that's not their only use.

There are a number of manufacturers who make fryers. One company that makes an electrical indoor/outdoor unit is Cajun Injector (see Sources). Their fryer comes with a 26-quart and a 16-quart pot—each of which has internal, easy-to-handle baskets to hold the food. This makes it easy to remove the fried food from the oil. If you use one of the pots to make turducken broth, as suggested earlier in this chapter, it also means that you won't have to strain the broth when you're done. Simply lift out the internal "basket" to remove the bones and any veggies you added to the broth for flavor. A fryer thermometer is also included, so you can make sure the oil's heated to the proper temperature before you add the food.

A Turkey Lifter is a simple way to remove a big turkey or roast from the roasting pan. Use this extra-large, nonstick steel lifter as a roasting rack for your turkey, ham, or roast beef, up to 24 lbs. Its handles wrap around the bird, eliminating the need for trussing. Handles fold flat for storage.

EVER WONDER WHY FOODS LIKE FISH POACHED IN OLIVE OIL DON'T TASTE "GREASY"? IT'S BECAUSE PROTEIN DOESN'T ABSORB OIL. IT JUST USES THE HEAT OF THE SURROUNDING OIL TO COOK ITSELF. LIKE WATER OFF A DUCK'S BACK, IT SHEDS THE OIL ONCE YOU REMOVE IT FROM THE PAN. (TRUE, YOU MAY NEED TO BLOT SOME OF IT AWAY, BUT YOU GET THE IDEA...) PUT SOME BREADING ON THE MEAT AND IT BECOMES ANOTHER STORY. STARCH ABSORBS OIL! KEEP THAT IN MIND WHEN YOU USE AN OUTDOOR FRYER TO FRY MEAT.

Sources

Grill Manufacturers
Broilmaster
Phone: (800) 255-0403
www.broilmaster.com

Camp Chef Cookers
Phone: (800) 783-8347
www.campchef.com

Char-Broil
Phone: (706) 571-7000
www.charbroil.com

George Foreman's Grilling
Machine
www.salton-maxim.com/
salton/

HealthSmart Contact Grill
Meal Maker Express
Contact Grill
www.hamiltonbeach.com

Sunbeam Outdoor
Products Company
Phone: (800) 882-5842
www.bbqhq.com

Viking Range Corporation
Phone: (601) 455-1200
www.vikingrange.com

Weber-Stephen Products
Company
Phone: (800) 446-1071
www.weber.com

Breadmaker
Zojirushi Home Bakery
Model BBCC-V20
www.zojirushi.com

**Broth bases, flavor
concentrates**
Minor's
AllServ, Inc.
Phone: (800) 827-8328
www.allserv.com

Crabs, soft-shell
Goldsmith Seafood,
Phone: (252) 473-5395
www.goldsmithseafood.com

Dough enhancer
Ener-G
Phone: (800) 331-5222
www.ener-g.com

Dried fruits
American Spoon Foods
www.spoon.com

King Arthur Flour Baker's
Catalogue
www.kingarthurflour.com

Nutty Guys
www.nuttyguys.com

Electric grills
Char-Broil
Phone: (706) 571-7000
www.patiobistro.com
www.charbroil.com

Electri-Chef Grills
Phone: (800) 442-7202
www.electri-chef.com

**Flexible molds/pans
non-stick baking sheets**
Flexipan, Silpat
Demarle Inc., USA
Phone: (609) 395-0219,
www.DemarleUSA.com.

**Ice cream & sorbet
maker**
www.cuisinart.com
www.donvier.com

Jam, cinnamon-pear
Queen's River Cinnamon
Pear Jam
Phone: (401) 783-4054
www.kenyonsgristmill.com

Lean beef
Laura's Lean Beef
1-800-ITS-LEAN or
www.laurasleanbeef.com.

Muffin pans, nonstick
Best Manufacturers
Phone: (503) 253-1528
www.bestmfrs.com

Chicago Metallic
Phone: (800) 238-BAKE
www.bakingpans.com

Kaiser Bakeware
Phone: (704) 588-8090
www.kaiserbakeware.com

**Nutritional analysis
software**
Nutribase 2001
CyberSoft, Inc.
Phone: (480) 759-4849
www.nutribase.com

**Reduced-fat but great-
for-melting cheese**
Cabot Creamery,
Phone: (888) 792-2268,
www.cabotcheese.com

Seasonings
Mrs. Dash
Culver Specialty Brands
www.mrsdash.com

7-grain cereal
Country Life Natural Foods
(616) 236-5011
www.clnf.org

**Smokers,
Stove-top, & oven**
Camerons Stovetop
CM International Inc.
Phone: (888) 563-0227
www.cameronssmoker.com

Soy sauce substitute
Bragg Live Foods, Inc.
Phone: (800) 446-1990
www.bragg.com

Spatula, heat-safe
Le Creuset of America
Phone: (877) CREUSET
www.lecreuset.com

Spice grinders
www.cuisinart.com
www.pleasanthillgrain.com

Spices, herbs
www.thespicehouse.com

Steamer
www.cuisinart.com

Sweetner, all-natural
Whey Low
VivaLac Inc.
Phone: (888) 639-8480
www.wheylow.com

Tailgating
www.tailgating.com
John Cahn's Monthly
online magazine about
tailgating.

Tailgating Grill
Grill2Go
www.grill2go.com

Turkey fryer
Cajun Injector
South Clinton, LA
Phone: (800) 221-8060
www.cajuninjector.com

Zesters
Microplane rasps,
Grace Manufacturing,
www.microplane.com

Glossary

If You Don't Know What It Means, Look Here

Basting Brush—A brush used to spread a sauce or marinade over meats as they cook.

Briquettes—The individual pieces of charcoal. They can also have special woods pressed into them for flavor.

Charcoal—The main fuel used in charcoal grills. Comprised of small pieces called briquettes.

Cross-Contamination—When the juices of uncooked meats get on cooking utensils or surfaces. These juices can contain harmful bacteria such as salmonella, or e-coli.

Diffusing Material—On grills, a substance such as lava rocks that allows the heat to spread evenly under the cooking area.

Grill—A device used for the cooking of foods. There are different types, like charcoal, gas, and electric.

Grill Basket—A handy item in which one can place several pieces of meat or vegetables for ease in turning throughout the cooking process.

Grill Cover—Usually made of vinyl, this protects a grill from the elements to keep corrosion from setting in on the exterior of a grill.

Grill Light—An attachment for a grill that aids the grill master in night cooking.

Grill-Safe Pan—Any pan without wooden or plastic handles that can withstand the high temperatures of the grill. The best is a good old cast-iron type.

Grill Thermometer—A device that relays the grill's internal temperature to help calculate precise cooking times.

Grill Toppers—An add-on for a grill used for cooking small or specialty foods.

Grill Umbrella—Keeps the food from getting drenched if a rain begins while you're grilling.

Grilling Mitts—Help to prevent burns on the hands, fingers, and lower arms during grilling.

Igniter Switch—A push button that causes the fuel to light on a gas grill.

Indirect Cooking—Cooking food on a grill without a flame or heat directly underneath the food.

Jerk—A special rub or seasoning that originated in Jamaica and the surrounding Caribbean.

Lava Rocks—A type of diffusing material. See also diffusing material.

Marinade—A liquid seasoning for meats, usually containing a tenderizer such as vinegar or citric acid.

Meat Thermometer—A tool used to determine the precise inside temperature of meats and the safest way to cook meats to avoid possible sickness due to bacteria.

Pit—A grill made out of a combination of brick, blocks, and mortar.

Roasting Rack—A special grill attachment for securing large meats, fish, or vegetables for indirect cooking.

Rotisserie—A device that aids in the turning process and is used for cooking a large piece of meat.

Skewers—Metal or bamboo "sticks" that allow the cooking of smaller pieces of meats and vegetables.

Smoker Box—A cast-iron box filled with wood chips to add flavor to meats as they cook.

Spatula—A flat-ended utensil with a long handle that turns flat pieces of meat and vegetables.

Tongs—A turning utensil for oddly shaped meats and vegetables.

Wood Chips—Used in smoker boxes or directly on charcoal briquettes to add smoke flavor to meats as they cook.

Index